THE
UNLIKELIEST
BACKPACKER

From Office Desk to Wilderness:
A hike along America's
Pacific Crest Trail

Kathryn Barnes

HORNET BOOKS©
PUBLISHING TALENT

The Unlikeliest Backpacker
Published 2019 by Hornet Books
Text © Kathryn Barnes
This Work © Hornet Books Ltd
Paperback ISBN 978-0-9957658-4-9
Also available as an ebook

Editor: David Roberts
Proofreader: Suzannah Young
Map: Leslie Hackmeier

Hornet Books
Ground Floor, 2B Vantage Park, Washingley Road,
Huntingdon, PE29 6SR

www.hornetbooks.com

info@hornetbooks.com

Printed and bound in Great Britain by
CPI Group (UK) Ltd, Croydon CR0 4YY

For Mum, my champion,
whose unconditional love
and support have always inspired me
to follow my dreams.

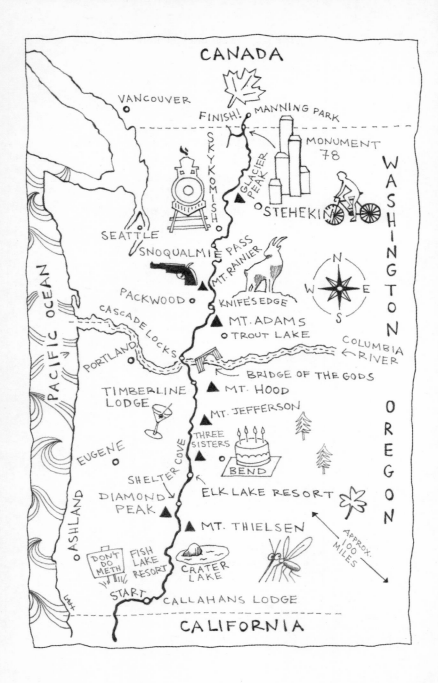

"The power of imagination makes us infinite."

John Muir

The National Parks and Forest Reservations (1896)

Prologue

The trail came to an abrupt end. On a precipice high above timberline, I gingerly peered over the edge. Nothing but a sheer expanse of silent, glistening snow lay beyond. It dawned on me: *this* must be Devil's Peak; what a fitting name. But while people had warned it might be a little sketchy, we hadn't met a single person who'd faced it this season.

Awkwardly releasing my hefty backpack to the ground, I further surveyed our surroundings. The mountain's northern aspect revealed a scene far removed from the shale and burnt trees of a few moments earlier. A sea of evergreen mountains stretched between us and Canada, yet we found ourselves stuck in a concentration of lingering snow.

"What happened to the trail?" I muttered, helpful as ever.

Without answering, Conrad reached for his phone to consult the GPS.

I began wandering the ridge, hands on hips, nervously looking up at the crisp sky. It was getting late. The afternoon sun drew long shadows, casting the snowfield into shade. We had reached the end. There was no possible way through. Just eight days into our Pacific Crest Trial adventure and this was it.

To make matters worse, our water situation was critically low. The last collection opportunity had been at a small hidden spring ten hours ago. According to the map the next water source lay less than a mile ahead; a place we should have reached by now. I instinctively checked for the reassurance of a phone signal. No service. As feared.

"Right," Conrad began hesitantly, pointing across the white carpet nose-diving down the mountain, "the trail is buried *somewhere* over there... no one's going through that, it's way too dangerous..."

We both began scanning for footprints. In the last two days of hiking through the Sky Lakes Wilderness we had met exactly two people. But they were professional hikers who had easily overtaken us hours ago. Surely they must have left some kind of prints to follow, if indeed they had even made it this far?

Without the cover of my pack I started to appreciate how cold it was. The wind hitting my back-sweat sent chills down my spine. Conrad walked back to the edge of the icy crag, peering over its steep drop-off.

"We need to get down there," he said, motioning a long way below to where the snow seemed to level out into wide pitches of nothingness, "the next spring can't be far."

Dread began building in my stomach as my mind raced through the desperateness of our situation.

He continued with a bit more confidence, "yeah, it's do-able, it looks like someone has skied down here."

I remained silent.

"Yeah, we can slide down, it'll be alright."

He was fooling no one. I shuffled over to share his view. It looked a long, perilous way down.

A defiant "F**K OFF!" – or words to that effect – formed my immediate response, assuming he was joking, but as he began shortening his telescopic hiking poles I realised he was not.

I could only watch as he strapped up before taking a seat in the snow. With his long legs dangling over the edge, he focused on calculating a route down.

The last words he said to me as he looked back over his shoulder did nothing to calm my nerves.

"You've got to control your speed, dig your feet into the snow, and DON'T let your poles get stuck, or you'll break an arm…. oh, and make sure you steer away from *those* trees!"

And with those reassuring words he was gone. I watched as his backpack-laden torso rapidly slid off into the distance, gaining momentum, a little rocky, but luckily managing an abrupt halt just before a row of pine trees far below. He was safe.

I did a quick mental fact-check. *No signal. No roads out. No water. No choice,* being the ultimate conclusion. I was completely alone in the still air. Conrad was not getting back up here. This was my moment.

I did the only thing I could. I buckled up my pack, grabbed my poles, sat down in Conrad's imprint, took a deep breath to steady my pounding heart, and pushed.

1

Call to the Wild

Mum looked at me, baffled. "You're going to do what?" Unable to wrap her head around it.

"Hike from California to Canada," I responded, with a growing sense of discouragement.

Okay, so deep-down I knew how crazy the plan sounded, coming from me, a self-confessed creature-comfort-loving city girl. Yes, I, who up until this very moment considered holidays lying beside a pool with a Mai Tai as an adventure. All the same, I felt a hint of betrayal with mum's doubt.

"Have you forgotten about the Brownies?" Mum persisted.

She was referring to my brief stint with the local Brownie pack, aged seven. I had joined to copy my neighbour Paula, the girl a school year above me with brilliant blonde hair who I looked up to with longing envy. I held mighty ambitions for membership: filling the empty sash with badges was the ultimate challenge; one that would piss my mum off because she hated sewing. But just weeks after forking out for the ugly yellow and brown uniform, Brown Owl announced the upcoming summer camp. That was it. I lasted perhaps a dozen sessions, earnt a couple of badges, but upon hearing the word "camp" decided to make a swift exit from a promising Brownie career. Mum was not impressed.

I certainly hated camping. I managed to avoid it for most of my life, with one exception. In high school I signed up for the Duke of Edinburgh scheme, a youth achievement award designed to enable teenagers to be the "best they can be" and give back to the community. In truth, my motivation was less altruistic; I did it purely to gain advantage on my university application form. Unfortunately for me, it involved a horrific expedition in the South Downs, ending with a team of six girls having a screaming match in the middle of a rain storm. Camped amongst mounds of cowpat in a boggy field with my gear soaked through, I shared a plastic survival bag with Louise Moses in one tent while the other four squeezed into the second. My sobbing 2 a.m. dash to a payphone begging to be picked up had proven fruitless. The next morning it transpired my lone companion had developed measles. What are the odds? Thinking back, I'm pretty sure that, while crying myself to sleep that night on the hard ground, I'd vowed: *never again.*

I guess I could see where Mum's doubt was coming from. But the more sceptics I heard who branded my husband Conrad and me as crazy, the more determined I felt. Stubbornness being a quality deeply entrenched in my soul.

Ironically, we couldn't have been further from living in the wild when the plan to hike the Pacific Crest Trail came into being. It was December 2015; we lay on a beach soaking up some much-needed winter sun in a five-star beach resort in Dubai. We should have been feeling pretty pleased with ourselves, but behind the façade the two of us were in our thirties, childless, and living in a small flat in London with a growing sense of restlessness. Conrad spent a large proportion of his days working in a bank purely to pay our mortgage, as two years earlier I had abruptly fallen off the career ladder. I won't bore you with the details, but life working in a high-stress, low-reward, competitive team of back-stabbers was not for me. With a deep sense of failure and shame, I sought medical help, culminating in months of counselling to deal with the event, but unlike with television psychology couches, no *eureka* breakthroughs ensued. I was left unemployed and empty, struggling to understand what my next move should be.

Growing up, I honestly thought I was going to be someone special. Perhaps all kids feel the same way. There's definitely a growing sense of entitlement amongst millennials today, but what I speak of is nineties optimism. I belonged to a generation who grew up with an ill-founded belief that we could have it all. And why wouldn't we think that? We'd grown up in a safe country, had access to world-class education, free healthcare, and became teenagers during the internet boom. The world seemed to yield infinite possibilities. For those coming of age in London in the late nineties, hopefulness was further endorsed by the appointment of New Labour, who blasted out sound-bites of D:ream's 'Things Can Only Get Better', whilst promising an opportunity-rich New Britain, as The Spice Girls sang about *Girl Power*.

It's no surprise I entered adulthood with high hopes. I may not have figured out *exactly* what I was going to be just yet – didn't have a clue – but I was sure it would be something *mega*-successful and high-powered. Failing that I'd probably just marry Prince William – he was about my age after all. However, this confidence slowly eroded throughout my twenties. The planes struck the Twin Towers during my first term at uni and, in the years that followed I discovered that the realities of New Britain centred around fighting global economic recession and fending off terrorism on the streets of London. As a graduate, I found myself in an unexpected game of survival, battling the real world of office jobs while trying to appear happy and successful in the face of growing online scrutiny. Facebook had come to Britain during my first year out of school, making an already competitive environment even worse. In essence, it wasn't quite the place my childhood-self had imagined.

Now, suddenly in my thirties and married, I wasn't feeling how people in my position are supposed to feel. For some reason I wasn't content with just getting pregnant, buying a house, a dog, and raising a family like everybody else. I didn't know why, other than to say that deep down I felt – and still feel – hopelessly young and wanted to shun the trapping responsibilities of adulthood. I mean, wasn't being married *adult* enough? I craved a change, I craved adventure; most of all I longed to be transported away from the distractions of my chaotic London life.

As I sat staring at the lapping Persian Gulf, my mind began to wander. I leaned over to Conrad, who looked worryingly red on the sun lounger next to me and blurted out: "We should hike the PCT."

He glanced back with a wry smile: "You know that involves camping, right?"

He probably thought I was just teasing for a reaction. He certainly wouldn't have dared say what he was probably thinking – that I was completely incapable of such a feat.

But I replied dead seriously, in a long and blabbering string of justifications: "I could deal with camping if I had to... big difference between this sort of camping and *choosing* to do it for fun.... it would be a challenge..."

My mind was still processing. "I mean... I don't mean doing the WHOLE thing... maybe just half of it. I don't wanna do the desert part, no way! I hear people have *died* from exposure and dehydration out there!"

Conrad's body language shifted. He slowly shimmied up, realising I wasn't joking – but was still amused. He was a far more adventurous traveller than me. After university he had taken a gap year and backpacked half the world, including very impoverished parts of India where he had lost a stone and a half after contracting a nasty food-related virus, but just like me he was no naturally "outdoorsy" person. Even his days of hostelling, he asserted, were well and truly behind him. After all, just look at where we were.

"You're so ridiculous," he teased, "you read one book, and out of the blue, you're off!"

So yes, predictably like many others I had just finished reading *Wild: From Lost to Found on the Pacific Crest Trail* by Cheryl Strayed. The movie starring Reese Witherspoon would be released just months later, inspiring thousands of would-be hikers to hit the trail, but at that point I liked to think of myself as an early adopter. Cheryl's tale was inspirational. And while I admit to being no natural born-adventurer or thrill-seeker, strangely the depiction of physical hardship, including the painful loss of toenails, didn't put me off. Instead, I became captivated by the sense of freedom she described. One line in particular resonated; I'd ponder it time and time again: "*How wild it was to let it be.*"

I wanted to be able to *let things be*, despite the fact that it undermined my uptight, perfectionist nature. So what if deep down I wanted to run away for a bit? Say *adios* to life's daily woes. To live my own adventure. Surely, I can't be the only city resident to have fantasised about teleporting into a quieter, simpler life? Even if it was just for a few months. As I went on to explain to Conrad, it might even provide the much-needed headspace to decide what we *really* wanted to do with the rest of our lives. Yes, it all seemed to make perfect sense.

On the beach that day we agreed to "look into it". At that point we knew very little about the trail and hiking in general, so were far from committed. Cheryl had hiked 1,100 miles of the trail, breaking up the sections due to bad weather, but at 2,650 miles in total, there was a lot of potential ground to cover.

***

Over the next few weeks, the more I thought about the potential life benefits of the hike, the more enthusiastic I became. Conrad and I had both dealt with health issues over the previous year and hiking would get us super fit, the fittest we'd ever been – and what girl wouldn't jump at the prospect of losing a few pounds? Better still, I could make shed-loads of money for charity, doing good for the world with every step. Upon returning from Dubai I'd immediately logged into Amazon and ordered us a couple more hiking-inspired reads, which we distributed between us, whetting our appetites each night with adventurous tales from the rugged Wild West.

For those unfamiliar, the Pacific Crest Trail is a national scenic hiking trail that navigates the western backbone of the United States. It stretches the entire length of the country, beginning at a wire fence marking the Mexican border – possibly to be replaced by a wall soon – continuing all the way up to Canada. Distance-wise, a European equivalent would begin in Amsterdam, pass through eight countries and end up in Istanbul. PCT hikers negotiate varied terrain, starting with arid desert in the south, leading up into the Californian Sierra Nevada mountains, through volcanic ranges and culminating in the conifer-clad Northern Cascades. The ultra-motivated people who attempt to *thru-hike* the entire trail in one go face a race against the changing seasons, which more often than not results in failure. [1]

For us Brits, reading about the changing weather was a rather foreign concept. As London is protected by the Gulf Stream, we

---

[1] Just 12 per cent completed the entire trail in 2017, based on 3,934 thru-hiker permits issued by the PCTA, versus 491 self-reported finishers. Due to informal reporting, statistics are unverified.

enjoy a fairly consistently-average climate of cloud-cloaked dampness. In the U.S. they have *real* summers. The kind where kids enjoy endless days playing on the beach, where coats and umbrellas are not required. Yet for hikers, the summer sun makes the Californian desert brutally hot to navigate. And by the time most reach northern Washington, the leaves have changed, signifying summer's end and the risk of visibility-limiting snow storms. Snow is the thru-hiker's nemesis. It can render the trail impassable in an instant, forcing hikers who have made it that far to quit in one very anti-climactic ending. The weather therefore creates an obvious window of hiking opportunity. With this in mind, it seemed sensible on our first overnight backpacking trip to avoid the desert. We couldn't afford to leave London until May anyway, by which time the desert would be relentlessly hot, with water sources scarce. I also felt troubled by the legal requirement to carry a bear can in sections of California, a sure-fire indication that bear activity was rampant.

Oregon appealed to me. Ever since road-tripping along its coast a few years earlier I'd wanted to return. Travel articles describing the beauty of the inland Cascade mountain range cemented the decision. All this eventually helped pinpoint a route: starting as close to the northern Californian border as possible, we would hike north-bound (NoBo) through Oregon and Washington, covering nearly one thousand miles.

Planning for such a long hike ended up being far more time-consuming and expensive than we imagined. After all, we were starting entirely from scratch. My day job became reading hiking blogs and gear reviews to know what to buy, and consuming endless YouTube videos on whatever I guessed would be useful, skill-related stuff to know. At some point, without realising it, we had become emotionally invested, having foolishly egged each other on. Just after Christmas we spiralled pass the point of no return by booking flights to San Francisco. A visit to the U.S. Embassy in London followed one rainy February morning. Our entire trip depended on gaining the all-important six-month tourist visa.

What is it about people who work in embassies? They begin

the intimidation tactics before you have even set foot through the door. Maybe it's in the hope that if you are some kind of fraudster or terrorist who wants to do harm to their country they'll psychologically crack you. At the airport-style x-ray machines Conrad was pulled aside and commanded to throw away a small travel padlock attached to his bag. What harm they thought we could do with it stumped us, but we weren't prepared to argue with the U.S. Military.

We sat in a giant beige hall crowded with hopeful faces until our number eventually appeared on the screen, summoning us to a designated window. The all-important visa interview took place with a stern female immigration officer, who sat eye-balling us from behind a Perspex screen.

She opened the exchange in an almost robotic voice: "What is the purpose of your intended visit to the United States?"

Conrad replied with caution, "we're planning to hike the Pacific Crest Trail."

"You do a lot of camping then?" she pressed, with a stern air of authority.

Oh crap, she's trying to catch us out!

Conrad's brain must have been processing overtime, but he quickly answered evenly. "We were in the Smokies, just six months ago."

A reference to our last trip to the U.S. – smart move. Without lying, or revealing what complete camping amateurs we were, he had cleverly managed to *allude* to our affinity with nature. He neglected to mention the fact that we had actually been road-tripping through Tennessee, so hadn't camped once, or that we didn't even own a tent.

Meanwhile I stood in stony-faced silence. Hyper aware of all the surrounding surveillance, I tried hard to look normal and law-abiding, even though I am normal and law-abiding. I was nervous about being unemployed as this was not my first rodeo with U.S. customs officials. I suspected they were likely to grill us on funding, suspiciously assuming that everyone wants to ditch their current lives and move to the "Land of the Free" to work illegally, spiralling America's economy into the gutter.

The questions came and must have been satisfactorily

answered, because she stamped some forms, and with it we were cleared. What an enormous relief.

With hiking permits from the Pacific Crest Trail Organisation easily secured, our last mission on the paper-stamping circuit was to gain permission from Canada to enter their country by foot. I couldn't imagine what scene would play out should we actually reach Canada. It felt like such a stretch. Would there be a giant maple-leaf flag in the soil? Or an official line to step over? Or a horse-riding Mountie to greet us and stamp our passports?

Unfortunately this step provided our only potential setback. Weeks of despair ensued when my permit returned as expected, with Conrad's nowhere to be seen. I teased him: obviously there must be a wanted convict or terrorist out there matching his name and description and it was only a matter of time until the Canadian men in black would swoop in to apprehend him. Finally though, to our relief, his permit arrived two weeks later. He now had no excuse to bail. Permissions granted.

Despite all the time spent on what we called "hiker-min", including the project management involved with putting our London life on hold, it still didn't feel real. At that point, even though I was excited, under the surface doubts were brewing. The reality of the situation intensified the closer we got to May. Friends started asking if we were hiking for charity and although it had been my original intention, the doubter in me suddenly became petrified we would fail and let people down. The charity element brought with it a deeper level of scrutiny; I hadn't even posted our hiking intentions online for this very reason. Failure would be a disaster. And anyway, as I justified to myself, failure was not completely within our control either; the weather, or forest fires were just two in a long list of reasons quitting may become essential. So I told people we simply wanted a challenge, and felt terribly guilty about it. I secretly vowed to donate a lump sum to a charity I had worked with a few years back if and when I got a real job.

In our remaining weeks in London I constantly analysed the cracks in our plan but wouldn't admit them out loud. It didn't help that family members were actually taking bets against our likely failure. Yes, they had that much confidence in our ability to survive! On this topic there were generally three schools of thought:

1) We wouldn't make it a week before realising our mistake – the over-whelming consensus.
2) We might just reach Crater Lake, our first re-supply stop, then decide we'd had enough and quit.
3) Stubbornness would carry us all the way to Canada – only my brother Tom believed this.

2

Gearing Up

We touched down in San Francisco on *Cinco De Mayo*, aka May 5th, a Mexican holiday dedicated to an important victory against the French back in 1862. The festival is still celebrated in parts of the U.S., though the meaning behind the day's significance has become overshadowed by an emphasis on eating tacos and drinking copious amounts of margarita, something akin to college kids in Cabo on Spring Break. This I learnt in the back of a speeding car driven by my cousin Chris on the way to his popular local Mexican restaurant, having just been met by him at the airport. Shame Chris hadn't actually had the foresight to book a table at a Mexican restaurant, on a Mexican holiday. After two laps of the car park and some wise-cracks from us, he conceded defeat and we all went for pizza.

Chris is my cockney older cousin, who fortuitously found himself living in America, having married Leslie, a red-headed Californian girl, ten years earlier. He held out for a few years but had long since forgotten how "pants" are actually called "trousers", "elevators" are indeed "lifts" – and don't even get me started on his pronunciation of "route". What a total sell-out.

The *Marshmeiers,* as I like to call them – a non-intelligent hacking together of their surnames – are very laid-back people. They probably didn't even consider the intrusion when agreeing to put us up for three weeks as we prepared for D-Day. I think Chris just welcomes any reminder of home, which we provided in the form of a suitcase laden with dried stuffing mix, HP sauce, and Hobnob biscuits. Perhaps best we don't tell the customs officials.

During our stay, the thought of Conrad and me hiking through the wilderness gave the Marshmeiers endless amusement. Usually over a beer or cocktail in one of their local dive bars, they would gleefully tease us, picking holes in our sketchy hiking plan, which when voiced out loud was undeniably pretty damn sketchy. It certainly involved a lot of "ifs" and "maybes". Since I can remember, Chris has always revelled in taking the piss out of me, like an older brother; his cheeks turn red and, just like his dad, his shoulders shift up and down as he chuckles. Chris' stance towards our hike firmly subscribed him to the "quit after a few days" school of thought. He liked to joke a lot about his impending trip up to Oregon to pick us up. Leslie was a little more optimistic, but fell short of absolute Canadian endorsement. I couldn't blame her.

They – or realistically I should say Leslie – were to be entrusted with a vital role in our mission: posting our resupply boxes. The hiker resupply box consists of certain food and essentials which, due to the relative isolation of the trail, would likely be difficult to buy. Some hikers choose to wing it, but not us. After all, I was the fussiest eater I knew, so needed this element of control. Contained in a spreadsheet in true management-consultant style, was an outline of *guesstimated* arrival dates and corresponding addresses of the places we aspired to reach entirely by foot. It all felt pretty finger-in-the-air, but we emailed it to Leslie nevertheless, alongside a statement reinforcing that our lives now depended upon her.

Our limited PCT training began on a day far too hot for a couple of pasty Londoners to be out walking, let alone attempting to scale a 3,000-foot mountain. It was Day 3 in California and we had taken an Uber to Mount Diablo State Park for our first attempted test hike. The backpacks we carried were mostly empty because we still didn't own the majority of the kit we needed – a fact I would later blame for much of our difficulties – and the shoes on our feet were old gym trainers, totally impractical footwear for the PCT. We actually didn't end up buying our final hiking shoes until the very last moment because it turned out to be an impossibly difficult, stressful decision to make. I mean, this was a big commitment. These shoes needed to carry us all the way to Canada. They needed to be comfortable for miles of repetitive all-day use, over unknown and changing terrain. And how were we supposed to decide whether to go with waterproof over ventilated? Boot over low-rise? And then there's varying toe-box shapes and instep support to worry about too. The possibilities and high stakes made my head want to explode.

Anyway, back to Diablo. Halfway up our climb, weary legs struggling, we welcomed the sight of a couple of picnic tables situated under the shade of a tree. We sat there and ate a couple of melted Snickers bars – stupidly the only food we had brought with us, thinking we would be quick – while watching a small party on the other table enjoying a full picnic feast. Yes, we had massively under-estimated how long it was going to take us to reach the summit. Thoroughly unprepared as we were, not only did we have little water left on a searing hot day, we had also been scaling quiet back-trails without a proper map assuming that our phone's GPS would be sufficient. It wasn't. We had been lost twice.

As we began making reluctant moves to continue, we caught the attention of the group.

"Are you guys training for something?" the gentleman shouted over in a friendly voice.

Once the three lady hikers and their male companion heard about our PCT ambitions they instantly struck up an animated conversation. They were a local hiking group on their way back down from the summit, so despite being at least thirty years older than us, they obviously possessed far superior stamina when it came to hills. The man who went by the nickname Shroomer, was a retired parole officer and veteran triple-crowner, having thru-hiked the Pacific Crest, Appalachian, and Continental Divide trails. With such hiking credentials, he began giving us tips about gear. Conrad and I took notes on our phones and were astonished when this stranger invited us to visit his home to walk through his full kit assortment. We took his details not quite sure if we'd attracted some sort of weirdo, and just as they were about to leave, Shroomer turned back to ask if we needed a map.

We looked at each other sheepishly, embarrassed to admit our obvious lack of forward-planning.

But before either of us said a word in response, Shroomer pulled a folded paper map out of his backpack and handed it over, reassuring us that he had loads of them at home.

Feeling indebted by his kindness, we thanked him and were wished "happy trails" by one of the departing women.

We finally reached the summit at 4:30 p.m. Arriving in the carpark of the small visitor centre where we had expected to buy snacks, we soon realised that it had closed just minutes earlier. The place was now deserted. Our only reprieve was a small water fountain, where one by one we refilled our bottles and chugged down much-needed hydration. As we stood there we witnessed the occasional cyclist arrive up the road, look at the view, then turn around to speed back down. At that point we didn't even consider the fact that it had taken us nearly five hours to hike just over seven miles. Our only concern was getting off the mountain before it got dark. My heart was jittering at the prospect of getting caught without head torches in an area, according to the warning posters, inhabited by mountain lions. At least we now had a map and gravity on our side.

Just before 7 p.m., in the rapidly-fading light we reached the park exit. The last few hours had passed in a blur of nerve-wracking panic, moving at marching-pace down an old fire road – a route selected in case it got dark or we needed rescuing. Its gravel surface had pounded my feet, buckled my knees, and a mile before the end a mosquito lodged itself in Conrad's left eye. We just couldn't get the bugger out, so by the time we reached the trailhead any passers-by would have seen a grown man cry. Tomorrow we vowed, whilst resting our sore limbs, to debrief all the various ways in which we had f****d up this little escapade in an attempt to learn from our mistakes. For now we just needed food, a shower, and a bed, in that order.

The thing about learning is it's a continuous process. Our first practice-camp a week later wasn't plain-sailing either. Back at the park's Juniper campground, we found our designated pitch complete with picnic table and fire ring conveniently located for the bathroom block. Yet before we even started to "make camp" like camping people do, Conrad thought it would be neat to film a time-lapse version of us putting up the tent for the first time. While he busied himself with a tripod I started emptying items onto the picnic table. But as our food bag came into view we got ourselves a visitor. The racoon looked cute enough, from a distance, yet his small pointy nose and bushy, striped tail became less endearing the closer the cocky little thing got.

"Why isn't he scared of us?" I anxiously shouted over to Conrad, who was still playing around with the camera.

"He will be. Watch." Conrad changed focus towards trying to shoo the racoon away, who in turn got closer, staring at us, completely unfazed through dark beady eyes.

"OK, it's not cute now! Get rid of him!" I started pulling the food back into my backpack before darting around to avoid the rogue, feral beast, who was, in my mind, going to bite and infect us with rabies. The fact that neither of us had opted for rabies vaccinations suddenly seemed a bad call.

Conrad changed tack and began throwing small rocks around the rascal, causing the adverse effect of drawing him even closer to sniff each rock thinking it was food. This went on for some time until he eventually seemed to get the message and disappeared to stalk another camp. This ridiculous episode in which two adults felt terrorised by a small animal, demonstrates that we didn't quite possess the *typical* long-distance hiker's affinity with nature. Up to that point, with the odd dog walk or jog in Epping Forest, I had considered myself a nature-*liker* at the very least. But then again, the scariest animals I had ever seen there were a pack of geese.

By the time Conrad finally got the camera ready for action, the sun was getting low. We had obviously learnt a lot from our first trip up the same mountain just days before. The final video of us erecting the tent timed our efforts at 46 minutes and resembled a Laurel and Hardy sketch. To be clear, this involved nothing more than putting together a simple tent consisting of laying a groundsheet, snapping together a one-piece frame, clipping onto it the main inner tent, before covering it with a rain fly and securing it. Yet we fumbled away, clipping things together, scratching our heads, un-doing, re-doing, while my frustration towards Conrad – whose job it had been to "test" the tent on the Marshmeiers living room floor – grew exponentially.

The next step in what felt like a theatrical play where we pretended to be *real* campers, was dinner. Now requiring a head torch to see clearly, I began lighting the stove to cook our pasta meal. Such a simple task proved to be a huge challenge. Using a small plastic measuring cup to pour alcohol fuel from the flask into the burner, I spilt so much of it over myself that the flame died before we could even boil a pan of water. Yes, on a one-night camp we had managed to run out of fuel and I now smelt like a walking petrol station. We ate our pasta *al dente* style, while keeping a watchful eye out for our pesky friend.

I felt deflated as we finally hiked out of the park the next day in dense morning mist. The night had been awful; neither of us barely got a wink of sleep. Who knew, after such a blisteringly hot day, by midnight the temperature would plummet so much we would be shivering in California in May? Our new and expensive sleeping bags with temperature ratings of minus-nine degrees had worryingly not helped. The reality of camping amidst the trees had turned out to be far less rosy than imagined. I wasn't sure if I could take another night of it, desperate to be back in a real bed, so I decided to mentally block out the inevitable back-to-back nights of wilderness camping required to hike the PCT.

In summary, the training was not going well. Casting aside our original intentions, we camped just twice more before hitting the trail. Once was in a highly-rated private camp ground along the Big Sur, complete with immaculate showering facilities, which we drove right up to. The other involved a five-mile trek and no showers, but crucially had a picnic table to sit at and other people around to provide a sense of safety. Both times we awoke after an awful night of sleep, packed up as quickly as possible, and made a beeline for the nearest diner.

About ten days into our stay at the Marshmeiers, our plan hit a snag. The big start date we had been counting down to for months was May 30th. This date had been decided mostly by fate, having managed to secure a two-night reservation at Crater Lake Lodge from June 7th. Crater Lake was to be our first key milestone, so the room would provide a rewarding rest after completing our first hundred miles of outdoor living.

Whilst in California we checked the daily weather forecasts to see how hot it was going to be in Concord. It was sweltering, and obviously not used to such heat, we worried it would be too hot to hike – or we were looking for an excuse not to anyhow. As we aimlessly surfed the web that day, Conrad stumbled across a site containing a colour-coded map detailing the current snow conditions for the west coast. Unsurprisingly, northern Washington state was still showing a lot of purple, the colour representing snow. Surely that would all be clear by the time we hiked there in late July, so we didn't think much of it. But upon further study, peaks throughout Oregon were also dotted with a lighter lilac shading. Conrad shared his findings and together we wondered what, if anything, it meant to our plans.

I took over the laptop and loaded The Crater Lake National Park website. The park's live webcam feed revealed the crater rim and visitor centre were both coated in snow. But from those angles it was impossible to tell how *much* snow and if it would inconvenience the trails. The sky looked blue, so maybe it would melt in a few days. We had little over a week to go.

I decided to call the park ranger station to get some professional insight. Perhaps the road closures outlined on the website were out of date. The phone rang for ages, then a voicemail instructed me to leave a message if I wanted a call back, so I did. All we could do now was wait.

"Ma'am, the trail is closed," said the polite but stern ranger who eventually called back.

Had I heard right? Trail CLOSED?! What the f**k?

Brushing aside what I thought sounded like an element of *you stupid idiot* in his tone, I responded with hope.

"Isn't there a way through on foot?"

"We haven't seen any hikers come through yet. It's been a high snow year. Crews still need to get in there to survey the trail damage. From what we've seen so far, there are over two-hundred trees down in the first half-mile section alone. That's going to take some time to clear."

My brain was confused, and from my worried tone, Conrad had started paying attention to the conversation, hovering over my shoulder.

Much to my dismay, the ranger continued, "we won't be able to get in there 'til after the roads are ploughed."

Of course, America prioritised clearing the roads so that

people could witness the natural wonders from the comfort of their giant SUVs. Completely flummoxed, I asked how long that would take.

"We can't say, ma'am."

"What about the Lodge? We have a reservation there on June 7th."

"The Rim Drive and North entrance are closed but we got a crew going through in the next coup'la days, so you should be good to drive there, 'least from the south entrance. We advise you check back with our website for the latest details."

Now completely crestfallen, I muttered some thanks and hung up. What a disaster. It hadn't even dawned on us that the PCT could be *closed*. I mean, it was summertime, wasn't it? And how could such a popular national park not be completely open for the rapidly approaching Memorial Day weekend? Even in England it's sunny in June. It's one of the few months you can usually stand outside a pub in the city. Yes, it may shower on you a little, and we're not really set up for *al fresco* dining, but generally, it's one of the more promising months. Where did this leave us?

After three weeks it felt like we had outstayed our welcome at the Marshmeiers. There is only so long you can clutter a person's house before it starts feeling a bit awkward. It wasn't fair on any of us; they needed their house back and I needed a night without Chris' snoring. Having made the reluctant decision to delay our hike start date by three weeks, which we determined was the maximum time we could wait and still make it to Canada, we booked a hire car. A plan quickly formed to hit the road on a circular road-trip, cruising west towards the coast, then south down the Big Sur coastal highway, before looping north up to Oregon. Trying to spend as little money as possible, our focus was on getting in some practice hikes, given our maximum daily distance was still only about seven miles, and completing a few nights of camping to test out the new equipment. In a stroke of luck we secured a cancellation popping up at Crater Lake Lodge, so as long as we could reach it by June 30th we had a guaranteed bed.

Not knowing where the last three weeks had gone, other than darting about between sports shops and supermarkets, we desperately spent our last couple of days inside the house, frantically pulling together our new kit and packing resupply boxes. This was a time-consuming and stressful job, because to be honest we didn't really know what we were doing. It was all guess work. How is someone supposed to know how much they can carry, versus how many days and how much energy it would take to hike each section weeks in advance? If we messed up our calculations and didn't pack enough, well, what then? And how much toilet roll does an individual get through in a five-day period? Mixing scoops of oatmeal (something I hadn't eaten since I was a child) into plastic Ziploc bags with spoons of sugar and powdered milk felt tedious. There was always a sinking feeling that all this effort could be in vain; that we wouldn't see the box again if we failed to reach the destined collection point.

Hoping we wouldn't be seeing them anytime soon – a sure-fire signal of our defeat – we hugged the Marshmeiers goodbye one oppressively-hot Sunday afternoon and hit the road. I remember hoping they wouldn't be the last family members to ever see us alive. What would they tell my mum?

3

Fear-Mongering

The night before the hike I didn't sleep a wink. Absolute, palpable fear held such a tight grip I felt like I couldn't breathe. It was surreal. After all the time spent planning and daydreaming from a flat in London, suddenly I found myself in Oregon with little more than the clothes on my back. I wanted to wake up Conrad and tell him it had all been a massive joke and he had idiotically fallen hook, line and sinker. In the worrying, I realised I shouldn't have secretly watched *Silence of the Lambs* as a child. Those kinds of films are rated 18 for a reason: they're deeply disturbing and can scar a child for life. This, and many other late-night Channel 4 films like *It* and *Hellraiser*, was inspiring my overly-active imagination to continually insert myself into a catalogue of gruesome endings, endings which now seemed inevitable. What was I thinking? Things had gotten beyond foolish. This was *dangerous*, and I was totally to blame.

Over the past months I had dedicated a great deal of brain power to developing a comprehensive wilderness fear list, playing out on internal loop, reducing me to a nervous wreck. Topping this list: bears and cougars. Just to clarify, I mean cougars of the *mountain lion* variety, not sexual-predatory older women. Thankfully we don't get bears or large cats in England, so I've never had to worry about them while walking through the woods. My ignorance was obliterated when, a few weeks before leaving England, Conrad Googled "cougar" and presented me with a slideshow of images.

"Bloody hell! THAT'S a cougar?" was my immediate reaction, glancing at the screen, "they're the size of a lion!"

"Yeah. Not quite what I pictured either," he conceded.

"But I thought they were more like big *cats*!"

"Yeah, me too." He continued scrolling through more pictures, "guess they're *really big* cats."

"Maybe the pictures are fake?" I suggested doubfully.

Conrad's eyes were transfixed on one particular image which portrayed a camouflaged hunter proudly flaunting a limp feline corpse at the camera.

"Nah, they're real. Isn't it sad to see them dead?"

I had to agree. Cougars are extraordinary-looking creatures. With piercing eyes and regal faces somewhat softened by long white whiskers. And those giant kitten-like paws! So cute. The cat in the photo looked a bit like teenage Simba from *The Lion King*. It was indeed sad; I hated those hunters. How could someone take pride in killing such a beautiful beast? Beautiful – but I still didn't want to meet one.

This belief became absolute certainty as Conrad continued: "You know they go for the jugular."

"What?" My anxiety level was rising rapidly. "You mean humans?"

"Just in general. This says they're *ambush predators*, so they stalk their prey, sometimes for miles, then leap from behind for the knock-out bite. Mostly it's young children though, or smaller animals."

I am only five-foot-four, so he had my full attention. "They eat people?!"

"Not many, but some. There's a few news reports of killings."

"Any in Washington or Oregon?"

He scanned down the screen. "Hmm, there's a couple of deaths in Oregon, can't see any for Washington, it's more dead pets and livestock. And non-fatal attacks."

I glared at him. "How many?"

"I don't think we need to worry about it," suddenly realising his error and beginning to back-track, "we're talking less than a handful. They're much more common in Canada. And they don't really *like* people. They usually stay away from busy places."

It was the thought of being in their crosshairs over a distance while they slowly hunted us down that sent chills down my spine. Conrad would be alright, he's over six-foot tall and skinny so they wouldn't want him. But me! Short and stocky, I'd make the best pork chops they'd ever tasted. I made a mental note to select a backpack that would tower above me to conceal my juicy neck, because with the average male cougar weighing 140 pounds there would be no contest if he decided to prey on us. I would forever remind myself of this while sitting on the trail without my pack on. Must watch my back.

Compelled by this startling new information I hunted online for some reassurance, but it really wasn't a good idea to start with the search phrase: "cougar attacks Oregon." Just that month a man named Malvin Jamison had shot dead a pouncing cougar about 200 miles east of the PCT in what he asserted was a "kill-or-be-killed" situation. And then there were stories where the cat was the victor. In 2004 Mark Jeffrey Reynolds, a 35-year-old mountain biker was struck, killed, and partially eaten by a cougar whilst bending over to fix his bike chain in Orange County California. And back in 2001, 30-year-old Frances Frost was slaughtered while cross-country skiing close to Banff National Park in Alberta. I wondered whether these were spontaneous kills or the result of a prolonged hunt.

I was eating this stuff up despite knowing how news reports love to sensationalise – "if it bleeds it leads"after all. Statistically I knew it was unlikely a cougar, mountain lion, or puma, whatever you call them, would attack us. Yet what a horrible way to go. I wondered about the pain, the fear, how long it would take to lose consciousness when being mauled by a beast, and considered those harrowing last moments of life. Following hours of research, the top piece of advice for anyone unlucky enough to come face-to-face with a cougar seemed to be: whatever you do, DON'T stimulate the cat's instinct to chase.

Bears are far more common on the trail than cougars. I found many hiking blogs and articles detailing bear encounters. Rather confusingly though, the instructional information out there outlines different tactics for dealing with black and grizzly bears, and sometimes black bears can be brown or even blond. I embedded to memory a few key take-aways. Firstly, black bears are skittish and should be more frightened of us. In theory anyway. Second, grizzlies are meaner. They are the variety more likely to attack, and if they do, the best option is to make yourself appear dead; think Leonardo DiCaprio getting torn to shreds in

The Revenant – that was a GRIZZLY bear. Next up, both bears are scavengers so will be seriously attracted to the smell of food, so we needed to be careful with storage and disposal of our precious supplies. And finally, whatever you do: DON'T SURPRISE BEARS. This is especially the case if they have cubs with them. They will not appreciate the surprise, and will likely attack if they feel threatened.

We had seen a couple of bears before. I had been frightened by a resident black bear on a quiet dawn hike in Tennessee's Great Smoky Mountains the previous fall. We were hiking in single-file following a stream which ran through a steep valley floor. Sun rays filtered through the gaps in the tree branches overhead. It was peaceful with the quiet sounds of birds singing and the soothing flow of water, until a loud clatter of breaking twigs abruptly pierced the calm. We both stopped in our tracks and shot a look towards it. Up on the opposite bank, less than 300 feet ahead, was an enormous black bear hunched over in the brush. He had spotted us too. For a few moments we watched each other. I didn't dare breathe. He was so much bigger than the mother and cub we had seen from the car the day before. Initially thankful for the water between us, I realised the stream at this point actually wasn't very wide or deep. Conrad must have been more confident the bear wasn't about to charge, because he started removing his small daypack to retrieve the camera. That movement seemed to trigger something in the bear and within seconds he galloped away up the steep hill, disappearing into the foliage. The episode was over before a single flash occurred, but for the rest of that hike I was on high alert, scanning the forest for anything that moved.

Back at home, I carefully scrutinised a map illustrating American bear habitats. According to the map, the PCT mainly runs through black bear territory, however the northern tip of Washington crossing into Canada showed potential for grizzlies. This was not the information I was hoping for.

Added to my fright list of reasons not to venture into the wild were those pesky hunters, or just crazies with guns in general. I'd certainly watched enough unnerving films and media coverage of mass shootings to understand the fact that Americans own guns, the licensing of which was a touchy issue that somehow remained contentious. After all, it's a protected constitutional right to own a gun, says the National Rifle Association in their convenient interpretation of the Second Amendment. I felt uneasy about this widespread access to firearms, with Americans able to rock up at their local Walmart with a driving licence and purchase a pistol. I figured if someone with bad intent pointed a gun towards another person, that person was entirely screwed. And with the isolation of the trail, no one would be there to intervene if we got screwed.

Despite terrorist threats across Europe, it's still rare to see an armed police officer on the streets of London; the good old baton or Taser is about the extent of their weaponry. If I do see a gun it startles me and makes me feel less safe, because I figure the forces must know something about a potential threat that I don't. Guns are not a rite of passage handed out like Smarties with every cop badge as they are across the pond. Only specially-trained officers are packing over here.

Of all my compilation of fears, those involving bad people haunted me the most. I had nightmares months before we left containing morbid snippets from the entire back-catalogue of a show I had happily digested over the years, CSI. I know all about the prevalence of murder, I thought. Perhaps our fate would be sealed by a knife-wielding maniac in the darkness of night like the plot from every teenage horror film, or we might just as well be tracked as part of a Hunger Games-style blood sport by hunters bored of killing deer. In truth, we would actually experience very little gun action on the trail, but I didn't know that at this point. One episode in particular stands out from Charlton Lake, but I'll get to that later.

Add venomous creatures, like snakes and scorpions to the mix and it seemed perfectly logical to cancel our trip and fly to Hawaii. My modern city life sure seemed safe in comparison to what awaited us in the wild. Yet I grew up in one of the most populated cities in the world. Surely the statistics meant I was far more likely to encounter harm in London than in rural Oregon! I knew that logically, but the thing about fear is it's all about perception. We each set our own fear thresholds, choosing whether or not to harness fear through telling ourselves stories of perceived dangers. They say the greatest fear to humankind is the unknown, and at that point the wilderness was *completely* unknown to me. To recap, we had just three nights camping experience under our belts before joining the trail, and on no occasion had we been completely alone. This left a great feeling of unease focusing on the night time. Anyone or *anything* could enter our tent; it was the equivalent of sleeping in an isolated, strange house with the doors wide open.

Thankfully I'm not a complete pussycat. Facing off against the voices in my head telling me we shouldn't, or couldn't, do this hike was my sane – or logical at least – mind. It would call out the negative thoughts with the odd "f**k you" thrown in for good measure. I rationalised that if we allowed our minds to be completely governed by fear we wouldn't do anything. Untapped self-preservation can easily slip into self-sabotage. Of course, not going ahead would have been the easy option, but I wasn't prepared to accept such defeat. There was something inside me I needed to prove; I had to see this through. Failure was not an option. Not yet anyway.

4

Friction in Paradise

It turns out Conrad and I held a unique selling point on the trail – we were *complete* amateurs. Yet, who would have guessed this would end up working to our advantage in those early weeks? This was because as novice walkers – I mean *hikers* – we had set ourselves tiny goals. Our plan was simple. We aimed to cover 10 to 12 miles a day until reaching our first milestone, Crater Lake, some 86 miles away. From Crater Lake we hoped to feel much fitter, so would add a couple of extra miles throughout Oregon, until attempting to average 20-milers across Washington. This pie-in-the-sky strategy lay at the heart of the expected arrival dates contained in Leslie's resupply itinerary.

Unfortunately, such slow timeframes come with a major downside in the form of extra food-carrying requirements. Food, it turns out, is heavy. And we had no clue just how heavy before it was too late, because neither of us had had the foresight to test our bags with five days' worth of food *before* hitting the trail. This oversight would light a fuse on our relationship and provide endless material to slag each other off with. We would rapidly discover that while arguments in the wild are short-lived, because they have to be, they also feel intensely upsetting as you have nothing but time to agonise over the tension and to analyse each bad word exchanged.

On 20th June we departed Callahan's Lodge, a hotel just off Oregon's Interstate 5, full of nervous optimism. That optimism didn't last long. Before we'd even made the official trailhead just a mile along the paved road, a realisation hit: our packs were too damn heavy. Despite padded hip belts designed to balance weight across the hips, the pain pushing down on my shoulders was relentless. I might as well have been lugging bags of cement. Every step was torture; I felt like my back was going to snap in two. I kept trying to readjust the various straps mid-stride but to no avail. Conrad was faring the same – although from his complaints you'd think much worse, with his repeated assertion that his hip belt had even less padding, but if he expected sympathy he wasn't going to get it; I couldn't have cared less.My mind was dominated by a single thought: *How the f**k am I going to lug this all the way to Canada?*

Our experience that Monday would have been completely different if it hadn't been for those damn backpacks and the tensions they created. After a token faked-smile selfie at the wooden trailhead sign to mark the official start of our trek, we followed a gently graded path through damp pine forest which looked like any other forest path, to be honest. There was the odd interlude of sunny meadows brimming with long grass and wild flowers, but mostly we saw vistas full of nothing but blankets of trees. In hindsight, such vastness was a real novelty for us, but my mind was focused entirely on the struggle, barely noticing the hum of birds and fluttering of giant black-and-white butterflies.

As our first day ended in a small meadow on the edge of another mountain, we didn't have the sense of being very far away. In the 12 miles covered we had met handfuls of other people, mostly day- or small-section hikers, and had heard for hours the purring of the interstate in the distance. Trying to think of something positive, I'd say my highlights were removing my pack for the day, and the little kick I got from watching the pointy snow-dipped beacon of Mount Shasta shrinking further into the distance, providing a visual sense of progress made entirely using our feet.

Our *bush camp* – anywhere that didn't contain proper bathroom facilities – sat in a meadow hidden just off the trail. Fortunately for the sanctity of our relationship, we found ourselves with company, so hit pause on the prolonged complaining competition. On arrival we were greeted by Maya, a very excited retriever dog who bounded over and liked to bounce. Maya was joined by her owner, Brandon from Tennessee, who rather bizarrely spear-headed a one-man camp that contained enough kit to host a small army. He was already perched beside a roaring fire cooking some sort of casserole in what looked like a crockpot. His comprehensive set-up baffled me, I mean did he air-lift this stuff in? Regardless, Brandon's presence in the meadow filled me with a deep sense of relief. Our first night in the woods would be beside a well-equipped pro, and a dog who could hopefully protect us against bears.

It remained warm and sunny until around 8 p.m. Having set up the tent we accepted there was nowhere convenient to cook and eat other than in the long, boggy grassland. I rolled my eyes as Conrad resumed his complaints, diverting them away from his hips to the importance of needing a seat with his long limbs. Who knew that it is apparently *impossible* for someone over six-foot tall to sit on the floor, or to cross their legs? Much to my relief Conrad left me to join another hiker, Micah, at Brandon's raging camp fire under the stars. Feeling the furthest from chatty I've ever been, I skipped the campfire and retreated into the tent to decompress, venting into my journal. That evening, June's giant, gleaming Full Strawberry Moon appeared, illuminating the tent; I barely noticed it.

Looking back at my first journal entry, it was mostly just one big whinge about Conrad. I wanted him to "man-up" and accused him of not carrying his fair share given our relative sizes. I hated the way he frequently made us stop to rest, taking ages to remove his pack and making a song-and-dance over strapping it back on again. My preferred hiking method was to just *get it over with*. My words may have been harsh and unfair, but our relationship was clearly being tested. Since leaving the trail Conrad has confessed how he honestly thought we were heading for divorce in the early weeks. I don't think I ever considered things as *that* bad, but I admit to the odd fantasy of pushing him off a cliff.

It was clear by day two we were hurtling along a steep learning curve. My frustration was complete when it actually took us two and a half hours to leave camp. In my non-diplomatic morning stupor, I blamed Conrad of course, nagging him for not being efficient enough. But really what we needed was practice to establish a routine. Despite our late departure we were still the first to leave, but within a couple of hours Micah – who had still been asleep when we had left – sailed past. Not long after, he was followed by Brandon who was carrying all his equipment in a

70-pound metal-framed mega-pack, with Maya up ahead. They both made it look so easy. Our slow speed infuriated me. I was, after all, accustomed to operating at a frantic London-pace, the kind of person who over-took dawdlers looking at their phones with a loud huff.

Other annoyances came from discovering my new pack was covered in irremovable, sticky tree sap after leaning it against a pine tree during a brief break, before coating myself whilst unsuccessfully trying to clean it off. Next I stabbed myself in the arm with my brand-new penknife. A key learning point to all here: it's never a good idea to attach a flick knife to the outside of your pack with a carabiner dangling around while moving! Conrad meanwhile, was experiencing what he referred to as "chronic butt-chafe issues," so occasionally had to stop to drop his shorts and coat the sensitive area in question with Vaseline. I'm sure the chipmunks were having a good laugh at our expense.

Bitching aside, we mostly travelled quietly, struggling to cope with the new physical exertion. It was a far cry from sitting at a desk all day. During these hours, and countless more, I would mentally switch-off to conserve energy, instead focusing on the present as we trampled over pine needles and cones from the surrounding fir forest. By late afternoon my feet started to overtake my heavy-pack-sore-back problem. At a creek next to Little Hyatt Reservoir, we met a guy named Joel, a Portland scout leader, taking a break to bathe his feet. We decided to follow his strategy; I could almost hear the sizzle as my sweaty trotters hit the frigid water. The soak felt amazing, but when I retracted my feet to inspect the root of the pain, I could barely touch my puffy soles. Aside from redness I couldn't see any obvious damage or blisters, so I put the discomfort down to my feet rebelling against the few extra stone my body seemed to have gained in the last 24 hours.

Possibly we were abducted by aliens on our second day, because there isn't any other logical explanation for how it managed to take us ten hours to walk just over 13 miles. The last frantic mile was an off-trail road diversion, marching along hot tarmac in what felt like the longest bonus mile of my life. The reason it was so desperate? Just north of the PCT sits a resort called Hyatt Lake, containing a kitchen due to close at 5 p.m. There was no way, even this early on, we could pass up the chance of forgoing dehydrated camp food for a proper hot meal. The very thought of a fried dinner had kept me going all afternoon!

By the skin of our teeth, we made it. Our efforts were rewarded with a nice greasy pizza and cold sugary drinks which tasted magic. As we sat in the small cabin-like diner staring out at the lake across the quiet road, the sun begun to fade, and with it our bodies unknowingly shut down. Feeling pretty dejected, we booked a cabin for the night to avoid having to hike to the nearest campground. The bed and shower went a long way towards repairing the day's frictions, and gave me something to finally smile about. I was grateful that Conrad, our unofficial CFO, had approved the unforeseen expenditure, not feeling even the slightest bit guilty. Well maybe just a little. But I figured there was no point in making this harder than it needed to be, right?

By the time we left Hyatt Lake the next day our improved relationship had already begun to sour. You see, even though we'd left Callahan's with impossibly-loaded packs, the resort owners at Hyatt Lake had been kindly storing half our food supply in an attempt to make the first two days *easier*. With full rations crammed into every cranny of capacity, our bags now appeared to be bursting at the seams, so we borrowed a set of scales for a final weigh-in. The results didn't seem right. I stood on the scales first, following a circus-worthy performance to hoist the pack onto my back. Minus my fat arse, the luggage came in at 33-pounds, but critically that didn't include any water! Conrad's was a couple of pounds more. These bags had been another difficult purchase. After returning three previous choices between us, both had ultimately been selected for their light-weight credentials, but the flip-side was less structure, meaning they were only designed to "comfortably" carry up to 30 pounds each.

I must admit, I expected Conrad to be carrying a fair bit more than me considering human biology, and the fact he has such a height advantage. I wasn't therefore very sympathetic to his endless rants concerning his load while I bent under the weight of my own pack. With each muttering I could feel myself getting more and more irritated. I mean, was this really the person I had chosen to spend the rest of my life with? He didn't seem like a solid choice of mate in the event of a nuclear apocalypse or something equally bad where basic survival instincts and brute strength were necessary. Yet, wanting to seem tough, I remained quiet. I let it bubble away inside, gradually feeding more coals into my furnace of seething rage. For example, before we even left the reservoir, I took the mental effort to calculate I was carrying around 30 per cent of my body weight, versus his 25. The grudge was planted.

Before my restraint could burst into a mid-trail showdown, we passed Brandon and Micah at their waterside campsite. They had teamed up with another hiker called Jessie, and decided to enjoy a day off to go swimming. This made me feel desperately jealous; we had lost our team, the only people we knew out there. Jealousy also stemmed from the fact that Micah was from nearby Ashland, so his dad had been driving up every few days with supplies, including special requests such as a box of wine for Brandon, and had picked up his son for a restaurant lunch the previous day. Surely that was cheating, I thought, completely contradicting my rationalisation of last night's cabin stay. Yet compared to these young guys we felt like a couple of outdoors fraudsters, playing at being hikers. I was embarrassed to admit we had just spent the night in a cabin and would have probably lied about it had it not been plainly obvious we hadn't made it from the diner to the campsite. As we reluctantly left them to their leisure I muttered to Conrad. "Bet they're laughing at us now, just like everyone else."

In the first two days on the trail we hiked a fair distance, considering our bodies were still in training. By day 3, we kept expectations low, deciding to aim for a state-run campsite called Klum Landing just 10 miles away. We found the forested trail continuing north deserted aside from a few timid deer, but by late morning tranquillity erupted into a heated *discussion*. You see, I had taken a bag of electronics from Conrad the day before when he complained the pockets of his hip belt weren't big enough. As I had larger pockets I offered to carry the battery pack, but for some strange reason Conrad handed it over with a surprisingly heavy bag of wires, chargers, and his Kindle – superfluous kit we later ditched at Crater Lake.

I will not drag out the gory details, because frankly they would make me sound like a real bitch, but resentment had built up inside me super-fast, even for me, culminating in a full on-trail hissy fit of accusations. Bad words were exchanged from frustration on both sides. Conrad countered my anger by blaming the design of his bag, but eventually conceded and accepted the bag back, along with the first aid kit as a goodwill gesture. Before going anywhere, we sat on a log and quietly munched our way through a bag of trail mix to further lighten my load. The trail mix itself had been another contentious issue, since I contended it was too heavy to lug around in the first place.

Walking past a sign with bullet holes in it, making me feel somewhat uncomfortable, but without much in the way of recourse, we reached our destination at the reasonable time of 4 p.m. We needed a time-out. I didn't expect us to find ourselves alone in the large drive-up campsite, but apart from the sound of distant boats on Howard Prairie Lake there was no sign of company.

While Conrad took a much-needed shower I sat at a picnic bench, airing my feet, reflecting on the day. It dawned on me that I had been so absorbed in my own agony, and in beating myself and Conrad up for being weak, I had almost lost sight of our reality. Just look where we were. That night we would be sleeping amongst a sea of waving trees beside a lake, with no sign of the *real* world even close. It was so delightfully departed from my norm, the surrealism was electrifying. We could virtually have been immersed in any age of time – minus the fully-plumbed toilet block. I wondered how old the trees were and liked to imagine myself back living in a simpler age, before phones controlled us and everything was instant.

All this open space sure felt like a far-cry from London; a place where I once got pissed on by a homeless man while descending a staircase from London Bridge. Yet given the tiring escapades of the last few days, my heart weighed with the knowledge Canada was still so far away. It was over-whelming to count all those remaining miles, so I vowed to take it day-by-day. It had to start feeling easier soon. Didn't it?

The campsite became eerie after dark. I couldn't help thinking our chances of meeting a gun-wielding madman intent on attacking hikers was higher in this location, with road access for an easy getaway. Still, the hot shower felt worth the risk. Feeling cleansed, we started a campfire in the fading light. The flames had a morale-boosting effect on easing tensions. Our marriage had just about survived another day. It helped that we concluded the night enjoying a treat of toasted s'mores under the starry sky.

5

Nature's Mocking Us

With access to a shower and somewhere to sit for the last two nights, we knew we'd been lucky. Such luxuries don't exist in the wilderness, so we sensed things were about to get tougher. We just didn't realise how much tougher.

It quickly began to feel as though Nature had it in for us. It felt personal. Crossing into Rogue River National Forest, increasing amounts of debris and fallen trees began impeding the trail. These obstructions got significantly worse the further north we progressed, with giant toppled timber often completely blocking the faint dirt path. Climbing over, under and around obstacles while heaving 30 pounds on my back wasn't something I'd contemplated as a potential hindrance to our lofty hiking ambitions. For a start, it was mentally taxing, as an offending tree would bring us to a complete standstill, losing any vague momentum we had, and requiring a visual analysis before we could put a foot forward to try and calculate a possible way through. Then, by the time we had figured out a detour around the offending blockade – typically through sharp thickets – we regularly struggled to find the trail again. The fallen trees made progress seem non-existent. It was so physically gruelling, we might as well have been taking part in an assault course to Canada with the SAS.

A forestry worker we later met at Fish Lake provided a brief explanation for this new hurdle. According to him, trees had been toppling in record numbers all over the state as two years of drought was levelled by an "unholy" – we guessed he meant atypically large – snowfall. Yes, the continental U.S. had enjoyed an epic ski season that past winter, thanks to increased precipitation from the Pacific Ocean, and now we got to pay the price.

Yet snow was not entirely to blame for the carnage. An

epidemic of mountain pine beetle hadn't helped matters. A plague of the black-shelled bandits, spurred on by the warmer, drier temperatures, was guilty of obliterating forests all the way from Mexico to British Columbia. Their process of larval feeding and fungal colonisation can kill even the most established of specimens in a matter of weeks. In true serial-killer style, the beetles, not satisfied with their conquest, then fly on to claim their next unsuspecting target. And thanks to the inconvenience caused, I couldn't help but think of Conrad and myself as being among their victims.

Yes, I was learning all sorts of new biological stuff in the wild. But while such titbits seemed fascinating on the trail – now I could look at trees and comprehend the tell-tale beetle pitch tubes – such lessons floated way over my head when I was a bored school student. Science, and geography too, just hadn't been my bag, baby. Yet being able to appreciate the practical applications in the natural world made me mad I hadn't paid more attention in class. Even Conrad seemed to know the different types of clouds in the sky, and could judge whether or not they indicated an impending thunderstorm; highly useful information when you're about to camp on an exposed ridge! If only teachers were required by law to give a brief upfront explanation, a prologue of sorts, to outline why the lesson they're about to teach may prove useful one day, kids like me might actually listen.

With lingering snow, most forestry agencies hadn't even begun the task of clearing official trails. This made us unwitting early-season "trail-blazers," re-discovering a path nature had unceremoniously commandeered during last winter. As a result, we averaged under two miles per hour on what the guidebook would have described as easy, flat terrain. Just to put this into perspective, most PCT thru-hikers add five extra miles to their daily average when they pass from California into Oregon. Some even take up the Oregon Challenge: an attempt to hustle the 446 miles between state lines in just two weeks.

At our current speed, based on a 10-hour hiking day, with no rest days and very few breaks, we were looking at over a month. And hiking day after day, with no R&R, seemed completely unsustainable.

Nature's trickery continued with the mosquito. Swarms of them to be precise. CRAZY, blood-thirsty, vengeful f*****s. Before Oregon I thought there was a tacit agreement between humans and mosquitoes: they stay away from the face. Well, the golf-ball sized bite that appeared underneath Conrad's left eye proved that theory wrong. The closer we got to Crater Lake, the more incessant they became. They were impossible to outrun, unfazed by the noxious insect repellent we doused ourselves in, and for every successful swat, five of their mates would appear at their funeral. They just kept coming and coming. There wasn't a second of respite from the buzzing, biting gang attack. It was infuriating, hindering even the simplest of tasks.

While squatting away, minding my own business during a quick off-trail wee, the nasty critters got me somewhere I hadn't even thought to protect. *Motherf*****s!* Not just on the cheek either, but in a particularly invasive spot of soft skin which stung like hell. They were quick, I give them that. Following said episode, every time I needed to pee I relinquished any remaining self-respect, as Conrad stood behind me swatting the air to thwart their strike. We had no choice but to hike with the added discomfort of head nets plastered to our faces, which despite buying, we never really expected to use. In the evening safety of our tent – safe only after killing those chancers who darted in with us – I would count and dress Conrad's numerous bites with sting relief and a guilty innate pleasure that came from knowing there was someone worse off than me!

We got through these trying times by laughing at ourselves. I mean, we looked *ridiculous*. I took so many photos of Conrad trying to navigate under colossal tree blow-downs, with his giant frame looking like it was about to snap beneath the weight of his pack, because I delighted in the spectacle. And snaps of him trying to eat without removing the mosquito net from his face, only to freak out when a rogue bug somehow got inside. And I can't forget the suspected tarantula bite on his left calf. We called it that because it seemed impossible the prominent mound could have been made by anything else. Oh, and I unknowingly rubbed my legs up against poison oak during an off-trail diversion, resulting in an itchy red rash that lasted for nearly a week. But

I just had to laugh; it was *insane*. The famous explorer Edmund
Hillary – the first person to reach both the North and South Poles
AND summit Everest – proclaimed a sense of humour as one of
the most important things on a big expedition, because in difficult
or dangerous situations laughter can ease the tension. He wasn't
wrong! "The Brits" modelled themselves as the walking epitome
of all the things that could possibly go wrong in the woods.

On the bright side, our low expectations were actually
working in our favour. We may have been travelling ludicrously
slow, but it didn't matter because *everyone* in the area was. At
least we carried sufficient rations to support such paltry progress.

Back on the trail through The Rouge River National Forest, after
a consistent uphill climb through thick woodland, we reached a
small timber cabin. South Brown Mountain shelter was built by
the National Guard in the early nineties to offer sanctuary to
lost cross-country skiers. We passed through the open doorway,
protected only by a PVC strip curtain, like the kind you see in
butchers' shops, into a darkened room. Inside, the smoky odour
of fires long-extinguished clung to the air. A sooty iron stove took
centre stage, surrounded by primitive wooden benches and piles
of firewood. It didn't take much of an inspection to decide we
wouldn't be sleeping inside. Though a bench would have been
preferable to hard dirt, the insects had set up shop, and our track
record of being bitten so far was not good. Even more worrying
was the presence of suspicious-looking droppings indicating
rodents, which I knew would crawl over my face and start
nibbling me to death whilst I slept.

Despite the shelter being a short detour off the trail, its novelty
attracts a number of visitors. I scanned through a tatty notebook
which seemed to be operating as the PCT register and recognised
a couple of names from hikers who had overtaken us. What I
was hoping to see were comments from south-bounders (SoBos)
proving the trail ahead was passable, but there was nothing
from this year. I signed our names and made some kind of stupid
comment along the lines of:

*"Brits travelling Ashland to Canada – who'd have thought we'd
make it this far nearly a week in?"*

While trying and failing to get the hang of extracting water from the very rare iron pump outside, soaking ourselves in the process, an elderly gentleman hiked into camp. Loren resembled an archetypal friendly park ranger-come-safari guide. Clad in khaki with a well-maintained white beard and a welcoming smile, he looked every inch the part. I slyly watched in amazement as his tent sprang up in no time at all. I wondered if we would ever master such tricks, gazing over at Conrad who was attempting to fashion a washing line to dry our socks, having spent an age fussing with the tent.

We naturally congregated around the picnic table at the entrance to the cabin. That evening Conrad and I marvelled at everything Loren did. Let's face it, this whole camping malarkey was still pretty new to us, so watching a *bona fide* outdoorsman at work was intriguing. For a start, Loren took real pride in preparing his evening meal. Whereas my camp cooking involved adding boiled water to a bag of non-descript dried ingredients, which all ended up tasting the same, Loren went to town adding all sorts of extras such as pulses and flavourings to give his meals some pizazz.

I felt inspired. He was efficient too, having cooked and eaten his meal before I had even managed to boil water. That's when I decided our cooking methods were out of whack; a new gas stove was obviously required to replace our brand-new stove. I was already looking for an excuse to ditch our alcohol burner anyway. The modest little piece of kit which looked little more than a crushed tin can was impossible to light without drenching myself in fuel. Come to think of it, it's surprising I hadn't set myself ablaze already.

Loren seemed to enjoy his new role as our camp guide, supplying us with heaps of useful tips and gear reviews. During our unofficial *how to survive in the woods* tutorial, I sat scribbling notes, asking him to repeat and spell out the bits I'd missed. To me Loren seemed to strike a sensible balance between carrying light-weight kit, whilst maintaining key items of comfort, the likes of which most thru-hikers would dismiss as superfluous. I was willing to action any advice he gave, so when he noticed me shivering in my hiking skirt and recommended I invest in some leggings I knew I needed to find an outfitter. After all, once the sun sets it gets bloody cold in the mountains!

The next morning while Conrad dismantled our tent, I joined Loren in preparing breakfast. I watched as he re-lit his stove after he'd already made coffee. He must have noticed that I was watching his every move with fascination, for he began explaining himself without a prompt.

"I like to give myself a little morning treat," he began, taking out a small piece of muslin cloth, and a plastic bottle.

"What's that?" I asked, unable to read the label.

"Doctor Bronner's peppermint soap. You've got to get hold of this stuff, it really wakes you up and makes you feel clean."

I watched as he squirted a small drop of the liquid soap into the cloth and ran it over his face and neck.

"Try a bit," he offered. So I gave it a go, wetting my face with my neckerchief. It smelt so fresh, and invigoratingly tingled on my skin. But something troubled me.

"What about attracting bears?"

We presently stank because we hadn't packed any toiletries containing fragrance, fearing it would attract unwanted wildlife.

Loren smiled, "it's only a small amount, and the bears can smell you over the soap."

Whether that was a good thing or not I wasn't sure, but I trusted Loren knew far more than we did, so the good old Doctor's soap got added to our shopping list.

Loren left a lasting impression as a very wise and patient man. Obviously in love with the great outdoors, he offered his spare time to lead a team of volunteers who maintain a section of the Washington PCT north of Hart's Pass. He left camp earlier than us, far more efficient in his morning routine, and with an appointment to meet a friend at noon. Together they hoped to summit Mount McLoughlin later that day. It might be the lowest in Oregon's chain of six major Cascade Range volcanic peaks, but they still had around 4,000 feet to climb before dark, and it still looked some way off on the horizon.

While we never saw Loren again, we kept in touch over email. A few weeks later we were surprised to discover he had aborted his intended hike to Timberline Lodge. His friend Joan aided his extraction by picking him up at Willamette Pass just north of Crater Lake. Despite being highly prepared, and far more motivated than us, he simply concluded the adverse weather and subsequent trail conditions had made hiking no fun. As a retired Washington native, he hoped to reattempt his hike later in the season. His email summed up what we were facing pretty well:

"The first three days were bug-free, but then as you know, the mozzies came out in force. I was almost running down the trail in front of a vicious cloud of them. One day I did 24 miles in less than 10 hours. At night I was a prisoner in the tent. The only morning I was safe was at Maidu Lake when I awoke to 36 degrees. The little blighters were too cold to bother me for a delicious hour...They certainly turned my hike into negative fun."

Loren was certainly right about the "negative fun" part. It didn't help that, adding to our list of woes was a common hiker problem: our feet were taking a hammering. Mine were swollen beyond belief, with a deep throbbing concentrated in the previously-soft balls. Maybe if I hadn't had so many pedicures over the years they would have proved hardier. My average daily walk to the closest tube station had clearly failed to prepare them for carrying a heavy weight while walking over such long periods. I guess I was lucky I didn't have blisters by this point. Less lucky was Conrad. "Megatron", as we liked to call it, had grown to great dimensions on his little toe, which was now deformed to twice its original size. There is a great deal of disagreement in the hiking community about how to treat blisters – whether you let them be or take a more invasive approach. Conrad chose the latter, each night cleaning the area with a wet wipe, before popping and draining it using a needle we deemed *sterilised* after wiping with a bit of hand sanitiser. Each morning, he would bind the offending toe with silver tape, which would inevitably get sweaty and fall off to reveal Megatron's return before lunch.

The morning we parted ways with Loren, we did so with a single goal in mind: reach Fish Lake resort in time for lunch. We didn't really know what awaited us there, but the note on our trail map indicated a cafe serving hot food and showers, the two things we craved most in the world.

Mile one went by with us feeling cold but motivated, mile two felt very much the same, walking through a constant non-descript forest tunnel, then came mile three where early thoughts we might just make our lunch date with a burger started to unravel. Old-growth forest had suddenly given way to the steep lava fields flanking Brown Mountain's great cinder cone. I treaded gingerly, with each crunching step feeling like I was walking over hot coals; my poor feet taking a pummelling. The lava was visually striking, with giant anthracite boulders providing a stark contrast against the wide, lush leaf-canopy below. Only once we emerged from the forest did expansive views present themselves, but I mostly focused on the ground to make sure I didn't break an ankle or worse – tumble down a mountain. I stole the odd glance toward the grand Mount McLoughlin, its snow-capped peak dominating the distant horizon. I wondered if Loren would make it to the top.

These days I know it's best to walk over lava fields when the sun isn't shining directly overhead. With hindsight, we really should have left camp earlier, as by noon lava rocks were attracting the sun's rays to create a giant human barbeque. Having just strapped our packs back on after climbing over yet another mammoth fallen tree, we met a trio of hikers sat on a ledge enjoying lunch. The sight of people with bags too small to be camping provided a welcome sign we had re-surfaced from the deep and must be edging closer to a road. Just like many others before and after them, they curiously probed about where we were from, and where we were headed. I tried not to stare at their sandwiches as we responded.

Upon discovering our nationality, the man's face lit up.

"Did you hear about the *Brex-it*?" he asked excitedly.

The foreign phrase snap-diverted my attention from his sandwich. I wouldn't say I felt the impact of being totally off-grid yet, but in the last handful of days with no phone signal or television updates, and an overriding preoccupation with our own misery, we had disconnected. It hadn't even entered my mind how important events were unfolding in the real world whilst we scrambled over trees and battled bugs. In unison we both confirmed we hadn't.

One of the other women quickly interjected before the man could get his words out.

"They voted for *Brexit*. Guess you two are going to be going home to a different country."

She seemed strangely delighted.

"I hope your passports still work!" the other lady chipped in before taking her final bite.

I honestly wasn't sure if she was joking or serious.

Conrad and I both stood in a state of shock. No immediate words sprang to mind. The fact that the British public had voted to leave the European Union after 43 years was unfathomable. It was the only political structure either of us had ever known. The news was entirely unexpected, with the impetus to leave the EU having originally stemmed from ultra-right British Nationalists, people who I thought no one really took all that seriously. Neither of us could have predicted this outcome so we struggled to respond.

While I was distracted in la-la land wondering what this meant to our immediate future, Conrad made diplomatic small talk, careful not to rock the political boat.

As we had departed for America too far in advance to qualify for a postal vote on the issue, neither of us had exercised our voting rights. Knowing this was going to be the case, we hadn't paid much attention to the months of debates on the subject, and to be honest I wasn't entirely sure which way I would have swayed. I understood why the majority had decided to take this stance, but without any obvious precedents, leaving Europe seemed a great unknown and therefore felt unsettling.

Then something else struck me: how surreal it was to be receiving a history-in-the-making UK newsflash in the middle of nowhere, from a group of Americans! Having watched the typically insular coverage of U.S. news networks in the past, I was impressed these people had even heard of the term "Brexit", *let alone* understood what it meant. They seemed thrilled to have been the ones to deliver the news. I was charmed to make their day.

Just as we turned to leave, Pat, Joan, and John mentioned they were about to head back to their car on Highway 140 a couple of miles ahead as soon as they had finished their sandwiches. They offered us a ride to Fish Lake Resort. *Hurrah!* This was fate; our lunch prospects were saved. But instead of just accepting the offer outright we tried to play it casual, muttering something about being grateful for a ride if we saw them further down the trail, but come on, let's face it – we were *desperate* for a ride! From there on, we continued walking at a deliberately slow pace, listening out for their voices behind, secure in the knowledge we had averted our first ever brush with sticking out a thumb on the side of a highway and hoping that a sadistic murderer didn't stop.

And before you think it, catching a lift off the PCT is *not* cheating. Not as long as you start right back where you left off. As we climbed into the back seat of their SUV, I leaned over to Conrad and gleefully whispered into his ear, "lunchtime!"

6

Don't Do Meth

Like a couple of excitable kids in Disney World, we pulled into Fish Lake Resort with eyes like saucers. Although a modest kind of place, the first thing I noticed about it were the row of huge RVs in the car park opposite. So big and shiny, they glistened in the sun, hotels on wheels made twice the size thanks to the giant awnings projecting from their sides. What I would give for my family to be trailing us with an RV right now, I thought. We had only been hiking for five days by this point but seeing these small signs of civilisation made me realise how disconnected we already felt.

After saying goodbye to our new friends, we took a seat outside the simple timber clubhouse, and quickly flagged down the waitress to get our food order in. Once that priority was dealt with, I trudged off through the tatty resort in search of a bathroom. Climbing the steps of the small green outhouse, my eyes became distracted by a noticeboard. In the centre, a *Life after Meth* poster prominently illustrated the harrowing transformation of a woman before, and after she had taken the drug. Her hollow, lifeless eyes were looking straight through me. I was transfixed. I found it peculiar that anti-meth campaigners had decided to advertise in such a scenic and remote location. But I had to give it to them: they made a compelling argument. *Must not do meth.*

Meanwhile, things sure seemed hectic from our seats on the resort's lakeside deck. Enjoying the free soda refills while waiting for our food, our whacky waitress, Missy, filled us in on the gossip. Recently, the resort was due to be sold, but for some reason the sale had fallen through. Most of the staff had since left or been fired; it wasn't clear which as Missy was kind of manic. There was nothing of her except skin and bones in denim cut-offs, and she made sure to repeatedly remind us she was juggling three jobs.

Perhaps it was too much caffeine, or too little sleep, but she did get me wondering about that poster.

Once lunch was finished, our attention swiftly shifted towards the next priority: shelter. I could have kissed the owner, Pam, when she offered us her last rustic cabin. That said, the clue was in the word "rustic", for only after paying and lugging our packs barefoot through the resort, did we discover what a real-life crack den looks like. In England I would call it a squat or bedsit. Resting by the edge of an otherwise idyllic forested lake, the room came complete with centralised waste disposal, in the form of an overflowing plastic garbage bin bang in the middle of the floor. The carpet it sat on was stained, and the bare mattress looked like it had seen way too much action over the years. For seventy-five bucks with no bathroom or electronic hook up, we returned the key, secured a refund, and disappointedly headed to the free hiker's campsite.

The campsite consisted of a tiny parcel of land with a single picnic bench, hidden among the trees a short way around the lake. We shared the site that night with six other hikers, probably more people than we had seen on our entire walk in the last few days.

One of those individuals was a man going by the trail name Park Explorer, who hiked solo, unless you count the companionship of his tiny Chihuahua, Ari. A feeble-looking tyke, Ari didn't strike me as an obvious choice of hiking dog. I asked his owner if he ever worried about mountain lions, to which he replied dead seriously: "it's the raptors that's the problem." Apparently, from the skies, little Ari appears more like a rabbit than a dog. His owner carried a special sling for when poor Ari's minuscule legs got too tried. I didn't get it. I mean if you're going to hike with the added responsibility of a dog to feed then surely you'd want one who could carry his own food, or perform some useful task such as warning off bears? But who was I to judge?

That afternoon I enjoyed the grimiest shower of my life. I didn't dare take my Tevas off to touch the dirty hair-clogged floor, as I frantically lathered my hair, feeding more quarters into the timer when it cut out mid-shampoo. At this point Conrad and I only carried handkerchief-sized micro towels. Mine had since been adopted as my "piss cloth" because toilet paper wasn't very practical unless doing a *number two*. I rinsed out my pissy towel to give it something resembling a wash, before spending an age blotting myself dry with it, one arm at a time, constantly having to ring it out while I stood in the tiny cubicle, shivering. If only my mum could see me now. It was a far cry from my usual bathroom routine.

At least I finally had clean clothes to change into, having just completed our first laundry. That said, the whole episode had been a very unpleasant one, which absurdly reduced me to tears. Conrad and I had thrown our dirt-encrusted clothing into a bin liner, and I had drawn the short straw to get changed into my only remaining clothing option – a waterproof jacket and matching bottoms – to do the honours. As I was swishing out of camp with a handful of quarters, Park Explorer spotted me.

"Are you doing laundry?" he shouted over.

"Yeah," I replied in my tracks.

With complete nonchalance he added, "could I throw in a couple of bits?"

I found this a kind of strange request, but in the spirit of hiker friendship I felt compelled to agree.

But I quickly grew upset as he began rummaging and throwing lots of grossly offensive items at me, including his stained underwear! I was unwittingly being treated as his maid. I felt cheated, as I over-loaded the washing machine thanks to him. Because of this feeling of injustice, and fragile state of tiredness, I got myself all worked up. By the time I returned to Conrad I ducked into the tent, bursting into tears. I don't cry very often. I can only assume it was exhaustion that drove me to it. Conrad instantly went into protector mode, wrapping me up in his arms and insisting on finishing the laundry.

"Don't have a go at him, it's not worth it," I feebly told him as I fished my journal from my pack. I retreated towards the lake with my tail between my legs, in need of solitude and an icy foot soak.

Following the stresses and strains of the last few days, and the awkwardness of always being in the shadow of another person, it felt good to just be me, sitting on a rock. I tried to reflect on the whirlwind of trodden miles, but struggled to comprehend the complex patchwork of emotions I felt in that moment. One thing I was sure of: this was tougher than I ever imagined. I wondered if we could really make it. I stared out at the water and sighed with heavy doubt, annoyed with myself for posting a photo of us at the trailhead from Shelter Cove. Now the world knew about the hike.

The irony of the current situation wasn't lost on me either: we had *chosen* to be there, footed a hefty bill in fact to be living in the dirt; no one had sent us off to war unwillingly. I tried giving myself a silent reality check about how fortunate I was, but like a total brat I couldn't muster up a sense of being *lucky* while stuck in this persistent pity parade. A tinge of guilt rapidly gave way to focusing on my immediate suffering, silently acknowledging every part of my body that hurt. This had all been *my* idea too. When I started considering the embarrassment and shame I'd face if we accepted defeat and returned to our families, my mind turned to despair. That was enough thinking for now.

Later that evening, due to the state of my now-bruised feet and rumours of deteriorating trail conditions ahead, Conrad and I decided to take the next day off. Tomorrow we would contemplate what to do next.

We found some familiar faces from our camp inside the resort's small diner as soon as it opened the next morning. Alfred – who went by the unlikely hiker name Speedball – was a tall, well-built hiker-come-maths teacher out to complete the Oregon PCT. He reminded me of Clark Kent, but that might have just been the glasses, dark hair, or the fact I was very tired. The previous evening, we had listened to him talk at length in a very matter-of-fact, deadpan way about the detailed contents of his ultra-lightweight backpack, which had a ridiculous base weight of just nine pounds. I couldn't help but feel very jealous.

Another figure in the diner was a guy in his twenties who went by the trail name Habit. It didn't take a genius to work out the nickname hadn't come from his choice of clothing. Habit was the first actual thru-hiker we had met. He resembled a skinny, hairy, tattooed Jesus, complete with long dishevelled beard and worn-out clothes. He claimed to have started in Campo on the Mexican border but was a little vague about his exact route to Oregon. Hikers were battling unseasonably heavy snow in the Californian High Sierra, so if he had taken the full trail, he really would have pulled off a minor miracle to reach this point. Perhaps he really was Jesus!

Sitting across from Alfred was a new figure who introduced himself as Dan from Kentucky. Over a hot greasy breakfast, the group chat centred around just one thing: snow. Dan showed us a photo on his phone taken by another hiker just a week earlier showing the Three Sisters Wilderness 150 miles north. All I could make out from the shot was white-out. It could have been taken in the Alps in the middle of February. This was not good.

Dan, it transpired, had hiked the trail all the way from Mexico to Mount Shasta in northern California the previous year, before deciding to take a time-out after 115 days. He explained with a hint of southern twang how he was "done", following huge weight loss and health issues, details of which he didn't divulge. He seemed pretty laid back overall – but was adamant he wasn't prepared to tackle the snow ahead.

"I'm not taking my chances, it's too risky," he stated outright.

He opened up the Google Maps app on his phone and began pointing out his planned *alternate* route to Mazama Village campground in Crater Lake National Park.

"It's 'bout 50 miles along Route140, passing Upper Klamath Lake, then due north up the 531. I got the option to detour east into Fort Klamath if I need it. Figure it'll take me two, maybe three days."

Conrad and I exchanged quick pessimistic glances, while Dan continued studying the map.

"All that road-walking is going to kill your feet!" I claimed, taking a mouthful of coffee. This was something I had direct knowledge of after following our one-mile road detour to Hyatt Lake Resort just days before.

But Dan didn't seem bothered. He was playing around with the screen, zooming into specific sections of the map.

"It's going to get hot on that tarmac," Conrad intervened. "I hope you've got sunscreen!"

Dan seemed to consider this for a moment without his face leaving the screen.

"Nah, I'll take it. Water might be slim pickins though. I'll carry four litres at least."

Neither of us had the heart to state it out loud, but Conrad and I were in complete alignment that Dan's plan sounded nuts! Were we not all out there to hike the PCT and see what it had to offer? And surely having hiked so much of the trail already, Dan must have faced snow before? Having unpredictable water-refill opportunities along a road seemed risky in itself. And with only a high-level map for navigation, who knew where he might safely camp, or whether he would get completely lost?

The diner folk were unanimous; Dan would be hitting the road alone. Well not completely alone; he would have to negotiate the tarmac with massive American trucks.

Alfred had kept very quiet during Dan's presentation. A very bravado kind of guy, he shrugged off the snow reports and left later that day. Seeing as other people were pressing on, and with no better excuses and a cabin waiting for us in Crater Lake, we decided to give it a shot and see if we could get through. Our Plan B – not too far from the forefront of our minds – was to turn around and hitch out of the mountains in search of a beach.

During this discussion we had drawn the attention of an older couple sitting nearby.

"Are you all PCT hikers?" asked the moustached man wearing a cowboy hat.

This was quickly established.

"My wife and I are out section hiking. This is Jan, I'm Scott."

A lady with silver-plaited hair smiled back shyly, while holding out her mug for Missy who was doing the rounds with a steaming jug of fresh coffee. We introduced ourselves with all the usual *where are you guys from* pleasantries.

"Nice to meet y'all," interjected Dan in his easy Southern manner, breaking away from the distraction of his phone.

Scott continued. "We overheard you talking about the snow. We're thinking of driving up to Crater Lake. Jan's having foot troubles, so she isn't comfortable with the snow."

The sound of a car instantly sparked my curiosity.

"Do you have a car here then?" I casually inquired, trying not to sound too desperate.

"No. We're going to rent one from Medford. Jan's about to call a cab and see how much it'll cost to get there."

"How far is it from here?" I asked, expecting it to be hours away.

"Well, only around 45 minutes west. Does anyone need a ride in that direction?"

Conrad and I looked at each other. Medford was a sizeable town with an REI, our gear mecca, and plenty of other enticing stores and food. We hadn't quite packed enough snacks for this section, expecting to easily pick up some additional supplies from the resort's store, but on arrival the tiny tuck shop was full of empty shelves, leaving us pretty miserable. Given this, how could we possibly resist?

Before anyone else could answer, Conrad quickly jumped in.

"Yeah, we could do with a trip to REI. We need some supplies if we're gonna be hiking in snow."

Alfred's detailed kit run-down had secretly convinced us we needed to replace our alcohol stove with a rapid gas-burner. With that changed up, and ice spikes added for safety, our bags would only be carrying about double his load. I seethed at the thought.

Less than an hour later, after saying goodbye to Speedball, we found ourselves racing through the mountain pass in the back of a cab. It was exhilarating to be travelling so fast. At our current hiking pace, it would have taken us three days to reach Medford, 37 miles away.

Before we knew it, we were back to where it all began: REI Medford. It felt like ages since our last visit just ten days before. We quickly picked up a gas stove, some larger light-weight towels, and I chose some Superfeet insoles which claimed to provide balance, support and shock absorption – all the things I clearly needed.

The final item on our list was proving tricky. A young sales assistant came to our rescue while we stared, completely clueless at the rows of hanging crampons. He seemed amused by the two English people before him, who obviously had little practical experience of backpacking, and were now out hiking the PCT in the snow.

"Those are the shoes you're hiking in?" he asked, gesturing to our trail runners in an obvious air of disapproval.

I jumped in on the defensive.

"Yeah, one of your colleagues in the Oakland branch recommended them for their breathability."

With this information he changed his tune and outlined why attaching micro-spikes to our rubber soles wouldn't be possible; they would tear up our shoes. It looked like we'd be facing the snow minus stabilising spikes.

Jan and Scott patiently waited during all this prolonged browsing. I was embarrassed to be holding up strangers through my own indecision, but on the contrary, they seemed to be enjoying themselves. *Who doesn't love a trip to REI, right?*

The couple, from a town in eastern Washington state named Walla Walla – it's a real place, I checked – joked they would now live their cancelled hike vicariously through us. Scott hoped to resume hiking with his dog for company later that season. We discovered this and lots more about our new friends as we sat down to a thank-you lunch at a Mongolian BBQ. Aside from the fact we were enjoying a well-earnt holiday from hiking, it felt wonderful to have someone other than Conrad to talk to. And Jan and Scott's young, fun-loving attitudes made them easy company. I wondered whether Conrad and I would discover our own adventurous, free spirits one day.

With our new light-weight luggage travelling with us in a backpack to Medford, I had rather hoped we would be checking into a hotel; there were so many more food establishments we had yet to visit. But sadly, this wasn't to be. We couldn't justify the $125 cab ride back to Fish Lake just to leave a day later, given Jan and Scott's offer of a return ride. So, after lunch and grabbing some groceries for the guys back at camp, we piled into their small rental.

I felt irrationally sad to be leaving the conveniences of town, but reluctantly accepted we were far from where we needed to be.

Our confidence level going to bed that night can best be

described by the text we sent to Chris and Leslie. It simply stated: *Hold off posting all future boxes until you hear otherwise.*

Following an essential fry-up, we felt a strange eagerness to re-join the trail the next morning. Actually, it was more a nervous mixture of excitement and trepidation at the prospect of reaching Crater Lake, our first milestone and official resupply point. Not forgetting the proper bed awaiting us. My feet were improving following long soaks in the cold lake, and I held high hopes my new $50 insoles would be a game-changer.

Upon departure the resort's owner Pam embraced me in what was a strange public display of affection for a British person, but surprisingly comforting. She warned us to "stay safe". A number of other hiking guests, including two young college girls, Tori and Michelle, had decided to come off the trail and bypass the next section. With no south-bound visitors passing through the resort yet, what lay ahead was unclear. But Pam insisted two north-bound hikers had left the resort the day before we arrived and hadn't returned. We took that as an encouraging sign. For now, we still followed the trail.

Jan and Scott waited to give us a ride back to the trailhead on Route 140. I loved those guys. As we loaded our bags into the back of their sedan, a U.S. Forest Ranger pulled up. He confirmed our fears; no crews had encountered the northern section of trail, but he seemed pretty proud they had heroically started clearing the southern section just yesterday. Not helpful timing for us. His only warning concerned bugs. Awesome, we thought. Surely the trail itself will be just fine then.

Scariest Moment Yet

Thanks to the lasting legacy of the U.S. Wilderness Act, Oregon's Sky Lakes Wilderness contains enough land to build over 46,000 football pitches. The Act describes wilderness as:

> "an area where the earth and its community of life are untrammelled by man, where man himself is a visitor who does not remain"

I'm going to give the politicians the benefit of the doubt they didn't literally mean just for *men*, when they set the very noble intention to preserve designated land as an "enduring resource" for future generations. As a result, Wilderness land is primarily shaped by the forces of nature, not people, leaving it rugged and, well, as the name suggests: *wild*. Conrad and I had visited some beautiful, remote corners of England over the years, but nothing would come even close to the feeling of utter isolation we were about to experience in Oregon's vast forests.

Sky Lakes can attribute its name to more than two-hundred pools of water dotting the landscape. A study in the nineties found several of these lakes had amongst the most chemically pure water of all lakes known to man (and woman!). I'm guessing their pristine contents has something to do with their inaccessibility. For hikers already carrying weighty packs, access to bountiful sources of crystal-clear water is essential. Unfortunately, the original PCT creators seemed to have masterfully carved a route almost entirely devoid of water. I'd like to thank them for that.

We left the trailhead with heavily-laden packs for the first 11-mile water carry. The mosquito nets went on instantly. The number of fallen tree blow-downs increased exponentially, creating a now familiar and challenging obstacle course which quickly began taking its toll. So in between all the *f-ing and blinding* we were doing it was obviously an opportune time to go and get lost.

Well, we were never entirely *lost*, just not where we should have been. At around four miles in, we had unknowingly taken the wrong fork – thanks to some awesome signage – and connected to the Mount McLoughlin trail. This we only realised after 30 gruelling minutes heading in the wrong direction. The warning sign outlining the dangers of climbing the mountain was the eventual give-away. We stood mid-trail whacking mosquitoes in the sticky air with a decision to make.

"I don't wanna go back up that hill." I stated, point blank, staring at my feet which were firmly planted in the dirt.

Conrad consulted our paper map.

"Yeah, agreed. There must have been over thirty blow-jobs in the last thirty minutes, I don't wanna do them all over again!" he moaned, whilst chuckling to himself over his witty word play.

"F*****g trees," he added.

He held the map out for me, pointing out our position asking, "how could we only be here?"

I shimmied over to the map.

"What the hell?! It feels like we've been going for hours, my knees are killin' me."

"How much water have you got left?" he asked, taking his pack off for a quick swig.

I uncomfortably contorted my body to retrieve one of my plastic Smart Water bottles out of my pack's tall side pocket.

"Urr, maybe three litres?"

He checked his other bottle, "I've got a bit more but I could down it all right now, I'm so thirsty, it's bloody baking."

My greatest fear, while consciously rationing our water, was that we would run dry in the woods, so this reality rattled me.

"What do we do?" I asked.

Conrad's attention was back on the map.

"It looks like this path leads to a forest service road. There's a stream there which looks like it goes to Fourmile Lake. We could get some water, eat lunch, and re-connect to the PCT further up here. Otherwise, we turn around and back-track."

Turning around to climb back over the same trees, uphill, felt heart-breaking. My vote was for the alternative, more *sensible* plan involving a big lake. We both agreed. Fourmile Lake, according to the map, contained a drive-up campsite, so with a road connecting it to the outside world we reasoned it most likely contained a shop or, even better, a cafe. And even though we'd left Fish Lake just hours before, any chance of real food was too tempting. It looked like a slightly longer route, but we figured road walking would be far quicker than dealing with trail blow-downs.

Walking down the primitive forest road in the searing mid-day heat, it was glaringly obvious we may have made the wrong decision. After the first quick but silent mile of regret we heard the hum of a vehicle headed in our direction. Without a second's hesitation I stuck my thumb out for a ride – the first time I had ever attempted this in my entire life – before watching the campervan speed on.

"What a dick! He had loads of room" I moaned.

We kept going in single-file, even more agitated. A few minutes later we heard another large vehicle, this one a big red SUV, so I tried again, making sure to smile. A crowded family whizzed past, waving apologetically. I huffed out loud.

We tried sticking to the far edges of the gravel lane with occasional pockets of shade, but the road was mostly exposed and did a good job of reflecting the sun. A road sign appeared, stating: "*Fourmile Lake 2.5 Miles*".

"What the F**K?!" I burst out, "I thought you said it was two miles tops! We've definitely done way over a mile already!"

"Yeah, well." He shut up, not knowing what to say.

"You should learn to read a f*****g map!" I shouted ahead.

Conrad stopped in his tracks, unzipped his pocket and threw the folded-up map at my feet.

"Be my guest!"

At that moment, during our roadside domestic, a large dirty-white pickup truck came into view. I flung my thumb out and forced a fake smile.

The truck's brake lights flashed as it came grinding to a halt just ahead. Rick was heading to the lake with a truck full of camping equipment, but offered us a ride if we could squeeze onto his tailgate. By that point, I would have lain on top of barbed wire for a lift. We bundled in, sandwiched between two kayaks, hanging on for dear life as he sped off, gravel throwing up a thick cloud of dust behind us.

We had survived our first, albeit brief, brush with hitch-hiking. But upon arrival at Fourmile Lake it didn't take long to ascertain that our hopes of a cosy little diner or sweet shop were unfounded. Overall the place was fairly quiet, with just a handful of RVs and super-sized campervans – most likely with their own fully-stocked kitchens and power-showers – decorating the shore. We decamped at a hot metal picnic table. There we sat in silence, gazing out at a couple of fishing boats while we consumed a highly disappointing lunch of tortilla wraps coated with packets of Nutella and peanut butter. *Oh, to be on one of those pleasure boats, bobbing away, soaking up the sun.*

By the time we eventually reconnected with the PCT with replenished water stocks, we calculated only a mile had been added to our day, thanks solely to Rick. Most importantly though, I had learnt a valuable lesson: do not entrust Conrad with map reading. To be fair, I should have claimed responsibility for the original wrong turn as I was in the lead. But I didn't.

The remainder of our day's walking was uneventful. In a tiny clearing amongst towering trees we called it a day. It was our seventh night since leaving Ashland, but the first time we found ourselves camping completely alone in desolate wilderness. In fact, we hadn't seen another soul the entire afternoon and it felt unsettling to us city folk. Thanks to the cloak of a thick tree canopy it was virtually dark long before sunset, creating an eerie enclosure.

While trying not to scratch today's round of mozzie bites – and still fighting off new ones – we concluded (once again) that this had been our toughest day yet.

"I'm *fack'erd*!" Conrad proclaimed, dropping his pack into the dirt. "Get it? F*****g-knackered – *fack'erd*!" he repeated, sounding proud of his invention.

I looked up at him through my mosquito net, dejected.

"I can't speak. I'm *ex-hausted*."

The air was abuzz with the biting menace, attempting a feeding frenzy on their stationary targets. It felt impossible to complete even the simplest task with them shrouding us, but we had little choice. Conrad rounded up our water bladders in search of the nearby spring. As soon as his figure disappeared, I realised how alone I was. Those few minutes of isolation in the woods gave me the heebie-jeebies, I was well and truly spooked. All my crazy fears of the things that happen in the darkened woods – which I seemed to have temporarily forgotten about – came flooding back. For ten minutes I stood rigid, just listening.

Much to my relief, Conrad eventually returned. We ate and retreated into the tent as soon as humanly possible to escape the relentless hounding. Mosquitoes had successfully made cooking a nightmare, eating intolerable, and any chance of a quick wash-down futile. Don't those guys ever sleep? After listening to a podcast, I turned to discover Conrad was already lifeless. It was just me again. I laid there beneath the creaking trees, detecting every last sound to determine whether it posed a threat. I eventually slipped into slumber, only to be abruptly woken at around 1 a.m. to the sound of movement on the forest floor. This wasn't just a chipmunk. The steps were heavy and coming towards the tent. I bolted upright, partly restrained by my sleeping bag, giving Conrad a shove.

"What's that?! Can you hear it?"

He sleepily cracked his eyes open and listened.

"It's probably just deer," he croaked, with little concern.

But I wasn't convinced. I was on high alert.

"You don't know that, it could be *bears*."

"They're not getting our food, I hung it in the trees. It's not bears. Go back to sleep." He closed his eyes.

Just that second, a gargantuan claw ripped through the tent, revealing the hot, snorting breath of a giant grizzly... Only joking; that was just a brief snippet of the scene playing out in my twisted mind as I laid awake. To my relief, the steps passed us by. A couple of hours later I was woken again by the same sound travelling the other way, after which I tensely remained awake, wishing for daybreak so we could get the hell out of there.

Next day, continuing with our rapid induction into the great outdoors, came snow trekking. In southern England, where we receive perhaps a week of light snow a year, it's easy to avoid. And after making the obligatory snowman or posting a few #snowday-s, I'd say the majority generally stockpile groceries and hibernate until after it's melted because, let's face it, in England you can't get anywhere when even the wrong type of leaves falling closes down train lines. What kind of catastrophe would occur if we received snow like the kind we were about to encounter beggars belief. So, when at over 6,500 feet we rounded the western face of Luther Mountain, what greeted us wasn't familiar terrain. Within metres, the trail transformed into steep banks of the white stuff, sharply sloping off the mountain edge into oblivion.

It stopped us entirely in our tracks, professionally kitted out as we were in nothing but glorified trainers. At that moment I recalled some advice I'd read in the *SAS Survival Guide* – a tongue-in-cheek gift from my brother. It stated:

"If not equipped with proper ice axes and crampons and skilled in their use, try to keep clear of mountain ice."

The book then went on to say something about the use of security ropes, but to be honest, not expecting this advice to ever be relevant to me, I skipped over that part. This now seemed an oversight; it didn't take a survival expert to understand the unavoidable danger facing us. One badly-placed step could have taken either of us plunging to our death on a valley floor far, far below. And a glance over the edge convinced me of the impenetrable nature of the densely-packed forest; there was no way Search and Rescue would ever salvage a body.

Now let me educate you in the delights of "post-holing". This happens when you lose a foot – or half a leg in my case – into deceptively soft snow. I had ventured less than ten feet before that new information got added to my reel of daily lessons. And while Conrad found it hilarious, being the person with snow now packed into my shoes, I couldn't bring myself to share his enthusiasm.

I had to give it to Conrad though, he took to the challenge with great patience, inching across the slopes deliberately. With each step he forcefully carved foot wells with his giant duck-feet, which I duly tracked.

"Just take your time," he coached me reassuringly.

"Have you looked down there?! We'd definitely die. It's like a bottomless pit," I remonstrated.

Conrad ignored me.

"I should tie us together," he sighed, "if you go over I might as well go too, or I'll have to answer to your mum!"

The very thought of that scenario did make me laugh –and went some way to easing up my rigid frame.

"But seriously," he continued changing his tone, "take it slowly, 'cos if you post-hole with too much forward momentum you'll break a leg."

Needless to say, a wave of relief followed as the precarious ice-traverse seemingly ended in an old burn-out zone. We followed the trail along an exposed shale ridge littered with the charred relics of tall, narrow tree-trunks, standing lifeless in the afternoon sun. The visibility from up so high was incredible, but away from the shade we found ourselves wilting in the sun. Despite our limited resources I was beginning to understand what was meant by the popular PCT phrase "the trail provides", with the appearance of a random ice deposit. Showcasing our new resourcefulness, we stopped at the mound to fill our hats and take advantage of its cold, hard surface; the cooling effect on my butt felt magic.

My adrenalin levels had just about recovered from the earlier snow section – in fact I was feeling pretty proud of our professional handling of a sticky situation – when after progressing along a few more hairpin-turn switchbacks we found ourselves stood at the edge of Devil's Peak. I'm sure my mouth dropped wide open with the realisation of what lay ahead. I thought we had just *conquered* Devil's Peak back there.

Devil's Peak clearly became a defining moment for me; pushing myself over the steep edge was undoubtedly the scariest thing I had done in 33 years of living. Some people would call that lame – the kind of adrenalin junkie who jumps out of aeroplanes for the fun of it – but I'm a great believer in self-preservation. If either of us had smashed into a tree whilst hurtling down the mountain on our butts at that moment, completely isolated from any road and with no phone signal, it would have been a tiny bit problematic. Thankfully that didn't happen.

My legs trembled as I dug my ankles deep into the snow to control my speed. With the cold air burning my cheeks, and some swaying that thankfully didn't tip me over, I made it safely down the slope, joining Conrad in the wide basin below. As I stood up, turning back to check out my tracks, I was flabbergasted. I couldn't believe what I had just achieved; what a nerve-quaking rush. My legs were soaked, my butt a block of ice, but I was *alive*.

We trekked through a sea of snow to reach camp thanks entirely to the help of iPhone GPS. The fright I received from Devil's Peak spiked once again, when on the way we passed a trail of fresh bear tracks. Well, what we determined were fresh bear tracks at least. We were no tracking experts but they looked legit, with five clear claw marks spread wider than my outstretched hand. Without bear spray, or any reasonable means of self-defence, my go-to solution to an inevitable bear attack was to simply make lots of noise in the hope they would sense a threat and scatter long before actually realising what little threat we presented. That night I embarked on a loud mumbling monologue detailing all the mundane camp-related actions I performed, as well as vocalising any random thought entering my head.

"I'm going to put my wet shoes next to the fire now to dry them off, I can't feel my toes... jeez, I stink like shit... I'm boiling up the water for dinner now, it's mac'n'cheese night, yum yum..."

While this must have been infuriating for Conrad it obviously worked: we didn't see a single bear!

From Devil's Peak, the PCT drops into Seven Lakes Basin, where it appeared the tap had been left on, with snow clinging to every rock and tree. Although we hadn't said it out loud, we both secretly hoped we could pull off a miracle and cover the remaining 23 miles to Crater Lake that day. But after four miles, thanks to the snow, we glumly accepted this wasn't going to be possible. It was at this point Conrad confessed a little something: that morning, just metres from our tent he had found two sets of big cat prints in the snow. They lay next to where our hiking poles stood in the ground, leading away towards our food bags hanging in the tree. After confirming the bags were untouched, he had taken the decision to scrub them out instead of showing me, from fear of triggering a freak-out. I was horrified. After all the hours of listening to the things that go bump in the night I had somehow missed the heavy steps so close! Although I protested his deception, I was secretly glad I never saw the tracks. I mean, how could I have possibly hung around long enough to eat breakfast?

While I kept looking over my shoulder every few yards, we sighted a tent right next to the trail. From it sprung the first person we'd seen since Fourmile Lake – Dave the *professional* traveller, slash drifter. Dave didn't strike me as your typical hiker, it was nearly 10 a.m. and he was still lying, half-baked, inside the inner membrane of his tent, with mosquitoes buzzing around him from a broken door zipper. Relieved to be reunited with his foam sitting pad which we'd found abandoned on a log where he'd left it after fleeing a cloud of mosquitoes, he prattled away relishing the company. I got the impression he'd been drawn to the trail because he'd no better place to be, which made me empathetic and meant we lingered there getting bitten for quite some time. He referred to the mosquitoes surrounding us as "maddening." He did seem quite mad.

That day we passed the last water source for the next 16 miles. The four litres we now carried needed to last until Crater Lake, including an overnight camp. The trail kept taking us from damp forested areas with patches of snow, mosquitoes rampant, to arid bush climbing above the shade. In these places, long stretches of open country caused by old forest fires meant we couldn't escape the sun. Here, in the Oregon high desert we caught our first faint glimpse of Crater Lake's famous rim. And unsurprisingly it was still sprinkled in snow.

Day 9 gained significance for another reason. Up to this point – much to Conrad's amusement – I had managed to live in the wild without once having to use the *bush toilet*. Using Conrad's words, I had not "dropped the kids off" outside due to flushable washroom facilities in Hyatt Lake and Klum Landing. It had to happen at some point, I guess, but typically I found myself suddenly overcome at a less than opportune moment. Dropping my pack, I leapt off into the brambly undergrowth, frantically digging a hole with a tiny plastic trowel as I struggled to hold it in. Shitting in the woods requires great balance while holding a deep squat, a seriously taxing workout on the quads. Thankfully, it gets easier over time, and what a relief it is, liberating even. Once I was done, I turned around to bury the evidence and was shocked to see the product of our new, dehydrated rabbit-food diet. *Must dig a bigger hole next time.*

Fifteen miles of vengeful mosquito-biting, snow-persisting mountain-climbing later, we decided to call it a night on the top of the strangely-named Goose Egg Ridge. Only after setting up camp did we notice a large number of animal bones scattered just feet away. The hairs on the back of my neck sprung up when I spied the crushed jaw-bone of what I guessed was a deer or an elk. We had officially established "Graveyard Camp" inside a cougar kill zone, basically baiting the bloody animals with our juicy flesh. Yet, although feeling rattled, it was a true testament to how drained I felt that I didn't suggest we do anything about it – let the lions eat us, I was done.

It was our third consecutive night wild camping. I felt grimy. The foul, ripe odour following me around was in fact me. Our test camping experiences before starting the trail had only ever involved a single night on the dirt, and not to mention two of the three occurrences happened in campsites equipped with hot showers. My hair desperately needed a wash, but given our water rationing, even if I did carry shampoo – which I didn't – it was futile. To top off my miserable mood, the flame on our stove went dead while I was boiling water to make dinner. Our gas canister had run out. At that point I wanted to cry. Jerky and a granola bar made for a shitty, unsatisfying dinner. Worse still, it was my own fault. When Conrad quizzed me about my cooking methods, I learnt gas burners are designed to rapidly boil water and are therefore not supposed to be set on a low flame. That just drains gas. Obviously.

The closer we got to Crater Lake, the more snow we faced. Hiking in these conditions wearing light-weight trail runners meant our feet were constantly wet. I cursed the REI sales guy who'd confidently advised foot ventilation was more important than waterproofing; what did he know? I couldn't endorse his logic on mornings where we had no choice but to hike out of camp squelching. Even a raging camp fire couldn't dry them out. I was becoming slightly obsessed with checking my wrinkled toes to check for foot rot, wondering what irrevocable damage I was causing.

Just in case I haven't already made this clear enough: hiking conditions of southern Oregon were tough. On the final morning push into Crater Lake I was experiencing what I can only describe as jelly-leg syndrome. My body was slowly going into shut-down, whereby one by one, each limb decided to become non-responsive and give up on me. Maybe it was just dehydration, but I was stumbling all over the place, tripping up and cursing my stupid self for being so weak.

Not long after passing a small wooden sign designating the park boundary, I came to a halt, throwing myself down into the frozen dirt. I laid there motionless, complaining I couldn't go on. Conrad removed his pack and planted himself with me. My body had never experienced such physical demand before. Muscles deep in the backs of my legs and butt I didn't know existed were screaming, my wet feet soft and tender, and my neck and shoulders strained under the alien pressure on my back. I had hit breaking point with five miles to go.

I hadn't considered making a scene; somehow by body acted unconsciously. I certainly wasn't one to relish amateur dramatics, so I'm not sure where the switch-flicking came from. While Conrad fished out painkillers from his bag, my mind spun all over the place. It wasn't supposed to be me who cracked. Between the two of us, I was the one who went to the gym most often. Of all the concerns I felt before joining the trail, I didn't consider the physicality of having to walk every day could be the greatest challenge. I was especially confident I could out-perform Conrad because just 10 months before he could barely walk due to a blood clot in his leg that developed after vascular surgery. Yes, thanks to a discharge nurse who decided to ignore the surgeon's instructions to give Conrad blood thinners after the op, he developed a clot, which a mad dash to the emergency room days later confirmed. Six months of anticoagulants followed, and we had to get a special doctor's note to confirm it was safe for him to fly to Dubai. His right leg still looked bigger than the left and ached from time to time. I think in some way his ability to recover from such a physical fright might have motivated him to this very spot. I bet he was regretting it now.

Conrad handed me his water bottle and a couple of pills which I swallowed without question, before he took it back and downed the same dose. We sat there in the frost, eating the last of our trail bars, staring into the white abyss like zombies. I eventually accepted we had to move. The snow become even deeper as the terrain evened out. And with it, the number of fallen trees grew, creating a maze of confusion. At one point, we hiked purely along tree trunks, jumping between them in the direction the GPS pointed to. We stopped around every mile to eat small bits of our dwindling food supplies for energy. After countless more steps, it suddenly appeared: Highway 62, the sun bouncing off its dark tarmac. *Hallelujah!*

Even more promising, a large van was parked directly across the road from the trailhead. This was surely fate. A slim blonde lady noticed us and started crossing the road headed in our direction. We must have looked quite a sight. I began feeling self-conscious, but this wouldn't stop me from biting her hand off for the ride she was about to offer. Or so I thought.

My heart sank the very second I heard the words: "Do you guys have cell service? We've broken down."

Faces visibly dropping, we both fished out our phones, turned them off aeroplane mode to check, before confirming we didn't.

"OK, thanks anyway, I guess one of us will cycle for help."

And with that she turned around, crossing back over the deserted highway.

8

Reaching a Milestone

To call Crater Lake National Park's Mazama Village a *village* is an exaggeration. As far as I could tell staggering into the parking lot, it consisted of a general store, an RV park, a few cabins, and a restaurant. It wouldn't exactly qualify as a village by the English definition – I mean, where was the pub? But still, none of that mattered. We'd made it, and I can easily say I have never been so glad to arrive somewhere in my entire life. What a triumph!

The parking lot was packed with vacationing families hopping in and out of their air-conditioned SUVs. We instinctively gravitated towards the picnic tables outside the rustic general store, home to a small gathering of hikers. Before we could even heave our packs onto the ground, Dave appeared with a can of beer.

"You made it then?" he slurred.

Conrad looked up and exhaled, "yeah, just about."

"Never doubted it. You won't bee-lieve it, they got dollar beers!"

Now, I'm not sure what time Dave had begun his drinking session, but he was very animated for 11 a.m. I found him intense in my fragile state. He referred to our collective group as "Hikertrash," a term I resented, and positioned himself a bit too close for comfort.

I sometimes wondered if Dave ever left Mazama. He seemed pretty content with his cheap beer and free campground showers. Unlike other hikers, who occasionally resurfaced further along the trail, we never heard any news of him again.

As soon as the resort's lunch service started, we slipped away for a well-earned burger. Our backpacks and trekking poles looked pretty conspicuous entering the casual family-fayre Annie Creek Restaurant, so I don't think it was a coincidence the waitress seated us way out in the back. Not that we cared. Sitting in padded chairs, slurping away on free soda refills, felt like paradise. We rudely sat in silence glued to our phones, finally having the opportunity to re-connect with the world over Wi-Fi after a four-day hiatus. I don't think I had ever been offline that long since getting my first smart phone back in 2007; a pretty sad self-reflection. Do you remember the time, *back in the day* when people would actually sit around, collectively debating life's perplexing questions, becoming increasingly animated over the course of many drinks, without the power of Google Search feeding instant answers? Well, those moments now seem to belong to a bygone era.

Back at the camp store, the group's numbers had grown. A couple of new, very smiley ladies called Laurie and Vicki introduced themselves as Toaster and Smudge and started discussing trail buzz. They had just witnessed the taxi departure of Alfred, aka Speedball, who had arrived the day before, resolved on quitting the trail. He said it was just miserable. I found the news surprising, and somehow satisfying. Alfred, so boldly confident and well-prepared compared to us, had quit. His actions seemed to validate our struggles and prove the gravity of the shit-show we had just overcome.

The ladies themselves were retired National Park employees and seasoned PCT hikers. Over the years, they had steadily walked the length of California, but despite the challenges of the High Sierra, they asserted this last section of Oregon had been the toughest they ever faced. They attributed this purely to the adverse conditions which gave us solace. I wondered if that meant conditions would improve, transforming the challenge into something manageable sometime soon.

While we were absorbing the sun in our hot rain gear – clothes in the washer – Dan from Kentucky arrived from his intense two-day road walk. He looked very tanned. He was joined not long after by Jesus-lookalike Habit, who brought further news from Fish Lake that Dirty Hippy had pulled out. For us this was perhaps the biggest shocker. This young, surfer dude-looking guy had arrived in Fish Lake the day after us with blood streaming down his face. Meanwhile, his mum had somehow gotten the contact details of the resort and called through to Pam, who placed a handset in his trembling hands. Through earwigging on his private conversation, we ascertained his injuries came from a fall while crossing the infamous lava fields. I'm sure it could have been a lot worse. He down-played the situation to calm his panicked mum, but from the look of it, his head had obviously taken a banging. A close call. As a super-fit 19-year-old training for the marines, he had been making record time from Mexico. He was even climbing extra mountains on the side with an ice axe just for the fun of it! His reason for quitting the trail? According to him: he just got bored.

The last trail casualty reached us later that evening as we waited impatiently for a take-away pizza. Yes, following burgers and a much-needed nap we were back for more nourishment. Micah, the young Oregonian guy we befriended near Hyatt Lake, walked into the restaurant. In fact, it was more of a John Wayne-inspired bow-legged hobble. He introduced us to his parents who were in tow with handshakes. An experienced hiker, he had managed the trek from Fish Lake using every hour of daylight to complete the section in just two days. It had taken us three and a bit. I thought we were broken, but the pain on his face was something else. He gloomily reported counting 803 trees obstructing the trail since Fish Lake. His parents were there to take him home. He was out. I couldn't blame him, but for some reason I felt disheartened to see him go, much more than Speedball. Before he left, Micah kindly agreed to post our Kindles back to the Marshmeiers. Yes – we had carried nearly a pound's worth of e-readers for the last 10 days and we hadn't switched them on even once!

We unexpectedly enjoyed two nights of rest and recuperation in Mazama Village, having managed to secure a cabin for an extra night and push our night in the Lodge back a day. The days whizzed past in a whirl of eating, sleeping, and socialising.

Conrad was initially disappointed our simple but clean cabin set amongst ponderosa pine trees didn't contain a television. Yet once I pointed out that he was free to go and camp with the other hikers while I enjoyed the bed and shower, he swiftly changed his tune and darted into the bathroom. As he worked his way through the clean towels, I managed to reach home over the faint Wi-Fi connection.

"It's Katie!" my mum shouted away from the receiver with excitement, presumably to get my dad's attention. She returned her focus back to me, sounding all choked up. "Where are you?"

My response was full of pride.

"We made it to Crater Lake. Well, not actually the Lake yet, but the main park campground, and we've got a cabin!"

It was so good to hear her voice. She fumbled with the phone before my dad joined her on speaker.

"Your mum's been worried about you," he stated. "Haven't you had a shower yet? I can smell you from here!"

I laughed, though I was sure I could hear my mum sobbing. If she was, I'm guessing it was just the relief setting in, as the last message she received from us warned of snow and bad conditions ahead. When I sent that text from Fish Lake it seemed like a succinct update, but now I realised I had caused her distress. *Must put a more positive censor on my correspondence going forward.*

The phone reception wasn't great, but I happily chatted away.

"It was the best shower of my life! We just picked up our first box, and we're just about to have a nap."

"You mean Chris remembered to send it?" Mum asked, half-joking, but also surprised.

As we had posted the first one ourselves, whether Chris was up to the job remained to be seen.

I talked them through some of our more colourful escapades from the last few days, and in return my mum provided family updates. She was just telling me about my brother's wedding plans, or lack of, when the call abruptly ended. Turns out Crater Lake National Park was having a power outage, so with nothing else to do we hit the hay.

That afternoon I added "best sleep ever" to my new list of simple things to appreciate. Neither Conrad nor I had been adapting well to life sleeping under canvas. To start with, wilderness camping is a far cry from the more typical *glamping* of pull-up camping, where families bring pretty much every home comfort bar the kitchen sink. Our set-up was compact and minimal. The first time we erected our tent, I couldn't believe that the manufacturer Big Agnes had gotten away with marketing it as a three-person. Dan had the two-person version in the same distinctive yellow hue just for him, so three-year old toddlers must have been used in the tent design process, which did nothing to help my claustrophobic anxieties. Given the limited headspace, Conrad generally got dressed outside, then awkwardly crawled in, unable to flex his body enough within the confines of the sloped roof. Shoulder-to-shoulder, exhausted, we desperately tried to sleep, but usually both followed the same pattern of broken hours stolen here and there. I blamed the three-inch air mattresses which resembled pool lilos. I just couldn't get comfortable, spending night after night tossing and turning, losing sensation down one side, re-adjusting, before repeating minutes later. Each time one of us shifted even slightly, our mattresses made a loud scrunching sound, like rolling over foil balloons, which meant we were acutely aware of the other's presence. Most mornings I would awake to the alarm groggy and miserable, with some kind of new neck or back ache from the night. The discomfort actually made me want to get up. Conrad was the same, so we only started communicating after drinking coffee.

Despite the last two nights spent in the park, we hadn't yet seen the famous lake. Five miles stood between us and the crater's rim.

We departed shortly after breakfast. With the contents of our first resupply box packed, we now moved fully loaded with five days of food. I feel like a broken record, but the morning's hike was hard-going. Thanks to its position at the crest of the Cascade Mountains, the park receives an average snow dump of 43 feet a year, and despite the late June sun, thick pockets of compacted snow clung to the shaded path. We climbed over 1,400 feet, relying almost entirely on GPS to navigate.

The mosquitoes continued their unrelenting terrorism. We couldn't stop. Pausing to filter water would have given them too much satisfaction, so we hiked thirsty. While covering such unpleasant buggy sections, Conrad liked to remind me of the various mosquito-borne infections that we were both now likely harbouring. West Nile virus and Dengue fever were uncommon in the States, but cases were on the rise.

"If anyone's going to get bloody *den-gee* fever," I stated to Conrad, point blank, "it'll be you."

Based on his track-record, he couldn't disagree.

As we trudged through the crunching remnants of winter, Dan appeared up ahead.

"Didn't we just see you at breakfast?" Conrad asked, puzzled.

Dan gave us a glimmer of a smile.

"I'm slack packing. Caught the 9 a.m. trolley up to the rim to crunch off the miles. It's real pretty up there."

Slack packing is hiker-talk for walking without a pack. I had to laugh!

"You're so jammy." I nudged Conrad in the arm, "why didn't we think of that?"

But secretly I was mulling over this cunning move. I couldn't decide if it was cheating or sheer genius.

"Thought I'd tick off the miles to give myself a better start tomorrow. Can't believe this snow. Think I've been off the trail more than I've been on it." He had an unofficial PCT navigation app called *Guthook's* open on his phone.

We assured him the snow got better lower down, with our collective attention suddenly turned towards the gathering mosquitoes.

Dan was first to respond. "I gotta keep moving, or they'll swarm me!"

We said goodbye, parting ways, Dan moving downhill much faster than we continued climbing.

It took us nearly three hours to reach Crater Lake's historic Rim "*Village*". At the ridiculously-understaffed cafe we rehydrated by guzzling litres of over-priced soda, while trying to avoid the chaos. It was the beginning of the July 4th holiday weekend, so the RVs were out in force. Animated kids chased each other over mounds of lingering snow next to passing cars while their parents happily ignored them.

Only a short walk from the touristy gift shop, a marvel

appeared. We stared down into a strikingly azure pool, deeply encased within the banks of a perfectly-formed volcano. The lake was completely empty, aside from a small, pointy island floating just off shore. It was utterly mesmerising, not just because of its spectacular beauty, but also because we were actually at CRATER LAKE – and we had walked there! The enormity of reaching our first milestone was huge. I didn't know whether to pinch myself or break down in tears of absolute joy.

"We made it!" I beamed, unable to contain my emotion.

I wrapped an arm around Conrad's waist and pulled him close in an unusual, sweaty public display of affection. We stood there admiring the volcano's caldera cone, its snow-dusted peaks and still, calming water. A tiny spec in the pool caught my attention. It was causing the only ripples on the entire lake. I watched it for some time before identifying a boat. It was heading towards Wizard Island, a name we discovered from an information panel, bestowed because the island resembled a wizard's hat. The island was actually a volcanic cone within the larger volcanic cone of Crater Lake, giving some indication of the sheer size of the monument.

It was such a great feeling to know the day's hike was already complete with the sun still shining for us to enjoy. After taking the obligatory round of photographs of the country's deepest lake, we went in search of some information on trail conditions. At the tiny visitor centre, fancily named an "Interpretative Centre", we tried speaking to a park ranger. The resulting conversation was staggering for the sheer lack of insight or information he was able to provide. Maybe he was new, or answers to trail conditions were not in his script so early in the season. Frustrated, we gave up and retreated towards an appointment with the very grand-looking lodge.

Crater Lake Lodge is an eye-catching property. Perched on the south-western edge of the volcano's rim, the green-roofed timber-and-stone building commands an unparalleled view of the lake a thousand feet below. It was built in 1915 to provide accommodation for those privileged enough to make the difficult journey back then to visit the lake. In the nineties it was virtually rebuilt, due to pressure to modernise, and the need to reinforce the structure against heavy winter snow. If it wasn't for the hotel's history exhibit, I would have been none the wiser, as the original design remains. It certainly is a charming building, with giant stone fireplaces and heaps of internal rustic woodwork.

I felt slightly embarrassed standing in the elegant reception area checking in. Hiking poles, dirty clothes and massive packs wasn't exactly the *look du jour*. But still, we were lucky to be able to afford a night there.

As we made our reservation months before we had been particularly careful to note the cancellation policy, given the seemingly likely event we wouldn't make it. But, lo and behold, we didn't cancel, and now faced an 18-hour mini-vacation to enjoy. Even better – without the backpack weighing me down I felt light as a feather. The new insoles and Epsom salt soak had worked a treat on my feet. I bounced around sending postcards and taking photographs of scenery that look super-imposed. We ended the day in rocking chairs on the hotel's veranda where we watched daylight slip away behind the mountains.

Reflecting on the intense journey so far, it was baffling for us that our hike had started just twelve days earlier. Time seemed to warp out on the trail. Each day we arose at first light and remained active until long after sunset. The trail demanded our focus, both on the surroundings and on every step, making for long, draining days. It didn't help that it felt nature was personally out to test our resolve. Yet, at that moment the thousands of mosquitoes and blow-downs seemed almost worthwhile as we stared at Crater Lake, a jewel of a reward. Look at us, I thought, we'd come so far, from smashing our two-hour record of setting up and dismantling camp, to getting familiar with answering nature's call "wilderness" style, and breaking in our hiking feet without breaking any bones. But, most importantly, we hadn't been murdered in our sleep. Not yet, anyway. And, in a personal triumph, I had washed my hair just once!

We studied our location on Google Maps, impressed at how far we had travelled physically too. Then we quickly realised what a paltry distance it was in the context of the Canadian border and went quiet.

British people have a tendency towards self-deprecation, we

can't help it, it's in our nature; we'll happily be the first to profess we can't do something, or to slag ourselves off. But in the last few days at Crater Lake, a decent number of strangers had stopped us to ask about our hike and to congratulate us. This was very inspiring. We acknowledged this with a glimmer of pride, gazing up at the stars now reflecting in the lake. Raising our glasses, we toasted to a safe trip ahead.

9

Time to Quit

With great apprehension, we realised it was time to leave Crater Lake. We had no idea what conditions lay ahead as we embarked on the next 26 water-free miles; the furthest distance we should have ever needed to squirrel away water. One thing we did know was that this haul would coincide with fully-loaded food supplies, testing the flimsy fabric of our backpacks to their limits. And let's not forget mosquitoes, aka the devil's spawn; every sign indicated they were waiting for us out there. Yet, despite these anticipated issues – or should I say "challenges" – we felt spurred on to continue by the very fact we'd somehow beaten the odds to make it that far. How much worse could it possibly get?

As the PCT is open to both hikers and equestrians, the official route bypasses the delicate heart of the park. Like many other hikers, we couldn't understand getting this close without seeing the highlight, so decided to take the popular alternative route to skirt around the crater's western rim. The air felt cool in the morning light, but the forecast predicted another scorcher so we made haste. With fewer people in the park in the early hours, the scenery felt majestic. Fluffy clouds littered the sky, reflected by the lake's giant mirror, and nicely framed within its castle-like crater walls.

The trail initially weaved up and down, hugging the crevices of the lake. We couldn't resist taking more photos of the enchanting views from each new angle. At the Watchman, the highest point the trail reaches in Oregon and Washington at 7,676 feet, the snow became solid ice, forcing us to retrace our steps through thick snow to the Rim Road. Of course, it being America the road had no safe pavement – or *sidewalk* – designed for pedestrians, so it wasn't ideal. As we walked in single-file, especially conscious of speeding vehicles on tight bends, the ploughed snow-pack

towered above our heads. Further up the road we passed a sign
for the Watchman trailhead. If we had continued on our original
route we would have crossed the Watchman trail shortly after.
From this side, orange warning tape criss-crossed the faint path,
with a useful sign advising the trail was closed.

Our strategy for the long waterless section was to carry a
massive five litres each and melt snow if required. Bent over
under the record load, it became abundantly clear that neither
our packs nor our feeble bodies were designed to carry that kind
of weight. The resulting day-long pain was a constant hindrance,
tenderising our shoulders, rubbing our hips, and hammering the
hell out of our feet. The extra weight felt so unnecessary, given
the tantalising cool lake below.

The lake's deep-blue hue stems from the fact it doesn't have
any natural inlets, relying on snow and rain to fill it, so the
water was inaccessible to us. I was caring less and less for the
beautiful sight each time I resisted taking another sip from my
limited supply. As most visitors to the park drive this road, with
various pull-outs and even a portaloo in one scenic viewpoint we
passed, I couldn't understand why there wasn't a single ounce
of drinkable water available. Not even a spigot. I mean, how
difficult could it be to install one?

Dan passed us shortly after we joined the road. He had saved
a heap of time by setting out intent on road-walking the entire
way, and by getting the shuttle bus to the lake let's not forget.
We had tried the *proper* route, but traipsing through snow was
slow and tiring, so we accepted Dan had the right idea. Dan had
started to grow on me during our time in Mazama Village. My
initial impressions at Fish Lake were that of a grumpy old guy
who liked to keep himself to himself. But it turned out he was just
more reserved than your typical American, and I appreciated his
dry sense of humour and sarcastic observations the more I got to
know him.

In a small, gravel road-side ditch, Dan gave us a brief update
on his day, solemnly informing us he was hauling seven litres,
before proceeding to march on until his distinctive red t-shirt
outline disappeared out of sight. I found it deeply frustrating

that we couldn't keep up with a 59-year-old. Given the snowy conditions and slow start, we quickly made the decision to copy Dan's plan and follow the main road out of the park instead of re-connecting with the trail.

It turned out the weather forecast was not wrong. The sun was making conditions worse, rapidly heating us into a pair of prattling prunes. How it could be so hot with snow still on the ground was beyond comprehension. It just didn't make sense. Hiking at this high altitude already made life more difficult – and coming from London, we consider anything above sea level "high altitude."

It soon became obvious we needed more water. I felt a sense of panic brewing inside. This was it, my worst fears finally coming into fruition two weeks in: I would collapse and die from dehydration, leaving my body to be picked clean by vultures. After we had left the lake behind, earlier snow deposits had rapidly depleted until only the occasional pocket remained. Desperate, we stopped on the edge of the road in a snowy bank and emptied out our stove. I was conscious we resembled a pair of lunatics, scooping up the dirty road-side snow with our new plastic Crater Lake souvenir flasks and dumping it into our cook pan, burner roaring, but we didn't care. To be honest, we both hoped that a friendly passing motorist would pull over to offer us pity water, which never happened. It took us nearly an hour to melt and filter a few measly litres – melting snow is not as easy as it sounds.

By late afternoon on the edge of the straightest, most boring, never-ending road, Conrad and I were stumbling along in a zoned-out state. Many an RV, full of excited July 4th weekenders, had zoomed past with their windows closed. I hated those people for their air-conditioning, and the refreshing beverages they no doubt consumed from the comfort of their ride. In the exposed arid heat, somewhere amidst an area called the Pumice Desert, I started to become really angry with each laboured step. How could we be walking through a National Park and there be absolutely no water facilities? I passed the time mentally writing a letter of complaint to the authorities at the National

Park Service. I'm sure they would have found my language very colourful.

After miles of road-walking in single-file, I started making something out in the distance. *Was it a mirage?* Heat reflecting off the tarmac was making the horizon wobbly. As we drew closer kiosks, marking the park's northern entrance station, appeared in the road. There was another structure too.

"Can you see that?" I shouted over my shoulder in Conrad's direction, with a sudden burst of enthusiasm.

His response was gruff. "Where you looking?" Obviously not in a joy-sharing mood.

"Just after the kiosk, to the left-hand side. Maybe it's restrooms. Or a shop." Whatever it was, *surely* it contained water.

"I wouldn't get your hopes up," Conrad replied gloomily.

But it was *something*, and I couldn't wait to get there to discover what. I guess I should have refrained from getting my hopes up, because it turned out to be nothing but another waterless portaloo. The northern entrance station consisted of a small toll booth flying the American flag, and a glorified dumping hole. A long line of stationary traffic snaked way back towards the highway.

I decided to walk past the cars wearing my most desperately thirsty look, encouraged by the previous kind people we had met on other days. The only people who acknowledged us were a couple of hippies who beckoned us over to their car window, only to ask what the hold-up was. *Thanks for nothing.*

As we continued, Highway 138 finally appeared. It was now nearly 6 p.m. and still ridiculously warm. According to our maps, there was a resort at Diamond Lake seven miles north. Given our horrific day we decided to try our luck hitch-hiking there, while slowly continuing towards the PCT trailhead in the opposite direction. The resort offered hope in the form of showers, pizza, and most importantly cold drinks, but much to our dismay we never made it; nobody was feeling hospitable enough to pick up strangers that day.

We found Dan sat in long grass at the highway trailhead. He looked frazzled. I was surprised to see him, expecting he would be miles ahead by now.

"What are you doing out here?" I asked. It was hardly a scenic rest stop.

"I'm tryin' to escape the damn mosquitoes! If I go in there they'll molest me!" He gestured towards the trail which led into the forest. There was something comical about his fragile state.

"Are they any better out here?" Conrad queried.

"There's a bit of a breeze, but I've still got a cloud of them attackin' me. I'm tryin' to cook, but all I'm getting is bitten."

I shared his pain. Since we had stopped, our mosquito issue had escalated tenfold. I dramatically filled Dan in on our day while watching him eating cubes of chicken from a questionable foil packet.

"I wanna die. I can't believe there was no water all day. Not even at the entrance station. They get hikers all the time, don't they? We wasted an hour melting snow! Not a single RV stopped to offer help. I'm so thirsty. This is torture!"

"Yeah, must have been 90 today," Dan conceded over another mouthful of chicken.

Conrad had to translate for me, 90 meant 32 degrees in the British language, yes aged 33 and I still hadn't manged to get my head around Fahrenheit.

"We just tried hitching to Diamond Lake, but no one stopped... so many tourists...I give up!" I moaned.

Dan was of the same mindset: "I don't care which way they're headin', I'll take a ride anywhere outta here right now."

Well, at least it wasn't just us pushed to the brink. We left Dan by the side of the road, hovering over his stove. We weren't sure if we would see him again if he was lucky enough to score a ride. But he wasn't. A short while later he traipsed back into the trees, setting up camp in a thicket not far from us. That night we remained in it together, an unlikely trio. Conrad and I were broken. So broken in fact, that instead of mustering up the energy to lament our dire situation, we agreed to "just sleep on it."

10

Snow Joke

Funny things happen in the woods. The very morning after we had hit our sleeping bags in pieces, desperate to be anywhere but there, the alarm beeped and we simply obeyed, with thoughts of retreating to the highway not even crossing our minds. Seeing Dan scamper off up the trail probably helped, at least subconsciously. And having passed out long before nightfall, we hadn't given ourselves the headspace to evaluate the proposition of quitting. I mean, logistically, say we did quit, we had no way of knowing how to get back to civilisation without the help of a phone signal. For now, we focused on just one simple concern: making it to the water refill 10 miles ahead.

Despite having improved the efficiency of our morning camp routine we left nearly an hour after Dan. Whereas hardcore hikers wake with the sun and knock out their first 10 miles before pausing for a bite, I don't function without coffee. As Conrad likes to say in a ridiculous high-pitched voice: "first I drink the coffee, then I do the things," to mimic me. So while boiling water I figured we might as well also start the day with the most important meal of the day too.

As I prepared breakfast each morning, Conrad would dismantle the tent. These were our defined jobs, making sense because I cared most about food and Conrad had an uncanny ability to whip the canvas off, thanks to his long arms. When we originally filled our resupply boxes, our typical breakfast rations consisted of a couple of days of porridge oats, granola, powdered milk, and the odd cereal bar. But by this point, I had concluded that only porridge – or "oatmeal" – would do. I actually went to bed looking forward to it, so that morning we had oatmeal for the morale boost, even though we couldn't spare the water to clean out the pan afterwards.

A glance at the map showed the trail was about to steadily

ascend to one of its highest points, cutting through the Mount Thielsen Wilderness. We knew this inevitably meant encountering snow. Imagine our delight when the initial miles began on a wide, clear, and mostly-level, forested track. We marched away, naively discussing how easy Oregon would be if it was all like this, until gradually, the odd spot of compacted ice appeared. They grew in coverage, shaded from the sun by the dense canopy of branches above. At around 6,800 feet we lost sight of the trail altogether, beginning to negotiate routes across slippery ice with hundreds of calculated decisions – *up-and-over? Straight across? Or down and rock scramble?* Whenever visible, we followed other footprints. Our progress dramatically fell to little over a mile an hour.

After a couple of painful hours, we found Dan sitting on a rock, eating a lunch of champions: crackers and peanut butter.

"You enjoying the snow?" I asked him with a smile, knowing how much he dreaded it. You see, up until then, he had managed to deliberately avoid getting himself into snowy situations, but that morning he set out with cautious optimism to see if he could manage it.

"Oh yeah! Those online people that said Oregon was *good to go* are talking a bunch of shit! They've got no idea what they're talking about from their armchairs back home!"

It was obvious from the irritated tone in his voice that he wasn't enjoying his day.

Conrad was staring at Dan's footwear, which contained additional metal chains over his boots.

"I see you've got spikes. Are they helping much on the ice?"

"Well, they give some traction; I'd slip and land on my behind if it weren't for them, but it's so damn icy I'm all over the place!"

I inwardly smiled at the butt slip I had experienced not ten minutes ago.

"Yeah, what is it about snow that makes it selectively pile up on the trail?! There's been some really sketchy bits with MASSIVE drop-offs," I quipped.

Conrad then pulled out the camera and started searching through it.

"I took a great picture of Kathryn fairy-stepping along a steep snow bank. You can see the mountain falling away at the edge!" Finding the referenced picture, he flashed it around.

"Nice one! Thanks for your support," I joked. *But I had to give it him, it was a remarkably tense shot!*

Dan was weary. "I'm glad I've got my beacon, 'cos this is dangerous! I wouldn't call what we're doin' "hiking" right now!"

He was referring to the emergency GPS spot beacon he carried, which he used to send generic *I'm safe* messages back to relatives each night and could be activated to alert Search and Rescue if he got into trouble. With safety in numbers, we joined forces. After all, Dan's emergency signal provided a glimmer of reassurance if the worst was to happen.

On a high outcrop, where the trail intersected with another, we came across three day hikers. They were sat on rocks, munching giant bags of crisps while carving doorstop sandwiches using an army knife and a block of cheese. The men were in fine spirits, happily chatting away, informing us of their plans to rock-climb the jagged shark-fin-resembling glacier above. But Conrad and I were distracted, completely mesmerised by their food. You see, we had started experiencing what's known in the hiking business as *hiker hunger*. With our miles generally increasing, and having spent the morning negotiating the snowy approach to Mount Thielsen, I was so low on energy that my stomach grumbled with appetite. Conrad focused on the crisps – his personal version of crack – salivating. While we all made small talk, I tried subtly complaining about living on dehydrated food, but sadly to no avail.

The day reached a heart-thumping climax high up on a steep frozen ledge. Dan stopped dead in his tracks, letting out a resigned "Aww, heck," as we eyed up the tall mogul-ridden ice field swallowing up the trail.

Conrad stepped up at this point, walking to the perilous edge to size up a possible route down. Meanwhile I turned my attention towards Dan. *"Throbbing Thrill Hammer"*, the very tongue-in-cheek trail name he had self-ordained the previous year, had already hiked 2,000 miles of the Californian trail, so I was surprised by his hesitance and anxious demeanour. My outlook lay somewhere in the middle of the two. Yes, I was scared, but fortunately thanks to Devil's Peak, this wasn't the Brits' first brush with human tobogganing. If you recall, Dan had road-walked that section, so while I nervously watched Conrad climb onto the chest-height ledge, I comforted myself in the knowledge that I was becoming particularly adept at taking tumbles in snow without breaking anything. More importantly though, and unbeknown to me at the time, I actually *was* getting a smidge braver by the day, with sporadic spikes in blood pressure becoming somewhat routine.

Our second butt slide down a steep ice chute involved a shorter, tamer slope compared to Devil's Peak, but also contained many more trees to potentially crash into. Conrad went first, with Dan standing somewhere in the background filming the event for his popular *Captain Dan* YouTube channel. Maybe that video would have gone viral if Conrad had suffered a gruesome crash, but thankfully we all eventually followed down without casualty. It was amusing – once I was safe of course – to turn around and see Dan's rigid frame following warily behind my own. From his fearful expression I realised I was doing pretty well. I have to say, I had handled this challenge with far greater confidence than the last – and would even go as far as to say I kind of enjoyed it. Who knew that facing fear head-on *before* giving it a chance to develop would prove so simple?

As the three of us arrived at the much-anticipated Thielsen Creek there was no sign of water. I froze, confused. We needed water. Anxiously, we left the trail and began trekking downhill while listening for clues. It took a few tense minutes before we registered a flowing sound echoing beneath our feet; yes, we had been walking over a fragile snow bridge. Looking ahead about a hundred metres from where it should have been, a melted break in the ice exposed a narrow stream of water. Relief poured over me.

Thielsen Creek was a prized break spot. In a small clearing beside the fast-flowing stream we settled onto a clear patch of dirt, removing our shoes and socks to bask in the sunshine. We took it in turns filtering water using the slow process of hand-squeezing the contents of the dirty bladder through our Sawyer filter, making sure to scoop it from the freezing current before bathing our stinking feet. Completing the scene were wet socks hanging from our makeshift laundry poles, and Dan bent over his stove. We collectively looked the epitome of what Hobo Dave had called "Hikertrash", even if I didn't want to accept it.

As we followed Dan's lead and began cooking an early meal, a lady appeared carrying a ridiculously over-loaded monster pack. We waved in recognition, but as she came stumbling towards us I could tell something was wrong. The woman was visibly shaking, her words impossible to grasp. It soon transpired that Ginger had just "fallen off the mountain," over the ledge we had slid down. Initially I assumed she was being a bit melodramatic, she was kooky, of an age similar to Dan, and physically didn't resemble your typical hiker. But then I noticed her ripped up, blood-stained trousers and stood to attention.

Dan really came into his own at this point, taking charge of the situation like a military pro. With his easy southern charm, he helped calm Ginger, before we heard the full story revealing her failed attempt to hike the chute before losing her footing and tumbling down the slope, planting legs first into a tree over 30 metres below. She was obviously in shock.

When I returned from a poorly-timed bush toilet a few minutes later, Dan was crouched beside Ginger, who was sat on a camp stool – yes, out of her monster pack must have come a seat – patiently studying her maps. He was helping her find a route out.

"You've got two options," he began with an army general's authority, "either 22 miles north up the PCT to the next forest road, or if you turn around and head back south, you can be out in 2."

Ginger screwed up her face not convinced, so Dan continued.

"We passed some mountain climbers at the last trail junction. I'm sure it was them we could hear hollerin' from the top of the mountain when we got here. They've got to be headed back to this parking lot," pointing it out on the map, "bet they'd be happy to give you a ride into town."

But Ginger was adamant that she couldn't face re-scaling the site of her fall.

"I already got a message from my huss-band. He saw me fall from my GPS. He messaged me right away saying: *You just fell, didn't you?* and asking if I was alright."

Those emergency beacons were clever little things. I guess that Ginger had a model similar to Dan's; I didn't realise they could be programmed to alert someone of a sudden drop in altitude.

She continued. "I've got this list my husband made me," producing a white piece of paper from a plastic wallet, which from my viewpoint looked like some kind of table of map coordinates.

"It's all the closest emergency extraction points, so I think I should go to the next one we arranged."

Dan didn't even flinch. He had just spent the last 10 minutes map reading for no reason, but hey, we hikers were a team. And how clever was carrying a list of emergency escape routes off the trail? Why hadn't an anally-retentive person such as me thought of that? The maps we carried were dedicated PCT *Halfmile* maps on A4 paper so, although essential and very detailed, they covered a very zoomed-in view of the trail and were not designed for those venturing onto intersecting trails or service roads. As far as we knew, there could have been a McDonald's just off the trail a couple of miles due west and we would have been none the wiser. That's a joke of course, Conrad would definitely have sensed it.

Ginger's – and Dirty Hippy's accident beforehand – served as a stark reminder of the dangers we faced. Just one poorly-judged step could easily lead to hazardous consequences; this was no Disney's Animal Kingdom.

A year later the trail would astonishingly claim six lives, with an additional young man from Ireland, David O'Sullivan still missing at the time of writing. These tragic deaths were each confirmed as accidental, with five caused by the hiker losing their footing in difficult conditions, including turbulent water crossings, ice chutes, and slippery rocks. The sixth death, of a man named Marvin Novo, was suspected to have been caused by heat-related injuries; the very reason I didn't dare set foot in the desert. Of course, I wasn't aware of this at the time, but knowing it makes my reverence for nature, first recognised on the trail, continue to grow to this day.

11

Smells Ripe

On Independence Day, fireworks echoed across America as Conrad and I created our own. We had spent the morning after meeting Ginger negotiating more snowfields, until reaching 7,560 feet – the *official* PCT highpoint for Oregon and Washington – where Dan had left our names and a giant arrow etched into the ground. Unfortunately, the arrow wasn't enough to prevent us from getting lost.

We wandered in zigzags across the glistening snow. Even the phone's GPS wasn't particularly useful; we'd wave it around to recalibrate it, but it failed to provide any feasible guidance to re-join the trail.

What people did before GPS I do not know. Navigation was another chapter I'd only skimmed through in the survival book. I'd given up after getting mightily confused about adjusting a compass for declination to work out orientation; I still don't get it. Luckily for me – or perhaps unluckily – I'd married a man who thinks an actual compass is redundant due to the power of his iPhone. If the battery ever dies he's f****d, but hey! Long gone were any sign of Dan's micro-spikes and all other tracks. So, tangled in a maze of snow-covered wilderness, it took us nearly two hours of bush-whacking to travel a mile. The same mile, I later discovered, Dan approached by screwing the map and walking in a straight line down a ravine to get off the mountain in no time at all.

The aforementioned fireworks came later that afternoon. Snow was beginning to melt as we quickly lost elevation, a welcome sight for both us and the mosquitoes. Yes, our followers loved the melting snow, laying their eggs in the cool, stagnant pools it leaves behind, so they were back in force and Conrad had finally suffered enough. Similar to my Crater Lake flip-out, he came to an abrupt stop mid-trail, but instead of collapsing he triggered a weird dancing freak out, flapping his arms and stomping, before throwing his sunglasses to the ground.

"What the *hell* are you doing?" I jibed unsympathetically. I could feel my eyes rolling without asking them to. I got it, the mozzies were a constant nuisance, but I was dealing with them by not taking the bait. In the grand scheme of things insects didn't seem the most significant issue to get worked up about.

Conrad started shrieking as if he'd just been shot. "They're driving me INSANE! They're making this trip *horrific*, they're gonna *force* me to quit!"

I was willing to ignore his little tantrum until hearing those last words which ignited something inside me – there was absolutely no way I was going to allow mosquitoes to be the reason for our failure; not after everything we'd already conquered!

"You're so bloody dramatic, I can't believe you threw your glasses on the ground like a f*****g baby! What are you gonna do if they break?"

"Stop being a *bitch*, they fell off my head, I didn't *throw* them. You don't get bitten like me, so you've got no idea, my skin is burning like hell!"

He was right to an extent, but I wasn't immune to their attack either. I had bites. Mozzies have their favourites though, and Conrad got their juices going. Maybe it was something in his blood – I once read they like blood-type O – or his musky smell perhaps. They certainly loved him, much more than I did at that moment.

I continued even more annoyed: "I can't believe you just said that! Pull yourself together, and just... just don't talk to me."

And with that I marched off down the trail, knowing it would take him some time to finish fishing the mosquito net out of his bag and to put it back on.

We hiked in silence that afternoon, hating one another. It felt very lonely. In the quiet I'd ruminate, dissecting every word of the spat, trying to understand who was most to blame. I hoped that Conrad wasn't about to quit, but just couldn't bring myself to apologise to try and prevent it because I really wanted to teach him a lesson, hoping he'd become more Bear Grylls as a result. I assured myself that any couple in the same situation would have had many more disagreements. I'm not actually sure how, or if the argument ever got resolved, but eventually we had no choice but to communicate. We simply had nobody else, and besides, neither one of us carried a complete tent so going solo wasn't really an option.

The bugs and physical demands were not the only struggles facing us. Since day one we'd both felt troubled by an impossible need to maintain a certain level of self-hygiene. At home we both showered at least once a day, sometimes more, we'd wear clean clothes, and I wouldn't dream of venturing out without at least a bit of makeup, deodorant and clean underwear. I had standards, after all, standards of hygiene not so easily preserved out in the wild. I knew from reading other hiking books and blogs that lightweight backpackers should ditch the deodorant and be satisfied with the occasional shower at rest stops, but we just couldn't let it go.

Our daily routine currently involved conducting a wet-wipe *wash* down before changing into night clothes and brushing teeth twice daily. This didn't really shift much more than the top layer of grime, and the wipes were unscented because I was scared of attracting bears, so we didn't smell great, but they helped bring a feeling of partial civility at least. I completed my nightly camp routine by using Conrad's multi-tool knife to dig the dirt out from under my fingernails. By maintaining a separation between our hiking attire and what we slept in, the inside of the tent and sleeping bags were protected from most of the muck.

I had two pairs of knickers on the trail. One pair I wore whilst the other was in some stage of bush laundry – which involved rinsing them out in a stream and hanging them off my bag to dry as I hiked. This looked really classy. I did the same with my two pairs of hiking socks. It wasn't perfect, but at least it was *something*. That something slipped the next day after completing our third night in a row of dry-camping. Standards were fast deteriorating. Water was so tight that I was forced to leave camp for the first time in pre-worn undies. This may not seem like a big deal to most, but to me, it was unbearable. The longing to feel clean contributed toward a general feeling of low morale,

so eager to reach the showers at Shelter Cove we opted to join
the Oregon Skyline trail purely to save seven miles. The OST is
a popular alternative PCT route shown on the *Halfmile* maps, so
once again it was not cheating. The trail was created nearly a
century ago to connect a collection of primitive mountain roads
and trails used by forest workers, native Americans, miners, and
trappers spanning almost the full length of Oregon. In 1968 it was
incorporated into the PCT, but with the trail rerouted many times
over the years, there now remain sections of the original OST that
are distinct.

Where the two trails diverge, the OST stays around a thousand
feet lower than the PCT all the way to Odell Lake where we
hoped to find our next resupply box waiting. That was if Chris
had remembered to post it.

We made quick miles on the relatively level terrain. Despite
feeling mis-sold by the name – there wasn't much skyline to see
– with no snow or blow-downs our speed doubled. Still, by early
afternoon it was clear that reaching Shelter Cove by smashing our
current 18-mile record with a 25-miler wasn't going to happen.
We decided to instead reward ourselves with an afternoon off
at Crescent Lake, stumbling into the first campsite we found,
owned by the National Forest Service. Not familiar with such
camps, I felt excited anticipation at the prospect it might contain
a shower. It transpired that my expectations of NFS camps were
wholly unrealistic, they are primitive affairs, but they did contain
picnic benches at least, a welcome break from sitting on the
ground.

We unloaded onto a bench in what appeared to be a completely
deserted camp, and began peeling off our sweaty shoes. Almost
as soon as I pulled off the second sock a less-than-welcoming
lady driving an electronic golf buggy came out of nowhere. She
was the camp host.

"Do you have a reservation?"

We looked at each other – *was she trying to be funny?* There
was nobody else there.

Conrad jumped in. "Urm, no, sorry. We're PCT hikers."

"Well, it's $20 per night. Cash."

This took us by surprise.

"Oh, OK then," I stated, unable to hide my gloom, "can we take a minute to discuss that amongst ourselves?"

She raised her eyebrows before turning away to play with some nearby recycling bins, all the while keeping a careful eye on us.

"What do you want to do?" Conrad asked, "the map says there's free camping somewhere around the lake, so maybe we should just go find that."

We weren't carrying much cash.

With a massive huff I couldn't hide how pissed off I felt. "I just took my socks off!" I scanned around before adding, "there isn't even anybody else here."

But between us we decided the sensible thing would be to just move on and find the camp we had set out for. But upon seeing us pulling our shoes back on, and about to re-hoist the packs, the lady returned with a completely new tune.

"Look. I suppose if it's just the one night and you don't leave any mess I'll let you have this pitch for free."

My face lit up! We had just received a gift of legendary trail magic. I had read about the term coined by long-distance hikers to describe unexpected acts of kindness received along the trail. When it happened to us it really did feel magical!

We didn't see the campground host again. She returned to her giant lakeside trailer, complete with its own satellite dish, shower and fridge full of food, no doubt. What a mighty sweet summer job that must be. I pondered if perhaps we should sign up for a similar position, until Conrad pointed out hosts are responsible for maintaining the lavatories and dealing with trash. No thanks.

The afternoon break was wonderful. Leisure time felt truly indulgent because typically, if we weren't doing our day-job of hiking, we'd be doing some kind of camp-related chore or sleeping. That day we finally kicked back to enjoy a well-deserved physical rest, besides a sparkling clear lake. My body was overjoyed. In fact, just a few hours of lazing in the sunshine without any deadlines or the usual artificial distractions of the outside world was pure joy. I don't believe our bodies are designed to be constantly "on" from the moment we wake until bedtime. They need time to rest and recharge. Putting my body into idle, true idle, not screen-swiping idle, was very calming on the mind. I read somewhere that allowing yourself time to become bored is brilliant for balancing mental health as it instils a sense of mindfulness. This time-out was just that. It was the gift of living in the present, though I wasn't conscious of it at the time.

After a long nap, we sat at our picnic table kingdom, eating dinner like proper people do, chatting away about the challenges of the last few days. It was amazing we had any chat left, considering the amount of time we'd been spending together. During the conversation Conrad encapsulated the mood perfectly when out of nowhere he innocuously stated: "Maybe we're just not outdoorsy people."

I couldn't control my laughter, spitting instant mash across the table. Conrad had made a valid point. We didn't really have a clue about the great outdoors, but then again, Einstein believed mankind still didn't know one thousandth of one per cent of what nature has revealed to us. All I needed to know was that Mother Nature could give back; I appreciated that peaceful moment perhaps for the first time.

12

A Stormy Outlook

A palpable energy of eager anticipation arose the closer we got to any place with supplies. We didn't expect much from Shelter Cove resort, other than perhaps showers, somewhere to wash our clothes, and a small store, where we'd hopefully be collecting our next parcel. By this point such simple things were more than enough to enliven our pace. I mean, what if the store sold ice cream? Or even fresh-baked pies? Hiking out of camp the next morning, such wishful thinking consumed us.

"Do you think they'll have cabins? I bet they have cabins, it's a fishing resort, and fishing men don't camp on the floor, do they?" I reasoned out loud.

Conrad was on the same wavelength: "If they do we'll rent one, I don't care what it costs, I need a bed. I just can't sleep properly on these shitty things, I spend the whole night tossing and turning."

"Yeah I know, I can hear you! A bed would be nice though... oooh, and a shower. I need boiling hot water to rinse this crusty layer of scum off me. I stink, and my hair feels rank."

Not listening to me, Conrad came to an abrupt halt.

"This doesn't look right. Are you sure we're on the Oregon Skyline trail?"

"What are you talking about? You're in the lead, I'm following *you!*"

Of course, according to Conrad our poor navigation was somehow *my* fault. With GPS it became clear we had taken a wrong turn immediately out of the lake, accidently following a horse trail headed in the wrong direction. Not the best start to the day. Annoyed, we back-tracked over a mile to correct Conrad's error. I would have liked to have made a wise-crack about using a compass but I just didn't have another barney in me so early in the day.

Hours later, after tackling many a blown-down tree, our surroundings transformed into a lush rainforest. After days of water-rationing we'd been transported into a distant land. Tracing a roaring creek through a grove of giant trees shrouded in hanging lichen, we finally exited the tree habitat into a wide clearing, containing a double set of railway lines. I paused, peering down the long, straight tracks, wondering where they could possibly lead. Once assured we weren't about to be mown down, I bullied Conrad into posing for a contrived photo holding his thumb out pretending to hitch beside the seemingly deserted line. Little did I know that in weeks to come we'd chug past that very spot aboard the Amtrak Coast Starlight sleeper train to California.

A handful of carved wooden signs guided us like breadcrumbs the remaining way into Shelter Cove, where a sense of euphoria awaited at the comforting sight of the lake, and markings of life dotted around its shore. We passed giant RVs dwarfing a handful of small wooden cabins, and a group of men who sat cleaning their fishing gear cheerfully acknowledged our arrival. As always, we gravitated towards the general store building on the promise of food and refreshments.

Sadly, the general store was a huge let-down. The cashier confirmed there were no cabins available to rent, before charging us $5 to collect our post, which had apparently arrived just the day before. Chris was cutting it fine. The store was more geared towards their fishing clientele, with plenty of tackle and tinned food useless to us. I got a Sprite, coffee, and ice cream all at once. Conrad opted for a suspicious-looking hotdog rotating in a glass carousel, Coke, and crisps. The only remaining hot food option was a frozen microwavable pizza which we agreed to reserve for a gourmet dinner.

Trying our best to mask our disappointment we asked about any nearby amenities. The closest town was clearly out of reach at 30 miles away. Another resort on the opposite side of the lake contained a restaurant, but with a 5-mile hike between us, we sadly concluded this was our lot.

We retreated outside to the allocated hiker area, which consisted of a couple of picnic tables sheltered by tarp, and some plug sockets; just enough to tempt smelly hikers away from the store.

We consumed our tuck as I rummaged through the box to remind myself what we'd stuffed in it so many weeks before. As we did, a white pickup truck pulled into the lot with the words "Odell Lake Resort" on its door. No sooner had I read this, than the doors opened, and out jumped Dan and Habit carrying foam hot-food containers. Before Conrad had any clue what was occurring I dropped my drink, and with a sudden surge of energy, sprinted over to the truck before it could leave. Hell, I'd have probably launched myself through the open window if it had tried!

Fortunately, the truck's driver, John, was the owner of the neighbouring resort. As soon as I had confirmed the resort served hot food and had a room with a bed available, I was summoning Conrad over and belting up. I didn't even pause to find out its customer rating or cost. I saw this meeting as divine intervention: we desperately wanted amenities and the heavens responded with John. I couldn't have been happier. We bundled in, crossing paths with the guys who were planning to camp. On the journey to the south shore John proudly explained his recent purchase of the property, which according to him dated back to 1903, making it the oldest resort in Oregon.

Odell Lake Resort is a simple, family-run operation, described online as an "unpretentious mountain lodge". Luckily our needs were simple: food, shower, bed. The main building operates as a small inn, with some additional attractive cabins and a campsite outside, none of which displayed anti-meth posters. As the resort was situated a fair way from the trailhead it wasn't really used to welcoming the hiker trade, meaning there was no laundry room. On understanding our predicament, John took our black bin bag of washing and did it himself, refusing to take any money for it. Trail magic had struck again.

With the resort containing the first television we had seen since beginning the hike, watching the news during our time there became a huge novelty. The upcoming U.S. Presidential election dominated the airwaves, with plenty of critique on the race taking place, all playing out like one huge circus. You couldn't make the stuff being said up, and this was on national TV! The spin! The hype! Hillary Clinton had just won the Democratic nomination, meaning journalists were not holding back, brazen in their criticism, but it was highly entertaining stuff, especially for people accustomed to British politics. Conrad and I became mesmerised by the carnage, intrigued by which way the polls would eventually swing. Rudimentary mention was made of Brexit, but no one really understood what it all meant yet, so nothing they said on the subject seemed of any significance. More riveting for us were the forecasts of bad weather on the way. Throughout the next day, we witnessed grey clouds forming, whipping up the lake, in an ominous and foreboding manner.

Our top priority on zero-days was always eating and resting. The resort was very proud of their new professional espresso machine, so after weeks without a decent cup of coffee, I was only happy to oblige. Jacked-up on caffeine, I was super-efficient at repacking our new food supplies and knocking out emails to just about everyone I had ever met. By late morning, having just updated social media with some comical pics, the only task remaining was collecting a parcel from back in Shelter Cove. Here we had to get creative as neither of us intended to walk there – it was our day off after all.

When we left the resort the previous day we did so before the arrival of the post, which hopefully contained our rushed Amazon order of bug spray and extra food placed from Crater Lake. First we tried loitering around the pine-clad lobby area, hoping to cadge a ride from a departing guest. When that failed, we spoke to one of John's relatives and got a deal on a tiny motor boat rental. Our luxury motor launch was in fact a rickety old fishing boat, but hey, it sure beat walking! Captain Conrad was particularly pleased, fancying himself as a day skipper. He opened the engine's throttle full blast, it strained in response, chugging along painfully slowly, yet in his mind Conrad was probably living out a grand James Bond adventure. It took 30 minutes to cross the open water at what felt like rowing pace, a journey that would have taken Bond less than five.

I have to admit, I enjoyed the ride. I watched as the thick-forested shore reeled by, occasionally closing my eyes to feel the gentle breeze and sunlight on my skin. I felt content, far removed from any problems back home. I've always thought the sun holds healing powers, from clearing up bad skin, to lifting moods; I miss its energising rays back home. I've begun noticing in recent years how much returning from our holidays, or should I say *trips*, is getting harder; I believe this has something to do with seasonal affective disorder. SAD is a condition believed to be triggered by changes in hormone levels brought about by a lack of sunlight. According to the support organisation SADA, around 8 per cent of the UK population suffer from the most serious symptoms, with a further 21 per cent impacted by lesser "winter blues". For me, it seems far less clear-cut than winter verses summer, it's during the overcast, grey days that my mood seems to darken and energy levels plummet. How different I felt now. Maybe it was a side-effect of the huge dose of vitamin D recently loaded into my system from spending so much time outdoors, but suddenly I felt very happy to be alive.

At the Cove, new hikers had arrived. Dan filled us in on his progress and his intention to stay put for a few more days to rest up and wait out the impending rain. Two new girls introduced themselves; as they did I was trying my best not to contort my expression at the sight of the blonde girl's face – she looked like she'd been punched in the eye by Mike Tyson. Her lid was red and swollen almost completely shut. The girls were awaiting a cab ride into the town of Bend to get medical help for what was apparently a mosquito bite. Those *sneaky* little shits. I'd never seen anything like it. As we wished them all well and retreated back to the boat I jabbed Conrad on the arm to quietly point out how lucky he was.

13

Dodging Bullets

It was highly tempting to stay at Odell Lake to wait out the impending rain. Overnight, the U.S. National Weather Service had upgraded the forecast for the Cascade region to "Hazardous". Rain was expected to hit by mid-morning, escalating to potential thunderstorms, showers, and sleet by the next day. Over coffee in the lodge's comfortable lounge, we sat debating what to do. As we did, we received a message from Dan:

I'm on my way over. Going to sit out the rain for the next 3 nights.

We stared at Dan's text with a mixture of emotions, bags already packed at our feet. Eventually, after debating the issue, and more coffee, we decided to reluctantly push on. Aside from making it to Canada, we needed to keep moving in order to reach Bend in time for Conrad's birthday in six days' time. And anyway, we reasoned it was highly unlikely we could avoid rain for our entire hike, so best get it over with.

Trail magic provided us a ride back to the trailhead from a British guy and his Australian girlfriend, who we met at the resort the previous night. Jamie and Marni were on a road-trip to Alberta, Canada, where they intended on starting a new life together. I found their plans all very romantic and felt excited for their future, if not a tad jealous of their young age and the possibilities it carried.

That evening, they planned on breaking up the drive by staying in the cool city of Portland; I would be lying if I said the thought of joining them didn't cross my mind, especially as the rain started before we even exited the car. As we disembarked, we spotted Dan on the other side of the highway. He stood on the tarmac in full fisherman-style waterproofs, thumb out trying to hitch a ride. We waved, but he didn't seem to notice us from beneath his giant hood. Upon explaining his predicament to Jamie, the lovely chap swung the car back around, crossing the carriageway to give a ride to another stranger headed in the opposite direction to Portland.

At the trailhead we ran into Toaster and Smudge, the two lovely ladies from Mazama Village. They were unloading from the car of a friend whose home they had stayed at for the last few nights. The ladies, it turned out, had a string of friends living in Oregon and Washington supporting their adventure. Vicki caringly enquired about Conrad's feet, remembering his blister issue from our first meeting. We never did take her up on her generous offer to dress his blisters, a small indication of what wonderful people they were. We wished them well, setting out just as the rain miraculously stopped.

With our recent rest and seemingly clear trail conditions, we initially seemed to be flying along. I felt confident that 20-mile days were set to become our new norm. We climbed away from the lake basin through a dark, dank forest with trees draped in green lichen candy floss. Occasionally a view of the distant lake appeared, but mostly we were in a green warren. We reached the set of small Rosary lakes, our first water source, to find them shrouded in a fluffy white mist. Maybe the rain will pass over us we hoped – it was already past 10 a.m. – the National Weather Service had obviously gotten their facts wrong. Then it started spitting. Constant drizzle ensued. Rain jackets and waterproof pack covers came out, and with them our optimistic moods were transformed. The mosquitoes rejoiced.

The deserted Maiden Peak Shelter provided a brief respite from the relentless rain. Much larger than the South Brown Shelter, it was dry, but pretty dark and creepy. I could definitely see the place being used as the inspiration for a teenage horror flick – *Murder in the Woods*, or something else involving unsuspecting backpackers. Studying the lynx and wolverine warning posters pinned to the wall didn't help matters. I frightened myself trying to make a mental note of the various paw print identification markings, while still in shock that a wolverine wasn't just a fictional *X-Men* character! With a couple more potential foes added to my list, we stepped back into the rain to clock off some much-needed miles.

Squelching into the backcountry area around Charlton

Lake later that afternoon, we had endured 11 miles of sweaty waterproofs and on-off rain. I couldn't see much with a biting cold wind bouncing off the misty lake, making it difficult to focus on anything.

Conrad set straight to work fixing our shelter while I began filtering stagnant water for cooking. I had just managed to light the stove's flame, after countless attempts with a lighter in the breeze, when a man appeared out of nowhere, startling me.

We hadn't encountered many people by that point, and those that we did meet were usually fellow hikers. But scanning him, the man didn't match that description. For a start, he didn't carry the obvious pack. He wore heavy clothing – a Castro-style khaki jacket, and... wait a minute.

As he got closer, I was paralysed by the sight of a dull piece of metal on his hip. What the f**k? This was it. My day of reckoning was here. We were about to be shot.

"You guys seen my friend about?" he asked in an uneven, gruff tone.

Conrad had been hoisting our food sacks into a neighbouring tree but stood to attention with the orange rope still in his hands upon hearing the unknown voice.

"We haven't seen anyone," he responded casually.

I wasn't sure if from Conrad's viewpoint he could see what my eyes were fixated on.

Irrationally, I quickly added, "we're waiting for a pack of our friends who are just behind us."

Safety in numbers.

The guy ignored me. With an air of frustration, he continued. "I'm camped down near Waldo Lake. He told me he'd be here."

There was something odd and shifty about his eyes. They darted around in an unsettling way like he wasn't concentrating on us as he spoke, instead scanning our camp and the water.

He began asking Conrad lots of questions about our trip, which made me even more nervous. Was he trying to figure out our plans, to decide if anyone would miss us? Or maybe he was about to rob us?

Moments later, a much younger guy appeared from the opposite direction and strolled over. He was clutching a tatty plastic bag and his trousers were patched together with duct-tape.

The old man barked at him, "where you been?"

"I'm on the north shore, man, over there," pointing across the lake, "I told yuh that." He sounded half asleep. He then turned to us.

"You guys hikers?"

"Yeah hiking the PCT," Conrad confirmed.

"Where yuh headed?"

"Canada."

"Holy shit, yuh don't say! Where yuh from? Ozz-tralia?"

We got that a lot in the States.

"No. England." Conrad politely corrected him.

"Yeah, I knew that," the older man interjected, "I was out there in the military."

Shit, now the gun made sense, he was a veteran. But did that make him an honourable person or a brain-washed lunatic unfazed by another killing?

The younger guy offered us some weed, which we graciously declined. They continued to make small talk with Conrad for a few minutes while I watched. At no point did I ease up. Something about that first guy chilled me. It was evident they were drifters, living on or close to the trail. It wasn't a nice day to be living outside. I hoped they were just innocuous stoners due another hit, but the tension created by the presence of a gun was palpable. I saw it in Conrad too, so he'd obviously spotted it. His body language was taut, protective even. I dipped my head into the tent to grab something, standing back up as the two men eventually headed off around the shoreline. I watched to make sure they were gone.

"What the f**k were you going to do with that?" Conrad mocked, gesturing to the penknife I had slipped into my pocket moments before, "the blade's an inch long!"

I opened it to inspect the blade with my finger.

"What you talkin' about, I could do some *ser-rious* damage with this, straight in the neck!"

I gave a cunning but strained smile. "Those guys *really* freaked me out. Do you think our food is safe up there? Are we safe?

Should we leave?"

"No. They're just harmless druggie douchebags. Probably living out here."

But I wasn't feeling convinced. I looked up into the tree where our yellow critter-proof food bags were swinging in the wind.

"There was something in his eyes. The older one. Something not quite right."

I couldn't get the image of the gun out of my head as I played back the scene. Aren't we supposed to listen to our instincts? Mine were telling me we weren't safe. If it wasn't for the fact the day was drawing in and it was still raining, I would have insisted on leaving. Standing there talking, I couldn't feel my fingers, so bitter was the breeze coming in over the water. I knew that hypothermia happens in the wild. So we quickly demolished another bland packet meal, before swiftly retreating into the flapping tent.

But I couldn't settle. Finally dry, after having changed into my non-hiking clothes, I made another vain attempt at suggesting we move on, but listening to the rain beating down I don't think I even convinced myself it was a sensible plan. I dared not venture outside again. The tent was our feather-weight sanctuary. Smashing another personal boundary that night, a plastic water bottle became our new in-tent piss pot. How depressingly mortifying it was trying to crouch over it without leaking all over my sleeping bag; I don't even pee with the toilet door open at home.

That night my knife stayed close to hand. I doubt I got more than twenty minutes of fitful sleep at a time. One minute I was awake, the next, vivid dreams played out in my mind during stolen moments of shut-eye, so I had no idea what was real. The younger guy kept returning to steal our food. One time he came into our tent. That one definitely woke me up, but I was too afraid to peek outside. It was still raining. I lay motionless, willing for daylight to come fast so we could get the hell out of there. It would be alright I told myself, as long as we weren't physically hurt. Losing our food supplies would have been a major setback – from this location it would have meant turning around and hiking 17 miles back to Shelter Cove on empty stomachs – but then again, some nights we camped days away from anywhere. And besides, losing our food was preferable to losing our lives.

When our alarm finally sounded I bolted upright, unzipping the tent with bated breath. Our sacks were still there, hanging in the tree! I cannot describe my relief. And crucially, we appeared to have survived the night. I probably shouldn't have done this, but the next time we reached a place with reliable Wi-Fi I tried Googling incidences of gun violence on the PCT, half-expecting to see the guys' mugshots. I only found evidence of a single gunshot victim. Back in October of 1988 a hiker on the trail just half a mile north of Highway 62 in Crater Lake discovered the body of Douglas Cracker. Yet contradicting my fears, Douglas had sadly shot himself.

That day we packed up a wet tent, put on wet shoes, and hiked through a monotonous green tunnel with our hoods up in the rain. It was miserable. We existed purely to count down miles.

We spent the next two days slowly descending into sodden despair. If there is such a thing as a mental wall, we had definitely reached it and proceeded to repeatedly smash our heads against it. What were we doing? I asked myself that question constantly. Positive attitudes were nowhere to be found. A thick white mist seemed to be following us through the bleak surroundings. In different conditions the area would have been great, with plenty of tiny lakes and ponds shown on the map, but I couldn't appreciate them now, or anything for that matter. Both of us regularly daydreamed about being back in the lodge, or anywhere warm and dry. Without the ability to stop and sit down for breaks, hot food fantasies played through my mind. I was really beginning to resent Dan, all holed up in a nice dry hotel room.

Between Charlton Lake and Elk Lake we came across just one other person on the trail, Ginger. We found her standing on the edge of a forest service road, still engulfed by her towering pack, wearing a cheerful smile. It was good to see a familiar face, or any face really. She explained how she'd gotten patched up following her accident, and remarkably not discouraged, had returned to hike various short sections of the trail over the past week. Her husband was about to collect her for a night in Bend. She offered

us a lift into town which piqued our interest, but tricked into a
false sense of optimism from a momentary break in the rain, we
reluctantly declined, only to regret the decision after the rain
returned minutes later.

Just as we couldn't feel any sorrier for ourselves, we passed
into the Three Sisters Wilderness zone, governed by a different
forestry agency who didn't seem to endorse the importance of
trail maintenance. Faced with an increasing number of slippery
tree trunks to climb over, I jumped from the top of another log
into a giant mud puddle. Shooting pains ran up through my feet;
the constant cold drizzle had softened them into hyper-sensitive
prunes. I held back tears because, let's face it, they would have
been pretty pointless tears and I likely needed the hydration, but
still, I was in pain. Maybe days like these are sent to deliberately
challenge our resolve, to make the good days better, and us more
appreciative. All I know is I kept pleading with Mother Nature for
a break in the rain, and it didn't come. The other thing I prayed
for was a minor miracle: a bed for the night, somewhere dry. I
knew this was highly unlikely because over the phone a few days
earlier, a receptionist had informed us of a family reunion who
had booked out all the cabins at Elk Lake Resort.

I tried to distract myself by creating a mental checklist of
things to be thankful for, but my mind kept swinging back to
despair.

"ONE: it's so cold that even the mosquitoes have f****d off." I
began muttering out loud.

"What you on about?" Conrad called back over his shoulder.

"It's my positive-thinking list... TWO: my feet can't get *any*
wetter. THREE: we're going to get a shower in the campground
tonight, and some hot food."

Conrad finally flashed a hint of a smile, "Mmmm, now you're
talking! I'm getting a burger. Maybe two. And I hope they're real
sloppy, with loads of fake American cheese and fries."

"Yeah, if we load up on ketchup we can get some vitamin
C back into our diet too!" But then my fake optimism quickly
turned sour.

"I just wish we could get a bed. Damn those reunion people!
Do you think they might cancel 'cos of the rain?"

On the final descent into Elk Lake, one of my shoelaces broke away from my trainer. A safety pin came to the rescue, a metaphor for my broken state. The forest had become a stick farm of dead trees, lopped to about 15-feet tall. It didn't look like a burn zone, so I wasn't sure what to make of it except it felt gloomy.

As we finally squelched down the muddy track into the campsite, I sensed we were close to breaking point. Then I heard something, somewhere off to our right, hidden behind a smoking barbeque, a man's voice sounded. He called out a magic siren call:

"Hey, do you guys want any food?"

14

Trail Magic

Travelling along the Pacific Crest Trail, we met some wonderful people. People who aided our journey, wanting nothing in return. But the generous charity awaiting our soggy, pity-party of two at Elk Lake literally saved our hike.

As we rounded the corner towards the man who'd just offered us food, a gathering of friendly faces and tantalising aromas greeted us. It looked like we had just entered a set for a Home Depot barbeque commercial. Children chased each other, weaving through small groups of adults, who drank while enjoying animated conversations, all oblivious to the rain. A patchwork of marquees stood together, sheltering a sea of picnic tables, each covered in bright check-print tablecloths. A line of barbeques smoked in the rain, supplying rows of shiny, catering-style buffet dishes full to the brim with hot food.

A slight lady layered in multiple fleeces and a green knitted top-hat signifying a distinct Irish theme bounded over to us, carrying a stack of dirty dishes.

"Hey there, I'm Janet. I hope you two are hungry!" Her friendly eyes sparkled as she offloaded the dishes into a washing up bowl.

Slightly uncomfortably, we confirmed our ravenous appetite and provided our names. I could only imagine how terrible we both looked, so I made sure to identify ourselves as hikers, just in case they had the wrong idea.

Despite being very busy, Janet was full of interest, asking all the usual questions.

"London. England," I offered. Never really sure if the England part was necessary or not.

Her face lit up. "Wow. Well, welcome to the Coughlin family reunion. As you can see, we're in a bit of a mess due to the weather, but we're doing the best we can! You've come at a great time, we just finished eating."

I glanced around, eyeing up the spread; aside from some used plates, you would never have guessed the family had even started eating.

Janet paused to give instructions to one of her small team of helpers before adding, "just throw your things down over there and help yourselves!"

She energetically began wiping down tables, while other helpers continued their allocated tasks in a whirl of activity.

Before we knew it, another lady appeared, pushing large plastic plates into our hands, which was our cue to release our bags and hit the buffet.

"Make sure you save room for dessert! We've got ice cream over there," Janet shouted back, to my utter delight. Ice cream just happens to be my favourite food of all time, a fact I blame my mum for. She loves relaying stories of her extreme pregnancy cravings, including the incident when my dad had to chase down an ice cream van on the A1. To this day she blames a calcium deficiency, so I'm going to go with that too.

Within minutes of arriving at Elk Lake we were happily chowing down on heaving plates, while a conveyer-belt of food kept appearing on our table. We consumed a veritable feast, starting with fully-loaded fajitas with a side of tortillas and dips, and another side of bread and butter, something I really missed on the trail.

Just as I'd declared that I couldn't possibly eat any more we moved onto fruit – well I didn't want to be impolite – before peaking with hand-scooped ice cream cones. I just didn't have the discipline to say no! By the time my brain caught up with my stomach it was too late – the pressure emanating from my swollen belly was truly painful.

As the two British strangers, we had unknowingly offered ourselves as the afternoon's star attraction. A gaggle of friendly people took it in turns to grill us with earnest curiosity. These were not the first Americans we had met who loved hearing about where we were from, and what we were doing, but I was puzzled as to why they would interrupt their big family event to host us. In return, they took great pride in revealing their home towns, and rounding up their kids to introduce us to their families. The atmosphere was electric. Initially, as outsiders I felt a true sense of British awkwardness, the kind that makes it hard to even make eye-contact with a stranger, but within no time we accepted ourselves as long-lost relatives into the Irish fold.

Family reunions, especially on this scale, are not common practice in the UK, so to us it felt like some kind of festival. The entire weekend had been organised with military precision, including a timetable of inclusive activities, enormous group meals all brought in and cooked onsite, and accommodation for a hundred men, women and children. Someone had even gone to the trouble of branding the green plastic water bottles with an Irish-themed leprechaun family crest. That someone was probably Janet, who, alongside her husband Pat, was responsible for bringing together family members from all over the country to join the celebration. It was a shame about the freak wet weather, but they certainly seemed to be making the most of their party. What a friendly bunch of cheerful people they were.

Janet was clearly a very special lady. Not satisfied with feeding us, like a mother hen she arranged showers and laundry facilities, invited us for dinner, and even allocated us a rustic cabin for the night that she insisted was now surplus to requirements. It was overwhelming. I felt embarrassed by the undeserved attention and generosity, but that said, I wasn't about to let pride get in the way of my own comfort. I mean, I was just about done with this hiking shit.

As we finished our food, Janet directed us across to cousin Colleen's large lakeside cabin. As we stood at the front door, filthy and wet, I felt nervous. We debated whether to knock or turn around and make a beeline for the campground. Maybe intruding on a family's private space would be pushing our luck too far. But I really needed a shower, so, warily I made Conrad knock. The door swung open to another smiley, energetic lady who introduced herself as Colleen and ushered us in.

Inside, the open-plan living area was full of life. A large excited gathering was getting ready for the next planned activity, a scavenger hunt. Colleen handed us fresh towels and pointed out the bathroom and laundry. I had the first shower, then, grabbing our heap of dirty clothes and wrapped in just a towel, attempted to dart into the laundry room next door without anyone noticing. But Colleen was sharp, insisting on helping me as if doing laundry on her vacation was some kind of pleasure! Wait a minute, that's exactly what my mum would do too; she's always delighted to discover an ironing board inside a hotel room closest.

Conrad soon joined me, and together we tried hiding away in the small timber-clad laundry to keep a low-profile and avoid interrupting family time, but Colleen wasn't having any of it. She called us back into the main room to join a pack of jovial adults who had remained behind, foregoing the games to drink. It was a bit strange standing in a room of strangers, discussing American politics wearing just a towel and a waterproof jacket, but they didn't seem fazed by us.

Colleen reminded me of my own mum, so far away, and in my weary state I wondered what Mum was doing. As we finally made moves to leave, arms full of clothes, Colleen jumped to her feet.

"Are you all set?" she asked, with an eagerness to help.

"Yes, we can't thank you enough." I replied, still feeling guilty.

"You're very welcome. It was my pleasure."

As Conrad exited, I quickly blurted out: "I can't wait to tell my mum about you, she'll be so happy to hear how we've been looked after, and so grateful for your help." I could feel myself slowly choking up.

Upon hearing that, Colleen beamed, assuring me it was nothing any mother wouldn't do. With that she flung her arms around me in a warm embrace and I happily succumbed. It felt comforting to receive maternal affection. Whilst I wasn't so sure if Colleen was right about any mother doing the same, I didn't dare contradict the sentiment. As she let go, she echoed Janet's invite to dinner later that night. I just about held in the tears. The last few days had been an emotional rollercoaster. Being welcomed into someone's family with such kindness felt overwhelming, and for the first time since leaving England I longed for home.

Feeling revived thanks to the bellyful of food and clean clothes, we ventured to the main resort building in search of Wi-Fi. Inside we stumbled across Vicki and Laurie (aka Toaster and Smudge) who, having just arrived, had already got the beer and burgers in. They filled us in on their version of the last few soggy days, ditching their hiking schedule to put everything they had into reaching Elk Lake a day early, just to get out of the rain. We all agreed it was miserable, but as with most things, it was much easier to make light of the situation after the event with the power of alcohol. Unlike us, the ladies both held naturally positive dispositions, yet unanimously they related to the sentiment behind Conrad's far-fetched summary:

"It was like God was stabbing my soul with a spear of spite and hatred!"

When the ladies described their freezing-cold showers, because the campground's boiler was on the blink, a spark of guilt over our good fortune ran through me once again. I explained our meeting with the Coughlin family, including their generous donation of a rustic cabin for the night. I hesitated because what I was about to offer was so meagre: the mezzanine space above the cabin, not much more than a tiny crawl-space in the shed's attic. I was a bit embarrassed to even mention it, but as I did, I was taken aback by the positive reaction.

"Are you sure?" Vicki replied in earnest, seemingly overwhelmed.

Conrad and I agreed in tandem. It felt good to be throwing something, no matter how small, back into the trail magic universe. I'm a believer in karma.

"That would be great, we'd really appreciate it." Vicky added, concluding: "We've been delaying putting our tent up because we couldn't face another night in the rain!"

It was agreed. That night, after a wonderful hearty dinner of spaghetti and meatballs with our new family, the four of us all hunkered down in the creaking timber cabin gifted to us. It was cosy, consisting of no more than a double mattress and small burner stove, with a ladder reaching up to the attic level, but it was toasty warm. I'm pretty sure the cabin was infested with mice, but I didn't care because my toes were finally dry. Our wet clothes hung off every imaginable nook and hook as we fell asleep to the sound of rain pelting the roof.

The care received from strangers in Elk Lake honestly

couldn't have come at a better time; I stand by the assertion that providence saved our hike. Never before had I met such warmly-welcoming, hospitable people. It felt unreal to be waited on, being asked if there was anything else they could get us while we ate as outsiders at their table. If any Coughlin family member should ever read this, I want to say *thank you* once again. The family probably have no idea how much our chance meeting turned our spirits around. It was like someone literally picked me up, cleansed me, gave me a healing hug and put me right back on my feet again. They blessed our journey and motivated us to continue pushing on towards Canada.

15

We Belong

After three days of intense rain, the sky let up. We departed Elk Lake as the sun magically burnt away the morning mist, its rays filtering hazy beams of light throughout the tall trees. Steam arose from the damp soil and the birds awoke in song. It was hard not to feel a sense of promise on a morning like this. Even for a self-confessed pragmatist.

The trail led us through darkly-dense firs before finally opening into a broad sun-filled valley, dominated by the splendid peaks of the Three Sisters. The volcanic peaks of North, Middle and South Sister sit unusually close together, forming an imposing string of volcanos that each tower over 10,000 feet. Having spent most of the preceding miles within the confines of the woods, I felt struck by the enormity of the landscape as we crossed an expansive grass basin underneath an even wider blue sky.

Of all the days we spent on the trail, the first day out of Elk Lake rated highly on our "most spectacular" list. I spent much of the day in a state of wonder and awe, watching striking vistas unfold, with snow-coated peaks passing in and out of fluffy white clouds. Nature's theatre was captivating, prompting the draining of an entire camera battery. But what really gripped me was the sense of space. It was a far cry from home, where I once fainted while standing on an over-crowded tube train during my morning commute, a scary event that helped prompt our rash move into the city while our friends bought houses in the suburbs. This finally felt like the trail I had set out to hike, and taking breaks lazing in sunny meadows complete with scented wildflowers and babbling creeks, I felt truly content. With such a complete turnaround in circumstance I had to wonder whether we'd caught the luck of the Irish.

Amidst this scenery and sunshine, we comfortably found our stride, so even after 11 hours and 19 miles of movement, we felt pretty good for a change. In fact, I'm sure I could have continued, were it not for us reaching the boundary of the Obsidian Limited Entry Zone; a no-go for camping for the next two miles.

Our 'Glacier Camp' was dwarfed by the shadow of North Sister's zig-zagging rock pinnacles and snow-covered glaciers. A raging stream gushed right beside us. That night's camp would be considered by most happy campers as ideal. Not falling into that category, I picked fault at the evening's tumbling temperatures as soon as the sun melted into the mountains, and at the sharp shards of glass littering the ground.

The next day, as chunks of ice floated in our water bottles from the overnight big freeze, I began to appreciate the beauty of the black glass we had slept on. It glistened like thousands of tiny mirrors in the early morning sun and on closer inspection – thanks to some kind of minor miracle – hadn't punctured our featherweight plastic groundsheet. These rocks are the namesake and very reason the zone is a protected area within the Three Sisters Wilderness. Millions (probably) of years ago, a volcano spurted lava over the land, which cooled so rapidly that it created this very shiny, brittle glass instead of the more typical pumice-stone by-product. The razor-sharp edges were once used by indigenous Americans to craft tools and even today, certain "enlightened" people would use the material to try and cleanse the aura of people like me.

We hiked all morning in the bitter cold, passing Obsidian Falls without so much as a photographic pause, because it was too damn cold.

It didn't take long before we entered onto a vast sea of lava, decimating our already relaxed pace. The stark landscape felt as though we'd been transported onto another planet. Anthracite and copper-coloured space rocks piled high, containing little vegetation except bare, silver-barked tree skeletons like those painted by Salvador Dali. We painfully edged up never-ending lava switchbacks, crunching over fist-sized, rolling rocks, wishing there was more between us than a pair of lightweight rubber soles.

I began to sense we must be close to the next mountain-pass road as the number of day hikers grew. Identifiable by their tiny, enviable, daypacks and a tendency to talk like they had all the time in the world, they would stop us to ask the same old questions. On hearing Canada was our final destination, people typically lit up, captivated by our mission – usually older people – and would follow up with even more questions. That day was unique though, for the two separate requests to take our pictures. I found this an odd one, coming as it did from strangers, but it felt rude not to oblige. On parting, one lady called us "superstars." I wasn't feeling particularly *superstarish* that day, but the irony tickled me nevertheless; who was I to question such American enthusiasm?

OK, so I shamefully admit that we might have had a small vested interest in taking so much time out of our busy hiking schedule to talk to people. Yes, secretly I hoped they might instinctively take pity, and offer us food! That day however was not a great one for donations to our cause, especially considering the amount of time we invested, but when one lady handed me her last chocolate-peanut Lara Bar I thanked her, grinning from ear to ear like a Cheshire cat bathing in a vat full of cream.

Food had started to become a real issue, or to clarify: the lack of food. Unfamiliar hunger pangs pierced the insides of my stomach, so I spent the day consumed in food-related fantasies. I like food. A lot. Even though I harboured hopes of losing weight during the hike, I wasn't prepared to languish for vanity's sake. Come to think of it, that's probably the very reason I'm a terrible dieter! Back in London I watch what I eat; I have done since I can remember, because I'm naturally dumpy. I've tried every fad weight-loss plan out there, from Atkins, to juice detoxes, to periodic fasting, where I discovered the most miserable version of myself *ever*. But suddenly food had become something different: fuel. And I was convinced that my body *needed* the nutrients from the foods I so badly craved at any given moment, which mostly seemed to be of the salty-carbohydrate variety such as bread (with butter obviously), baked potatoes, and chips drenched in vinegar. In truth, I'm sure we carried a bounty of food compared to the majority of hikers on the trail who travelled 30 miles a day on nothing but protein powder and adrenalin – but knowing that offered no solace. I wasn't even trying to be a die-hard thru-hiker after all.

Up to this point our trail diet consisted of a fairly decent breakfast of oats or granola, followed by snack bars or trail mix during the day, rounded off by some form of dehydrated meal – usually pasta- or rice-based – for dinner. Yet the feeling of deprivation was insatiable. My mind craved everything I couldn't have; I never felt satisfied. Like a spoilt child I naturally sulked as a result, before catching and chastising myself for it. It reminded me of an episode years before when I'd worked in the operations area of a London bank. One of my colleagues, a very laid-back Australian guy, had listened to me complaining about the delivery date of my new car being delayed before silencing me by calmly stating: "Kathryn, there are children in Africa dying of starvation." I shut up immediately, shame swallowing me up with the stark perspective. I'll never forget that.

These were our trying times, however, and keeping up an appearance of good behaviour was proving tough. By mid-afternoon the constant ankle-rolling and jarring movement from walking over lumps of lava had developed into shin pain. With battering winds coming over Mount Washington, it seemed like as good a time as any to confront Conrad about the hunger situation.

"Why am I the only one who seems to be hungry? It's making me *so* miserable. Don't you even *care* about food? Why aren't you *suffering* too?"

Much to my surprise, Conrad abruptly stopped in his tracks. He turned back to look at me with a perturbed expression peeking from under his woollen beanie.

"I'm *constantly* hungry. In my stomach is a *massive* black hole. I just don't see the point in complaining about it as much as you do!"

I was taken aback, not knowing how to respond. It was like mosquito-gate in reverse. Hiding my emotions wasn't something I was familiar with, but I couldn't let Conrad seem more resilient than me, so I buttoned up. Withdrawing into a more muted internal sulk, we continued along the endless path of pain.

Our aim to reach 21 miles that day fell three miles short. The lava finished us off. We made camp amidst a burn zone of spindly silvered timber which we lovingly named "Desolation Camp".

The alarm echoed around the dark tent at 5:30 a.m. As I laid motionless, my brain switched on. It thought of just one thing: breakfast. Thanks to our hiking shortfall the day before, seven miles now stood between us and Big Lake Youth Camp, where we hoped to join their 9 a.m., hiker-friendly breakfast. Desperate for something other than our dwindling supply of paltry cereal bars, we hiked with a crazed, silent determination. The first few miles were all uphill with plenty of blow-downs, so I became increasingly anxious we wouldn't make it. There was no time to pause. So, when my stomach started reeling with the all-too-familiar pang of cramps, I swallowed down a granola bar and triple ibuprofen chaser mid-stride and hoped for the best.

Bright green ferns lined the trail, but I still couldn't make out a lake. I prayed we hadn't taken a wrong turn given our record speed and the long waterless section. Eventually we joined a narrow spur trail, hoping it was the right one, and continued for a mile of hungry anticipation. Finally, a foreign noise penetrated the forest. It was the sound of children singing somewhere in the distance; it felt like a siren call. As we stepped into a hidden clearing, a number of small buildings and a dirt-track road appeared. A big, colourful sign made of yarn woven around giant pins welcomed us with the message: "*You Belong*".

Yes, please, I thought, *sign me up. I'll subscribe to any place serving hot food; soup-kitchen or cult.* While congratulating ourselves for arriving twenty minutes early, Conrad realised he had left his bum bag half a mile back up the trail where he'd stripped off his long-sleeved top. This bag was a relatively new addition to his kit, helping to "balance him out", but crucially it happened to contain our key valuables, such as camera, credit cards and phone. Engaging some kind of hidden energy, he sprinted off up the trail, knowing his little oversight could be responsible for seriously screwing us up. Meanwhile, I went in search of a man named Noah, wholly relieved it wasn't me who had to walk the extra distance.

Apart from in the movies, I had never seen a real American summer camp before. In appearance, Big Lake Youth Camp exactly resembled the music camp that Michelle attended in the *American Pie* films. Small, A-framed wooden cabins, with sloping, chalet-style roofs were arranged around a main Headquarters building. A tall bell tower stood in the central courtyard, surrounded by various flags hanging limp off huge flagpoles in the still morning air. Conrad re-joined me with the bag, gasping for breath. A group of kids passed by, holding new Cannon cameras for their nature-photography club. Beyond them, another group was coming back from the lake following a morning water-sports session. Why hadn't I grown up as an American summer camp kid? I wondered whether they had any idea how lucky they were! Don't worry, I'm fully aware how old that makes me sound.

Although it stated on the Christian camp's website that they welcomed PCT hikers to share a meal, I was still blown away by the friendliness of everyone we encountered. Each of the staff – or "camp counsellors" – went out of their way to greet us, often hanging around to chat. There was an obvious trend in the Seventh Day Adventist Church's recruitment criteria: young, wholesome, and super-friendly. Toby from Eugene had just graduated as an aero-mechanic, which I thought sounded awesome, but he had since begun to re-consider his career aspirations to work with kids. Jeff, from Tillamook, the pretty, cheese-producing coastal town, was about to start his third year of a Biblical studies degree. While I was fascinated to learn more about how the camp worked and their backgrounds, I was first-and-foremost preoccupied with my breakfast.

Up in the staff mezzanine area overlooking the large dining hall below we sat eating the best bagels I had ever tasted. And oatmeal. And vegetarian patties. All washed down with a full pot of coffee. Yet no amount of coffee could have helped me deal with the pandemonium downstairs. Kids bursting with energy would spontaneously break into song over their food. I wish I could have been that enthusiastic about anything at that age. *What were they putting in the water?* I didn't care. Hunger really does make everything taste *a-mazing*. I had never enjoyed a bagel as much in my life. Without even thinking about it, I had loaded my plate with every topping option the buffet had to offer, proceeding to polish off not one, not two, but *three* bagels, each heaped with butter, peanut butter, cream cheese AND jam. At home I don't even eat bagels because I consider them too dense and unhealthy!

After a long hearty breakfast, we helped clear away the plates, left a donation, and returned to the main building to retrieve our packs and utilise the novelty of bathroom plumbing. A number of other hikers had arrived. While Conrad used the rare Wi-Fi service, I entertained myself watching the others opening their resupply post. With a tinge of envy, I determined each individual had larger and more interesting daily rations than us. It dawned on me that, although there was an obvious limit to the *overall* amount of food we could carry, if we started pushing ourselves to make a few extra miles each day – like them – we could reduce the number of days between stops, and therefore eat more *per* day. Now this may sound glaringly obvious, but upping our miles wasn't even a consideration until weeks into our hike. This notion of "saving" days, so we could eat more, only came within the realms of possibility once our fitness began improving.

Bounding out of camp towards the promise of town we found ourselves in unsurprisingly fine spirits. I could almost hear the 'Kum Ba Yah' of tonight's inevitable camp fire singing us out. We felt giddy with excitement – and probably high on sugar – at the thought of reaching the town of Bend. Apart from the impromptu and speedy side-trip to REI in Medford, we hadn't been anywhere even resembling a town in almost a month. I tried passing the five miles daydreaming about all the awesome stuff we could possibly do there, including what we should eat first, but there was a greater issue I could no longer ignore.

This morning's cocktail of painkillers had begun wearing off, *big-time*. I called out to Conrad to keep going, before pulling off the trail. My suspicions were right. It was unavoidable I suppose, but for me the monthly visit from Aunt Flo involved a whole new kind of pain, pain that made all other pain seem trifling. You see, I was diagnosed with endometriosis in early 2015 after years of trying to persuade doctors that I wasn't just a big fanny; that the pain I was experiencing was not normal. Endo reportedly affects 1 in 10 women of reproductive age. It's a huge problem, but one seriously under-estimated by the marvels of modern medicine because no one has yet figured out a cure. The condition causes cells which should be found inside the uterus to grow elsewhere in the body, so each month as they break up and bleed, instead of being naturally released from the body in the form of a period, they have nowhere to go. The consequence is inflammation, scar tissue, hormonal imbalance, and ultimately a f**k load of pain akin to your insides being pulverised by a meat grinder.

Had it not been for my first laparoscopy to remove the affected tissue over Easter that same year, the idea of hiking the PCT may never have come to me. You see, after the surgery I had caught an infection – thanks, NHS – meaning it took some time for my tummy to heal and for exercising those muscles to become a possibility again. Belting up a backpack would certainly have been out of the question for a number of months, and with doctors warning me of the possible life-changing complications to pregnancy, I felt out of control. Just like some people respond to recovery by training for the marathon, I decided I needed a reason to want to get back to the gym. The heart-sinking problem with endometriosis is it's highly likely to grow back, and it did. I would later go on to have another, more-invasive surgery, but for now, all I could do was pop more pills and accept the pain. I felt a great deal of comfort in the knowledge that I was just hours away from a bed and bathroom facilities.

We finally reached the highway, known as Santiam Pass, just before noon. Now just one thing stood between us and a short side-trip to civilisation: catching a 40-mile ride there. Even though we had travelled in a couple of strangers' cars to detour destinations by that point we were far from hitch-hiking pros and I suddenly felt uneasy. Watching vehicles whizzing down the long, straight road I began to wonder if anyone would stop, and if they did, whether we would ever be seen again. I could see the trailhead we would hopefully return to in a couple of days on the other side of the road; I sure wasn't ready to pass through it yet. But would you know it, within two minutes of me holding up my homemade *"Bend please"* cardboard sign, a blue pickup truck stopped. I like to think that my fetching hiking skirt might have helped.

The driver was a man named Carl, who was on his way to the nearby town of Redmond, and luckily for us was in no apparent rush. Conrad spent most of his time zoned out on his mobile trying to book a hotel, so I got the semi-awkward task of keeping the conversation flowing for nearly an hour. Luckily Carl proved fairly easy company. Something had rattled my initial instincts when he started talking about his hunting trips and hiding ammo in the woods. That and the fact he was an avid Donald Trump supporter, led me to deduce it was highly probable he was carrying a weapon and maybe even a couple of spades. Still, I think I did a good job at remaining politically neutral, not wishing to incite any bad feelings, with Conrad annoyingly offering very little input. Despite my irrational fears, Carl proved a very wonderful person who had also taken a risk with us – and took a diversion out of his way to drop us safely in downtown Bend. We had arrived. Trail magic strikes again!

16

Bend Birthday

Conrad and I agree that in the highly unlikely event the U.S. President decides to start randomly handing out visas like Smarties and give us some, Bend is the place we would live. This fantastic small city, so conveniently located for outdoor pursuits, claims to receive 300 days of sunshine a year. If true, that's approximately 90 per cent more sun than London, a sure-fire remedy against seasonal adjustment disorder!

Pulling up in Carl's pick-up on a Wednesday afternoon, we arrived to buzzing streets, the scene of a vibrant local food market. The sun was shining – obviously – with plenty of happy faces out enjoying a stroll in the town's riverside park, laughing, eating, and playing ball games. As Carl turned down Main Street I felt like a child on Christmas morning, pent up with excitement. Yet having spent nearly a month living with relatively scarce resources, the sudden surge in choice felt overwhelming. Where do we even begin?

We thanked Carl, not quite sure of the appropriate hitch-hiking etiquette for departing a person's vehicle.

"Should we have offered to buy him a beer do you think?" I whispered to Conrad as we walked away.

"Only if you want to endorse a DUI," he quickly retorted.

"Come again?"

"Driving. Under. The. Influence." he mocked, as if I were the dumbest person in the world for not knowing the American acronym. But, that aside he did have a valid point.

After checking into a very-overpriced chain hotel, because it was close-by and we felt desperately hot carrying our packs, we took quick showers and slipped back into dirty clothes. Securing food was always of greater priority than looking clean. Our first stop at the imaginatively-named Bend Burger answered Conrad's recent prayers. As it wasn't busy we lingered for quite some time, recharging our nutrient shortfalls, taking advantage of the novelty of air conditioning and Wi-Fi. It was refreshing to feel the absence of a schedule. Although very aware of it, I did a good job of ignoring the glares of the two young employees watching us, even though attracting such looks would usually make me run a mile. George Orwell was definitely onto something when he wrote "clothes are very powerful things". Let's be honest, people judge other people based on what they look like, even if they don't mean to. I'm aware of this and usually take a degree of pride in my appearance, so it didn't come naturally to let things go a little and accept the downtrodden, dirty look. When I shared my concerns with Conrad he laughed, but the next day his scraggy hiker beard was gone.

Much to my delight, we had made it to Bend in time for Conrad's birthday, our next "*let's just try and make it to…*" milestone after Crater Lake. After lunch I made the excuse of needing an "essential" pedicure to ditch the husband and dash around the shops looking for something resembling a present for the big day. The options were of course severely limited by our luggage restraints. That year Conrad would receive trail bars, a nice soap to use while in town, sweat-wicking foot powder (hint hint), and healing cream for his mystery stomach rash which the ammonia from his piss had failed to clear up. Yes, I left that little gem out – he really did piss on himself!

We rounded off the evening at a Latin bar looking slightly more respectable following a laundry run, but still of course wearing our hiking clothes. Over "medicinal" mojitos we held conference, reflecting on the trip with the kind of clarity that only copious amounts of tequila can provide. Mostly, we laughed at ourselves, reliving the most trying times of nearly quitting – episodes much funnier in hindsight from the comfort of a bar – munching free nachos. We revelled in the mind-boggling satisfaction of our achievement. Two-hundred and seventy miles may not sound like a lot to avid hikers, but to us it was *preposterous*! We also couldn't paper over the hardship. It was intense. We had faced and conquered so many personal challenges, and as recently as just that very morning it all felt *impossible*, yet somehow, much to our amazement, we were still going! This gratification wasn't a familiar feeling, so when we passed out onto a king-sized bed before 9 p.m., we slept like babies.

On Thursday 14th July Conrad turned thirty-three. Just being off the trail with a bed was a triumphant birthday treat in itself. In fact, I'm sure doing nothing all day other than lying in bed, watching TV before ordering a take-out would have felt like a party. But I wouldn't allow the special day to pass in such an unceremonious way, so Conrad had no choice but to get up and enjoy the glorious sunshine.

The plan I sketched out focused entirely around a hiker's best friend: food. We were just getting dressed to go for our first sitting when I made the mistake of turning on the television. You see, Bend was one of only a handful of places where we had the chance to catch the news. Today's breaking story did little to instil any birthday cheer. Closer to home in Nice, France, a 19-tonne cargo truck had just hours before ploughed into crowds of people who were out celebrating Bastille Day. We watched as faces of horror and desperation filled the screen. Nobody knew this at the time, but 86 people would go on to lose their lives as a result of that senseless attack. We sat transfixed on the edge of the bed. It felt somewhat ironic that the people who died had probably done so in what they considered a safe, familiar environment. It made me not only feel lucky to be alive, but stupid too for all my complaining and fretting over living in the wild unknown. Why is it that it often takes real tragedy for people to find such glaringly obvious perspective?

After breakfast, we took advantage of the hotel's free bike rental to ride south through a series of quaint residential streets to the Old Mill District. There Conrad got his real birthday present: a trip to REI. We took it in turns to pose outside the huge store frontage, adding to our touring collection of REI locations, before picking up some more packets of dehydrated food and, most importantly, exchanging my broken shoes. REI are a membership-based cooperative and have an excellent reputation for customer service with a no-quibbles return policy; a policy that would surely be abused beyond absurdity back in the UK. This wasn't a quick trip, what with having to re-visit all those trying decisions about footwear options, but I finally came away with a different pair of more cushioned Merrill Moabs.

Conrad's patience was rewarded with a giant pizza lunch, complete with cheese-loaded garlic bread on the side, justified because we figured we *needed* the extra carbs. Our return journey took us along the wide Deschutes River through Drake Park. It was there, while watching excited people tubing downstream, that we agreed to add Bend to the top of our list of U.S. towns to inhabit. Our rationale for this decision was three-fold. Unlike London, it seemed buzzy enough without being crowded, it enjoys a prime position on the eastern edge of the Cascades for year-round access to the great outdoors – this we deduced from the mountain views and from studying maps of local hiking trails and ski resorts in REI. And finally, it had character, packed full of cool independent stores and restaurants. Later that afternoon we discovered perhaps the best of these food outlets: Bontà Gelato. The rich smoothness and intensity of flavour was a sensory joy, forcing us re-visit twice more to test out a comprehensive assortment of varieties.

We capped off the evening looking even more out of place in a fancy Cajun-American grill. The food was divine, but our bodies seemed to have decided to shut down early that evening. Maybe it was the result of all the painkillers we had both been popping over the last few days, or perhaps the adrenalin fuelling us had stopped pumping with the rest day. Even scarier was the thought that our brains might have finally registered how exhausted our bodies had become and were flipping the kill-switch. That certainly would help explain why, the next day, we felt even worse. I was beginning to wonder if taking two zero days was a massive tactical error. Would we ever make it back to the trail?

Over the hotel's breakfast buffet, we started our second zero day with a quick analysis of where we were injury-wise. Conrad had been suffering with a painful hip, which he attributed to the combination of a heavy hip belt and sleeping on the ground. His mystery rash just below the belly button was also showing limited sign of recovery. We tried to self-diagnose it online without success. I was pretty confident he wasn't carrying

Lyme disease, even though it was reportedly on the rise; I made a mental note to start checking my legs for ticks. In fact, the wound's location seemed strange for it to be the product of a brush with a poisonous plant or a tick. I suggested that he tried to see a doctor while in town, but like a typical man he shrugged it off, preferring to instead vent to me about it for the foreseeable future. What is it about men and their inability to ask for help?

In comparison, I seemed to be faring pretty well (lady problems aside). The balls of my feet had evolved to develop a new layer of hardened skin – which I made sure was left untouched during my maintenance pedicure – so swelling and constant foot pain was, I hoped, now a thing of the past. The itchy leg rash was all gone. And I appreciated the relative convenience of my monthly business, which hopefully would be mostly over by the time we re-started our journey.

On the subject of bodies, a key hygiene matter was addressed in Bend: our pong. I hadn't realised how pungently offensive body odour was before the hike, having used deodorant without fail since I can remember. Online thru-hiker wisdom preached light-weight strategies which indicated no room for such trivialities, so we had taken their advice and left the deodorant at home. I regretted that move by the end of day one. Enough was now enough; no longer was I prepared to hike feeling physically repulsed by my own aroma. The new mini stick deodorants we picked up would became a game-changer, worth every ounce.

Another strategy adjustment taking place involved food. As you will probably remember me mentioning previously – and moaning about extensively at the time – food had really started to be an issue. Hiker hunger from long days on our feet made for misery. The insight gained into other hiker's supplies at Big Lake convinced us to reassess our own. After all, the resupply packing back at the Marshmeier's was all guesswork, and our assumption that we could just buy extra stuff as we went along was proving ill-founded. It turns out that Amazon don't deliver everywhere, and our shopping options so far had been very limited.

Fortunately, Bend had plenty of shops and was one of the only places we hadn't sent a resupply box to. We just needed to pick up enough food to get us to the next box – hopefully –

waiting at Timberline Lodge. I thoroughly enjoyed this shopping challenge because it meant I could pander somewhat to our current list of cravings. Also, American grocery stores sure put my local UK Tesco Metro to shame. I have seen employees in Whole Foods even polishing apples before carefully stacking them into towering pyramid displays. In Tesco they don't even bother taking fruit out of the plastic shipping crates. We therefore headed to Bend's answer to Whole Foods, a shop named Market of Choice, which most definitely contained choice. Too much, in fact, because we were in there for near-on two hours, wandering the aisles wanting to buy everything, but having to stringently calculate the weight-versus-benefit pay-off.

Despite all the endless decision-making, we still ended up leaving the store with more food than we could feasibly carry. Our new strategy centred around upping the number of dedicated freeze-dried hiker meals, which contained more protein and calories than the packets of dried pasta and instant mash we had leant heavily on before. To these main meals we added dehydrated vegetables and small bags of couscous to bulk out the contents, and hopefully fill us up. On a recommendation we switched the milk powder we had previously used with powdered goats' milk because it contained more fat. The irony of this was not lost on a serial dieter who only ever consumed almond or skimmed milk back home! The milk was added to bags of oatmeal, dried fruit, nuts and sugar to make breakfast awesome. Lastly, we sought out more savoury-based daytime snacks such as crackers and hard cheese, having seriously had enough of protein bars. Unfortunately, the Ben & Jerry's wouldn't have travelled well, so I had to eat that immediately. On a side note, Cherry Garcia tastes much better in the U.S. than it does back home; it's much creamier and even a different colour. Why is that?

By the time all this new food was decanted into Ziplocs, and half of it boxed up and posted onto locations further down the trail, it was time to eat again.

According to the official "Beer Town USA" visitor website, no trip to Bend is complete without sampling some of the local micro-brews. The town proudly boasts one brewery for every

4,500 people, which is the most breweries per capita in the state of Oregon. What a shame Chris and Leslie hadn't come to meet us, as visiting every location on the Bend Ale Trail could have been a personal pilgrimage for Chris. Not a beer drinker myself, we settled on a predictable trip to the most famous local drinking hole: the Deschutes Brewery Pub, where Conrad sampled the IPAs over our last supper.

17

Vacay's Over

It was time to say goodbye to Bend. Unsurprisingly we found the prospect of abandoning rediscovered creature-comforts, to hike all day in the searing heat, before spending the night on hard ground caked in our own sweat, somewhat unappealing. And with 150 miles of Oregon trail still before us, Canada remained unbelievably far away. Even so, somehow we were slowly beginning to consider ourselves as *vaguely* capable hikers. Don't get me wrong, this confidence was a far cry short of *we're-going-to-reach-Canada* confidence, but it felt encouraging that our ever-changing goalposts were widening. Back in June we had begun with: *let's just make it to Crater Lake*; followed a few weeks later with: *wouldn't it be awesome if we could just make it to Bend*. They now currently progressed to a *let's-at-least-finish-Oregon* vibe, which in our books felt like real fighting-talk.

Fortunately, we didn't face the stress of hitching back to the trailhead. Following a series of calls the previous day to listed trail contacts, we got lucky and Uber Ducky – real name Brian – offered us a ride. Brian is one of a large network of trail angels, people of a different breed, who graciously provide assistance to hikers. From Facebook groups dedicated to providing real-time help and advice, to selfless individuals who pull up at trailheads to give out free refreshments or rides into town. Some people even put hikers up in their own homes. I'm not sure how extensive this is, whether the gift is unique to the U.S., or the Pacific Crest Trail in particular. Even so, it seems there is a whole altruistic trail culture out there, wanting to aid the safe passage of others, and to share a role in their adventure.

Brian was a local angel who talked passionately about his involvement in extending the adoption of disability legislation in the public spaces of Bend. I bet the small businesses being ordered to adapt their storefronts may have been less enthused by his work, but it all sounded very commendable. The conversation took a less welcoming turn when we unloaded at the small trailhead carpark.

Brian had previously mentioned paying him gas money over the phone, which we thought was fair. But as I struggled to re-extend my poles and Conrad dealt with the parting pleasantries, things became uncomfortable.

"Thanks again, Brian," Conrad stated extending out his hand for a shake, "how much do we owe you?"

Brian shook Conrad's hand stiffly. His manner had become very serious.

"Whatever you think is fair," he replied solemnly.

Conrad looked to me for support. We had been expecting him to quote a figure for gas. Given he must have made this journey lots of times before, I assumed there would be a standard fee. While we very much appreciated his time, the current dilemma felt embarrassing.

Conrad excused himself from Brian for a moment to confer. His uneasy body language reminded me of Mr Bean.

"Urmm, what do you think? I've got no idea how much we should give him," he stressed.

"Me neither. I don't know how much petrol costs around here." I hated this uncertainty, eager to get going but not wanting to be rude. "I guess it's a tax-free state, if that makes any difference? But I don't want to be tight either because he's taken time out of his day to give us a lift."

Conrad was looking through the uniform-sized American notes in his makeshift Ziploc wallet, struggling to identify what each one was.

"If we give him a lot more than the price of gas we probably should have just taken a cab or hitched for free," he reasoned.

"Maybe we're reading this all wrong. He's a trail angel, so probably he just doesn't want to be out of pocket."

We agreed that $25 seemed a fair amount for the 80-mile round trip. Were we tight? Were we fair? To this day, I still worry whether we reached the right figure. I'm stressed just thinking about it now. Nevertheless, it put a dent in our petty cash, a serious risk if an ice cream van was to pop up somewhere deep in the wild.

By the time we started hiking into the Mount Jefferson
Wilderness it was nearly noon. The sun beat down as we began
a steady ascent through a stunted forest of old burn offering no
shade. Amethyst-coloured wildflowers attracting buzzing bees
flanked the rocky path. Like a broken record, I cursed the weight
of our newly-loaded food bags, compounded by the fact we had
to hoard water for the next 10 miles. Why didn't it feel any easier
yet? Annoyed with myself for never having done any weights
work at the gym, I vowed to change that if I ever made it home.

As it was the weekend, we found ourselves sharing the trail
with lots of clean-cut day hikers. And the more fatigued I grew
in the heat, the more envious I became of them. These people
were out enjoying exactly the same scenery as us, but that night
they would be returning to hot dinners, showers and a bed.
Meanwhile, we faced camping for the next five nights straight.
The husband of a young couple who passed us by summed up my
sentiments perfectly when he moaned: "it just gets old," referring
to the chore of camping night after night. In my low motivational
state, a tiny voice inside would attempt a random pep-talk. It told
me to focus on the epic sense of achievement I'd feel if we could
just make it through those five nights, completing Oregon in little
over a week. I was reminded of the hotel comforts at the end of
this section, with a legendary food buffet, and hopefully another
resupply box. And maybe, just maybe, if we could make it to the
Bridge of Gods – Oregon's northern border – it would spur us on
to Washington. And surely, Washington would be a breeze in
comparison. Right?

That afternoon we partially climbed and navigated around
the western face of Three Fingered Jack, a jagged mountain
named quite literally. Some of the scree slopes we crossed were
seriously dubious. Wash-outs from mountain torrents had left
little of the trail but loose rocks which gave way under foot. The
hard, sharp terrain gave me the ultimate chance to break in my
new hiking shoes. At this rate I might as well pre-order the next
pair, I groaned. Thankfully, just when I felt myself about to trip
into the rabbit-hole of despair, the trail provided some comic
relief.

"Well, I've seen it all now!" I whispered to Conrad, eyes

wide in prudish disbelief at the sight of the figure ahead of us. Loincloth Man wore nothing but a small piece of fabric wrapped around his waist, and a backpack with extra anti-chafe padding between his bare shoulders and the straps. I'm pretty sure he would have been arrested for public indecency in London, but out here anything seemed to go.

"Why is it never the young, buff ladies who feel the need to get naked in public?" Conrad smiled back.

I agreed with the valid point. Nudist colonies are jam-packed with old guys wearing beer bellies over their tiny Speedos. I instinctively tried taking a sneaky photo as the man passed, but he was moving too fast so the image shall instead reside stained on my mind.

We later met another memorable individual while balancing on rocks filtering water at Koko Lake. The young hiker couldn't have been older than 21, with a nymph-like figure that seemed to effortlessly hop along, blonde hair blowing in the breeze. Now, I don't want to betray the sisterhood, but honestly, I was shocked to discover this woman was hiking alone. I mean, she was much younger than me, fragile in stature, and Swedish-model attractive. I instinctively feared for her safety. Most women we had seen on the trail hiked in pairs, and typically the partner would be male. That said, I shouldn't have been so surprised to find her alone, the number of female hikers is on the rise. Back in 1993 when the trail was officially completed, just 15 per cent of finishers were women. Last year this figure had grown to around 32 per cent.[1]

Perhaps society has conditioned us to see women needing male protection. After all, it wasn't really that long ago when social norms dictated that women be chaperoned, so venturing off into the wild alone would have been unthinkable. To promote further progress we must stop telling girls they *can't*. Teach them instead how to take care of themselves, and continue promoting the trend towards equal access to the outdoors. Companies are already catching on, directing entire marketing campaigns

[1] Figures based on the number of completers reporting back to the PCTA, so exact numbers are impossible to verify.

towards outdoorswomen, and finally developing products in colour choices other than Barbie pink.

I realise my bias upon seeing a lone female hiker was borne from my own fear. Let's face it, if Conrad had refused to hike the PCT I honestly wouldn't have attempted it alone. This didn't stem from any doubts regarding physical prowess or stamina either, in fact one could even argue that generally women make up in stamina what they perhaps lack in natural strength compared to a man. No, of my list of initial fears previously discussed, the one that daunts me the most is the human-factor, most notably the little-talked about added vulnerability I believe wouldn't cross a man's mind. It's the danger – no matter how small – of physical violation, which in my over-active imagination somehow feels even worse than being shot dead, and the reason I never should have watched the film *Deliverance*. Part of me feels like a hypocritical coward for admitting this out loud, knowing we shouldn't let fear limit our possibilities. But in reality, I sense this unspoken female factor is widespread.

I looked at the young lady standing before us and wished I could be brave like her, brave enough to one day hike into the wilderness alone. Yet the more I thought about it, the more I came to wonder whether I would actually ever *choose* to do just that. The endeavour would certainly *prove* me capable of going it alone, but then again, I could have chosen to hike solo all day on this trip and reconvene at camp but never found myself more than a few feet away from Conrad. I realised the benefits of comfort and companionship I felt from having a partner outweighed anything I personally needed to prove to anyone. All the same, I knew deep-down that if I ever really *needed* to, I could go it alone.

After a brief exchange of hiker chat, our new friend enthusiastically exclaimed: "You GOT this," referring to our ability to reach Canada. I couldn't help but laugh out loud at her words and the gusto with which she proclaimed them. In the few minutes she had known us we had pretty much spoken of nothing but the hardships of camping. But I had to give it to her: there was something contagious about her American can-do-ism. I left feeling rather inspired by this young woman who had the tenacity to haul around a two-person tent, continuing her journey after her boyfriend had found it too hard and jacked it in.

We concluded the day on the edge of Rockpile Lake, far enough from the highway to return to deserted backcountry. As we struggled to set up camp in a strong wind, a large grazing deer appeared out of nowhere, staying surprisingly close by, staring at us with menacing eyes while he ate. Weeks later, and hundreds of miles north, that very deer came up in conversation with another hiker. At least I assume it was the same animal he spoke of as he described the presence of a lingering deer. The famous deer of Rockpile Lake apparently stalks campsites to graze on any wet patches of dirt, addicted to the salt found in human urine! The crazed look in his eyes now made perfect sense.

That night, a howling arctic wind picked up, and a thick mist enveloped the lake as the sun went down. I wore two pairs of socks to regain the feeling in my toes. But when I woke to the call of nature (the worst part of camping by far), I stepped outside to a brilliant sky full of stars. I checked the time because it felt like I had awoken in some kind of alternate dream world; it was 2 a.m. The moon had completed a full cycle since we had begun hiking. Its shiny round surface reflected in the lake, illuminating the camp as if it were morning. Never before had I quite appreciated the splendour of the night sky.

When morning finally did come, the trail led us along a narrow ridge running high between two cinder peaks. On one side Mount Jefferson beckoned, its almost perfect conical shape resembled an oozing walnut whip; I related everything to food. In both directions steep slopes coated entirely in trees stretched into the horizon, with a distinct contrast between dark burn zones and verdant life. With the dominance of 10,000 feet of stratovolcano, Mount Jefferson made a good natural feature with which to track our progress. The mountain's sheer slopes, mantled by five still-eroding glaciers, causes a craggy, scarred appearance all the way up to its snow-covered crown. Its peak, so far away a day ago, got closer and closer until we were circling its base. A satisfying feeling I never tired of.

From high vantage points such as these the trail would inevitably lose elevation. This time as it did, the trail twined through a transformed canvas of bright green ferns and grasses. I was busy listening to the noise of crickets and frantically-flitting hummingbirds as we rounded a bend, to be startled by a forestry worker. He was alone, wielding a hammer on some rocks.

"Oh, wow, you made me jump!" I blurted out. "We weren't expecting to see anyone." Sometimes I baffle myself with my stupidity, I mean, it wasn't as if we were in our own back garden.

He stopped banging and looked up, wiping his brow with his sleeve.

"Afternoon. You PCT hikers?"

"Yeah – well, some of it anyway," Conrad replied matter-of-factly.

"Do you have permits?" he asked.

"Yeah, do you want to see them?" Conrad offered.

This would be the first time we had been requested to produce our permits, which were now buried somewhere in the bottom of my bag.

"No, that's OK. But can I take your names and destination?" he asked, in a seemingly formal tone, taking out a small notebook from his back pocket.

Conrad obliged.

The guy scribbled away before adding, "where from?"

"Interstate 5, just outside of Ashland." I stepped in, attempting to make myself useful.

He scribbled down our information, then just when I thought we were good to go, he began THE lecture.

"Now I'm going to tell you something I tell all the hikers. Do you know what "*Leave No Trace*" means?"

"Yes, absolutely." I quickly blurted out, like I was standing in front of the headmaster trying to impress. "We always carry out our trash and bury our waste."

Maybe he didn't believe me, or maybe he just hadn't spoken to anyone all day, so he decided to give us a detailed reminder anyway. For those unfamiliar, "Leave No Trace" is a set of ethics endorsed by conservationists to limit people's impact on nature; in essence, we should leave the land as we found it. Adequate waste disposal is one of the seven key pillars. We all eventually have to *go* in the wild, but it was pretty mortifying to be stared in the eye while being instructed to bury my poo at least six inches deep. The man struck me as a little strange, but then again, it must take a certain kind of person to choose a job that involves living solo in the wilderness for days on end.

The man rounded off his briefing with some cautions, which included seeking shelter from the thunderstorm forecast later that evening.

It didn't take long before we reached the location of another of the ranger's warnings. He warned against crossing the bridge of ice now directly in our path; "it won't hold up much longer," he urged.

Our trail map flagged Russell Creek as a potentially dangerous water crossing too, but just how dangerous depended on how deep and fast the water was flowing. Standing on a ledge looking down at the white water below, I could feel the spray in the air. Arching over the thundering current stood the aforementioned and questionable-looking bridge of ice, clearly showing advanced signs of deterioration. We walked up and down the water's edge, sizing it up. There was no doubt we had to get across somehow. Our only choices seemed to involve a steep uphill scramble over boulders to circumvent the ice before wading through at a slightly narrower crossing point, or trying our luck with the bridge.

Conrad went right up to the edge and peered underneath the arch.

"It looks pretty solid to me; I think I'm gonna chance it. What's the worst that can happen?!"

That was a stupid remark, I thought, as my gaze followed the water cascading down the mountain into apparent oblivion. The answer to his question was surely *death is the worst thing that could happen*. And death following the most foolish last words ever, given the situation. I wasn't convinced, but then again, I didn't regard the other option as particularly safe-looking either, so I just stood there, tensely watching as he carefully, but swiftly traversed the ice just below the main trafficked point, before jumping up onto the bank on the other side.

"It's fine," he shouted across the water, "just give me a sec, I want to get the camera out."

I still wasn't happy, but I waited for him to give me the

go-ahead, then held my breath while precisely following his footsteps, making sure not to look down over the edge.

"Looks like we're going to live to hike another day," I exhaled with immeasurable relief as I joined him.

Conrad ignored me, still playing with the camera.

"Shit, look at this," holding the camera's screen out for me to see, "the ice is so much thinner from this side! It looks like you're walking on water!"

I could have punched him.

The predicted storm never came. In its place, we began experiencing such a changing array of weather that our photographs look like they were taken on different continents.

The next day started in the Baltic. I unzipped the tent to an encasement of freezing cloud, so I quickly zipped it back up again. Within 30 minutes of leaving camp we met a passing hiker who queried whether we'd been caught in last night's lightning storm. Mountain weather is so localised it's baffling. According to the U.S. National Weather Service, an average of 27 Americas are killed each year by lightning. I knew going into the woods that lightening was a possibility, but how I would have actually handled it remains a mystery because the advice was confusing. General guidance advises you to get off exposed ridges and seek cover once 30 seconds or less separates lightning from thunder, and to stay away from metal objects (obviously), but I also read that most people struck by lightning are standing under trees at the time, so the chances of avoiding a strike in a densely-packed, high-elevation forest seem precarious.

We crossed the boundary into Jefferson Park, entering a scene shrouded by early morning mist. Having spent the first couple of weeks on the trail in low- to mid-elevation coniferous forest, these new higher-altitude pockets of glaciated, volcanic peaks rising above subalpine meadows felt wondrous. I concentrated on gazing through the thick haze, vigilant for anything resembling a bear, but the landscape was still. Instead, a spectrum of colourful wildflowers circled tiny pools, piercing the otherwise grey morning. Further along the trail, outside the park, we ascended Park Butte, reaching nearly 7,000 feet in just a couple of miles.

Patches of snow became more concentrated, the vegetation more barren, with streams of melting ice criss-crossing our path. At one point, with the running water and grey, wet mist everywhere, we could have easily been in the Brecon Beacons in November. We shot tonnes of photographs because it seemed bizarrely comical to see our silhouettes barely visible in these July conditions. Giant stone cairns helped us navigate through desolate snowfields towards the mountain's summit.

Our photographs suddenly teleport us into summer as the sun appeared, entering the Mount Hood Wilderness on the descent. On this side of the mountain the snow had all but disappeared, and bright green shoots poked out from between the rocks. I felt happy to be alive. Going downhill was always easier effort-wise after all, until mile three of the rocky course when my feet decided to register their disgust. I cursed at replacing my old hole-ridden shoes – everyone knows you have to break a new pair in, ideally without a 30-pound mega-pack on your back. But I had to laugh. Just when our bodies should have been feeling fitter, stronger, some unforeseen ailment would knock us back down! And one injury could impact another: my arms ached from over-using my hiking poles the previous day trying to compensate for the impending blister hotspots on my feet. Added to the complaint list, I discovered two blisters at camp that evening. On the plus-side, Conrad's aching hips were beginning to feel better, so I guess we sort of balanced each other out.

The highlight of the day – maybe even week – came in the form of an ice cream from Olallie Lake Resort's general store, with crisps for Conrad. The secluded lakeside resort was only a short diversion, well worth it for food. I found visiting these tiny places, so scenically remote, charming, and not like anything I'd seen back home. The resort at Olallie Lake dates back to the 1930s, retaining much of the original primitive feel, with no gas, internet, or electricity. True, this meant there would be no hot showers for us that day, but washing didn't faze us after securing the last two ice cream sandwiches, cold fizzy drinks and Pringles, which we polished off on the creaky front porch, while watching people fishing out on the lake.

We camped at Jude Lake, just inside the Warm Springs Indian Reservation. A confederated native tribe self-govern the area, maintaining their rights to harvest and hunt the land and waterways. PCT hikers are authorised guests, having right of way along the trail, but unable to step more than 200 feet from it. We shared the lake water with a friendly lobster and met the first south-bound hikers who had started their hike just days before us from the very place we sought to reach. The attractive young couple appeared much fitter than us, something I noticed as they explained how they traversed Washington's Northern Cascades in early June with the help of ice axes and spikes. Our only hope was for those peaks to be melting rapidly, as we were clearly not equipped to do the same. They asked us about the store at Olallie Lake so I automatically mentioned our ice creams. The girl's face lit up as she excitedly repeated "ice cream" back to her partner. I didn't have the heart to tell her.

18

Canada: 550 Miles

It had taken us a month, but we finally broke a 20-mile day upon entering Mount Hood National Forest. Twenty-one miles may seem lame to most on the PCT circuit, but considering the weight on our backs, the elevation change, and our minimal experience, I felt pretty impressed. Our bodies were gradually becoming machines, albeit slightly rusty, painful ones.

The previous day we had reunited with Dan after finishing early to take advantage of an opportune campsite beside the Warm Springs River. This strategic move allowed Dan to catch us up after his prolonged stay at Odell Lake waiting out the rain, and for us to take a refresh to air out the tent and our feet. Upon his arrival, Dan's way with words provided its usual comic relief. He outlined his genius "alternate" route through the snowfields from the highest point and detailed how earlier that morning he had managed to shatter his phone's screen by dropping it not onto rocks, but into a patch of soft dirt. His "life-line", as he referred to it, was now kaput, and due to doubly-bad luck his last resupply box hadn't arrived, so he now had no backup paper maps either. What a pickle.

"Lucky it didn't happen in the snowfields," I told him, "or we may never have seen you again."

"Eventually they'd find my red shirt. This baby's' never goin' to de-comp!"

The decision was made that Dan would tag along with us, purely for our GPS guidance and not, according to him, for our company. After a morning trek through shaded firs, we arrived at Timothy Lake. The 1,500-acre lake took some time to reveal itself. Weaving through thick trees, we heard the soft sound of water lapping against the shoreline and a motorboat in the distance, before seeing its glistening surface. Unlike most lakes we passed, this one had road access and was located only 50 miles south-east of Portland, so served as a popular recreational destination.

Yet sadly it still didn't offer any facilities we deemed useful, such as showers or a cafe. We contented ourselves with a circle of logs around a blackened fire ring to decamp for lunch.

Over pita bread and jerky we learnt more about Dan's colourful past as a meteorologist in the U.S. Air Force, on secondment with the UN in Africa, and more recently as a retired Costa Rican house-sitter and wronged husband to a "bitch" ex-wife. It's true that Dan had taken some initial warming to, but the more I got to know him, the more I appreciated that when he opted to sit in his tent and read alone he did so because he was tired and naturally reserved, not unfriendly. When he did share, his warm and gentle character really shone through. He appreciated many small things we often overlooked. For example, when we complained about tree blow-downs in Sky Lakes he explained that mechanical tools were not allowed in wilderness areas, so any trail maintenance in these parts would be by hand-saw. Seeing the sheer size and thickness of fallen trees after that, I really started to appreciate every speck of fresh sawdust on the ground.

As Dan came from Kentucky we naturally teased him about the connection to KFC and his resemblance to the franchise's figurehead. He always had a story to tell, and this was no exception.

"I met the original Colonel once. He came to our little mountain college in Kentucky, handing out scholarships."

Conrad and I looked at each other delighted. I mean, the REAL Colonel? What an honour!

Eager to know more, I pressed him. "Scholarships for what?"

"Pre-engineering."

"American education is amazing," I laughed. "How can you pre-learn something? Don't you just *learn* it?"

Dan stared at the lake blankly. "I didn't learn a thing. Eventually I dropped out."

After sticky, relentlessly-uphill hours, we paused at a tiny spring for some much-needed water. It was 5 p.m. and we had completed 18 miles, but instead of setting up camp, we decided to copy Dan's afternoon recess strategy. Seated on a log, he fired up his stove and proceeded to cook an evening freeze-dried meal while simultaneously downing as much water as physically possible, a process he called "camelling up". Eating early made sense in theory as, for one thing backpackers are technically supposed to cook and eat at least 200 feet down-wind from camp to avoid lingering odours attracting unwanted wildlife, namely bears. Not luring bears with tempting human foodstuffs doesn't only make sense from an *I-don't-want-to-be-mauled-by-bears* perspective, it's also for the safety of the bear. When stupid campers bait bears, they become accustomed to associating humans with food. This reprograms the bears' behaviour so they become more confident and aggressive. This usually results in rangers euthanizing the creatures to mitigate the risk to humans. Now I may have been terrified of encountering a bear, but I didn't want to see them killed either, not as long as they left me alone.

We ate a meal, going against my usual method of getting the day's miles over with as soon as possible before rewarding ourselves with a cooked meal. The 30 minutes' rest probably did us good. We left carrying three litres of water each for the next 12-mile climb. In areas devoid of regular water sources such as these, the unpredictability of locating our next refill opportunity continued to cause me anxiety; I was petrified we would get lost and perish from dehydration.

Dan set out ahead of us, believing we would soon catch him up, but instead we spent the next four miles stumbling through old-growth Douglas firs in a weary haze. My legs had already given up for the day so they didn't appreciate those extra uphill miles. Our one saving grace was that the temperature had cooled down a little. To get through the slog we plugged in our headphones and cranked up the music, something that we hadn't done much of up to that point because I was usually too busy listening for bears. My anthem for the day was Cat Stephens', 'Wild World'. I sang out loud, wobbly and tuneless, to ward off any threats, and because I was going a bit insane. Dusk was fast approaching, a scary time in the darkened forest, so I was relieved when we stepped out onto an exposed ledge. It was here that we caught our first sight of Mount Hood across the deep valley. The peak stopped us in our tracks, completely taken aback by its magnificence. Oregon's tallest crest was shining like a beacon in the late-afternoon sun.

Its lofty tip, dipped in snow, surfaced proudly from a bed of solid-green forest, reaching up into the clouds. It looked far away.

Resurfacing at Wapinitia Pass, we crossed the highway and virtually fell to the ground at Dan's feet. His tent was sitting on a tiny triangle of land between the trail and a path leading to the trailhead parking lot just off the road. Dan was relaxing on a solo picnic table.

"Hi y'all," he greeted us as we approached, "well, I'm all settled. Got me a table, and some *sh-it!*" He was gesturing to a massive pile of horse crap right next to the table.

"Oh yeah, nice! What a scenic spot!" Conrad congratulated him dryly.

"Some jackass must 'a taken the horses specially off the trail to hit this spot! Classy move," he continued.

I was peering into the rest stop beyond him, obscured by the trees. "Is there anything of interest over there?" I asked, hoping for a cheeky McDonalds.

"Only a porta-potty which I intend to wreck in the morning," he confirmed with a twinkle in his eye.

"Nice. We'd better button it until Timberline Lodge then." Conrad responded.

But there was already no chance I was going anywhere near the block, having developed something of an irrational fear of chemical pit toilets over the years. When forced to use one I can't be the only person who hovers – holding my breath for the smell – a foot above the hole to go as fast as humanly possible, while panicking a snake, or some other, even worse creature might ooze its way out of the muck to attack me. Right?

My attention diverted to figuring out where I could unfasten the pack and officially call it a day.

As I scanned further up the trail, it dawned on me how creepy it felt being so close to the truck stop. "I bet you get some right weirdoes pulling up late at night."

Dan was quick to respond. "Heck, if they do, they'll get me first!"

"Good to know," I frowned back cynically.

That evening we slept close to the road. *The Complete Idiot's Guide to Backpacking and Hiking* advises backpackers to never camp within sight of roads as a safety precaution. It was true, I certainly felt less safe in this and any area where delinquents had easy access to our vulnerability. Ironically, I came to feel more protected the further into the back country we roamed. This night was by far our worst campsite, not only for the fear-factor, but also for the sound of trucks and their airbrakes thundering along Highway 26 into the early hours. Knowing our bodies couldn't have progressed any further, I popped a blister and a dose of what Dan referred to as "Vitamin I" – ibuprofen – before retreating into the safety of our fabric shelter.

Rudely awakened by our beeping alarm the next morning, I could barely stir given the disastrous night's sleep, but then it struck me: 11 miles to real food. My eyes shot open. As long-distance hikers *love* talking about food, at least a dozen people – some hundreds of miles ago – had relayed accounts of the Timberline Lodge buffet. It is one of a handful of legendary PCT must-stops. So, with high expectations we packed up in record time, foregoing the usual hot breakfast to ensure we'd make the lunchtime buffet. It didn't strike me then, but how superbly simple life is when making an appointment with a buffet is your paramount concern of the day!

Dan had left camp without us, confidently close enough to the lodge. I'm sure he shared our excitement about the hot food, but his chief concern revolved around trying to catch a ride somewhere to replace his phone, without which he was going crazy. Aside from the food fantasies, I had without a doubt reached my absolute personal limit for going without a shower. At the hotel, a room reservation, and hopefully a resupply box containing toiletries, awaited us. I say *hopefully* because I was feeling an impulsive pang of anxiety over whether anyone had actually remembered to post it, my mum having told me from Crater Lake how Chris was driving around California with one of our boxes in his trunk, last thing she heard. Perhaps I should have sent a copy of the resupply spreadsheet home so Mum could have phoned The Marshmeiers to hassle them on the days preceding a designated drop-off.

Much of the slow climb through dense, shaded forest was

spent listening to podcasts. Mount Hood reappeared in the final two-mile approach as we stepped onto a scraggy alpine tundra. Without trees to protect us, strong winds whipped up, making hats impossible, and the dirt-mulch trail transformed into fine sand, making us sink with each step forward. On the other side of a deep canyon, nestled into the western face of Mount Hood, stood Timberline Lodge. Willing our way towards it, we began to make out something leading up the mountain ahead. Only when close did it become apparent that the ski-lift was moving, with tiny dots gliding down the snow. Yes, it was the end of July and people were skiing down Mount Hood! Who knew the resort has the longest ski season in North America? In a good year it can last into September.

We passed a sign that read: "*CANADA 550 MILES*", to which we just looked at each other blankly, before walking down the paved pathway leading to the strangely familiar-looking hotel. In the 1980s the building was made famous by providing the exterior shots for the iconic Overlook Hotel in Stephen King's film *The Shining*. I remembered watching the film when I was probably too young and feeling terrified as the young boy climbed out of a third-storey window to escape Johnny's axe by sliding down a snowbank.

Stepping through a wide doorway engraved with a colourful feather-headdress-wearing Native American, the building was busy. Gaggles of tourists wandered around marvelling at the historical interiors, reaching out to touch intricate carvings. The level of craftsmanship there was stunning. The lodge, opened by President Franklin D. Roosevelt back in 1937, owed its creation to the New Deal. Under the program, local people in need of work were given the opportunity to showcase their skills, and in return they really went to town. Chunky hand-crafted wooden furniture, striking shiny mosaics, and detailed wooden carvings populated every nook and cranny of the charming building. Over-sized twisted ironmongery adorned every door and stairway, reminding me of a medieval castle. I could see why the tourists drove all the way here just for a peek: the whole place was a work of art.

On arrival we did the most logical thing possible and headed straight for the buffet. The timber-rich Cascade Dining Room held an air of formality, but I was happy to see lots of people in ski wear, so our dirty hiking clothes looked less conspicuous. We sat with a view out across the mountains, with Mount Jefferson just about visible in the far distance. The buffet was, of course, excellent – but then again, anything would have been compared to hiking slop in foil bags. Usually my approach to buffets involves making a beeline for the desserts, but that day I was particularly enthused by the variety of salads, the tasty homemade cauliflower soup, and the fresh bread. Overall, our consumption was disappointing; we failed to get good value for our buck. In fact, we probably ate a fraction of what other people did before feeling instantly bloated. Our stomachs had adapted to eating little and often, not responding well to such a rich feast. I obviously hadn't learnt a thing from binging at Elk Lake.

Now in a food-coma, all I wanted to do was pass out on a soft bed. Unfortunately, we were informed by the stern receptionist that our room was not yet ready. When a very crafty Dan, who had not pre-booked like us, managed to secure a cancellation and trotted off with his key, I was not impressed.

"I got *lucky*, alright! Three-hundred-and-fifty dollars' worth! Priciest hotel room I've ever stayed at," he stressed, defusing my complaint.

With time to kill, and unable to fill it by putting anything else into our mouths, we did the next logical thing and went in search of the laundry room.

Down in the basement, we stripped off in the tiny changing space attached to the broken sauna. There, we took turns to cleanse off layers of dirt in the shower, sharing a single micro-cloth towel no bigger than a handkerchief to dry off. The laundry was located in a snug opposite. As all our clothes stank, Conrad checked the coast was clear before darting out across the hallway, towel barely covering his modesty to load the machine. With no lock on the door, we sat butt-naked in our little timber-clad cubby-hole waiting for the wash cycle to end. Luckily no one felt inclined toward a sauna that afternoon.

We spent two nights resting at the lodge. Our timing couldn't have been more fortuitous, as a storm hit the Cascade region the evening we arrived. With his expensive room and no easy hitch into town, Dan elected to take a zero day too. He would have to wait until the next stop at Cascade Locks before he could address his phone problems, so we donated our paper maps to enable him to go "old school" in the meantime.

Having successfully, and much to my relief, received our third resupply box, we set about reconfiguring our provisions. It hadn't taken long to tire of many of the snacks we had packed back in Concord.

"If I see another Cliff bar I'm going to flip," I warned Conrad, as I created a small mountain of donations to the communal hiker box.

Our tastes changed often throughout the weeks, usually moving towards *more real* or *fresher* foods, so we began to restock from small grocery stores whenever possible. We expected to reach the next one in a couple of days.

Thick clouds hugged the mountain tops, so visibility didn't reach beyond the carpark while Conrad and I cozied up in the grand, hexagonal lobby bar.

We gazed out at chair lifts disappearing into the mist as we caught up with world happenings. It was now official: Donald Trump was running as the Republican Presidential nominee. As ignorant outsiders Conrad and I had always assumed that Trump's superfluous and shamelessly disrespectful campaign was a mere farce. Even when it was beginning to look increasingly likely he might win the primaries, we expected that an eleventh-hour saviour would swoop in and restore sense. But no. The Republicans had spoken, and Trump was apparently their best shot at The White House.

With the joys of food, internet access, and fuelled by alcohol, the hours melted away.

"So, this is what leisure time feels like," I mused.

Conrad shot me a look of annoyance. "Are you joking?! Every day is holiday out here. You don't know how lucky you are!"

"*Holiday?* This hiking malarkey's a full-time job. If we were in Hawaii, or lying on a beach somewhere THAT would be a holiday. This is a far cry from that."

He shook his head. "You should try getting a real job down the coal mines."

"You're one to talk!"

And it continued much like that, getting more raucous. At least with the power of Google Search, we had the tools at our disposal to settle any arguments, such as whether drinking at high altitude makes a person get drunk quicker. I was adamant it did, blaming altitude on the fact that I was showing advanced signs of impairment after just two cocktails.

"It's something to do with the decreased oxygen in my blood."

"If you had less oxygen you'd die." Conrad countered.

"I'm lookin' it up. You'll see."

Eventually I had to concede that at only six-thousand feet, and surely acclimatised by now, any slurring was more likely the result of me being a lightweight.

Fully lubricated, we made sure to tick off some outstanding but vital tourist business. We took commemorative photos of each other holding a replica of the famous "*Here's Johnny*" axe by the giant fireplace – which, in hindsight, we should have done before the drinks – and sent postcards home to mark the near-end of Oregon, inserting them into what I hoped was a genuine post box, but looked more like a tree trunk.

Tomorrow would be time to finish Oregon, but for now we chowed down on late-night pizza before passing out in a glorious bed.

19

Beam Me to The Bridge

With 50 miles of Oregon remaining, we departed Timberline Lodge the next morning, regretting the large buffet breakfast and last night's blueberry-infused cocktails. Dan had sensibly sacrificed breakfast to leave at first light, armed with two cans of Mountain Dew, so was now likely hours ahead. We never knew whether we'd see him again, the elusive man in red.

Hiking with a belly-full of pancakes was indeed a rookie error. Sluggish in the heat, we spent the day slowly traversing in and out of Mount Hood's precipitous western canyons. I couldn't believe my eyes as we rounded one particularly steep downward switchback. Coming towards us was Joel – aka Scout Master – the guy we met on our second day near Hyatt Lake. Back when we bid him a safe trip with our feet dangling in the reservoir, Joel marched off intent on completing Oregon in just twenty days. Unsurprisingly, we never expected to see him again.

"What are you doing here?" Conrad beamed, shifting his poles into one hand to shake Joel's hand with the other.

"Hey, it's the Brits! Good to see you guys are still goin'," Joel responded, returning the handshake. "I'm south-bounding now, started out from Cascade Locks yesterday, headed to Shelter Cove where I left off."

"What happened to your twenty-day plan?" I asked, standing to one side as a small-sized group of day hikers tried to squeeze past.

"I just wasn't enjoying it. Weather was terrible, the conditions were not what I expected."

Conrad chipped in. "The blow-downs you mean?! They were insane in Sky Lakes!"

"Yeah, they were slowing me down so much I decided to take a time-out for a few weeks, I'm glad I did, yesterday was glorious!"

I smiled back, with a tinge of jealousy knowing Joel would

likely be encountering a trail far improved compared to what we had endured.

"Yeah, wish we could have done the same," Conrad sighed, "but we'd never make Canada if we lost that kind of time."

Sadly, he was right. Our slow-and-steady hiking method sure took perseverance.

It was comforting to see Joel hadn't lost his positivity. His bright pink t-shirt read: *"Powered by Joy of the People"*, striking me as a fitting testament to his cheery disposition. We exchanged standard trail information and took a photo together, before wishing him luck with the mosquitoes.

Following days of limited water, we now had too much of it thanks to the run-off from Mount Hood's dozen glaciers. Carefully, we edged down a steep, narrow path that crumbled away as we trod into the mouth of a ravine. At the base, we clambered across sand and large rocks until we reached what our map warned could be a dangerous river-crossing. Sure enough, the Sandy River was gushing. Thanks to a thunderstorm back in 2014 the original bridge had been washed out while carrying a person across. That person sadly drowned, and for some unknown reason the bridge was never replaced. We took our time sizing up the silty water, before fixing on a couple of dead tree trunks tangled together around 30 metres upstream. As always Conrad went first, cautiously inching across, holding his poles up so they didn't touch the water and drag him in. Seeing him make it safely across gave me just about enough assurance to follow. A deep sense of relief was waiting for me on the other side, just like with every water crossing before.

By mid-afternoon the oppressive heat showed no signs of relenting, so we opted to take the shaded Ramona Falls alternative trail. The two-mile scenic detour transported us into a vivid-green mystical world belonging to the pages of *Narnia*. I was half expecting to see pixies perched within the tentacle-shaped tree moss cloaking the moody forest. Ramona Falls burst from the mountainside. A group of day hikers gathered in its wake, snapping photos. I was already beginning to feel pretty intolerant towards idiot tourists as I watched two teenagers attempting to climb up the slippery rock-face, inconsiderate of their own safety and anyone else wanting a photo of the falls without their skinny arses in it. Call me selfish – and many probably do – but I wanted these natural wonders to myself. For a lot of this trip we had just that, by roaming beyond the beaten track, until we came within reach of a road and the spell was broken.

Wanting to escape, we continued further and within minutes the forest fell silent, bar the soothing sound of flowing water. The trail twined through a lush, fern-filled oasis. We kept stopping to take photos of unusually-shaped fungi and the green canopies above. As always, the pictures failed to do the place any justice.

"I think we're in Middle Earth," Conrad mused, as we followed the meandering creek until we re-joined the PCT and crossed the Muddy Fork river over a high, thick log footbridge.

Thanks to the buffet breakfast-induced late start, we didn't make it to our intended campsite 17 miles in until nearly 7 p.m. On arrival, there was a problem: the steep, rough terrain wasn't suitable for our modest three-person tent. Never before had we encountered such an issue with the camping spots designated on the maps. Feeling desperate, I leaned back onto the mountainside behind me to relieve the pack weight, while we assessed our limited options. We could either turn around and walk half a mile back to the site we had passed 10 minutes before, or push on to the next one four miles ahead. Given the time and our fragile state, the sensible choice was turning around. But mentally we couldn't accept the idea of walking extra distance AWAY from Canada, so elected to push on into the rapidly fading light.

It was unsettling hiking in such low light. The dark provided ample cover for a cougar, out on its evening hunt to ambush us, so I told myself. My usual late-in-the-day stumbling became replaced with an adrenaline-fuelled pace I hadn't seen before, ferrying us to Salvation Spring in just over an hour. Scrabbling down towards the water, the unwelcome sight of a sea of colourful rip-stop nylon confronted us. At least seven tents crammed into the small spring recess, with a single campfire blazing at the centre. As people gathered around its warmth, laughing, I could virtually feel my jaw hitting the ground. Scanning the area it was plain to see the large group of women had claimed every square foot of the ample flat space with an extensive array of crap littered everywhere.

I could have cried, or maybe punched someone. I certainly felt a surge of anger which quickly gave way to despair. I stared at the women as they relaxed by a campfire, hot chocolate in hand, ready for bed. Then I got a grip and snapped into survival-mode, grabbing my dirty bladder and bending down to the spring.

I left Conrad to participate in friendly, idle chit-chat that largely centred around their weekend jolly, while I hurriedly collected water. I wasn't noting any offers to make space for us, so I knew we needed to keep moving before it was pitch-black.

It turned out that we did get to walk back on ourselves after all. Nearly a quarter of a mile back, we pitched our tent next to Dan's under the faint glow of torch-light. Clambering into our shelter we didn't even stop to eat dinner, we were THAT done.

As dawn broke, and with aching joints, we made an early start along Waucoma Ridge. Within a couple of miles, the shaded green tunnel ended, and an epic view emerged before us. From our craggy vantage point, overlooking a deep valley far below, we could make out the vertical rocks that funnelled together to form the mouth of Eagle Creek. Further ahead stood a giant crater-topped mountain. Moments later another more-pointed peak appeared, also covered in snow but a bit hazy. While I was seeing to an emergency pee break, Conrad consulted the map and identified them as Mount Saint Helens, Mount Rainier, and a third peak, Mount Adams, further east. This was our first glimpse of Washington's giant summits which we fully expected to be passing within a couple of days. Yes, without us even realising it our goalposts now extended beyond the Columbia River into Washington.

Upon reaching the old abandoned Indian Springs campground, my heart leapt. A man with a dog and a huge pickup truck was setting up what looked like a giant cookout. What wonderful timing for a trail angel, I thought, stomach suddenly lurching. But no: Paul introduced himself as the brother of one of the seven women camped at Salvation Springs. On their three-day hike he had driven up a primitive dirt road to bring them an on-trail feast. Oh, and he was currently erecting a canvas structure hosting a pump-action *shower*! I could feel my jaw hitting the ground once again. I should have befriended those ladies, I reasoned! We sat at the other picnic table slowly filtering a few measly litres of water scooped from the spring, whilst watching Paul fussing over more and more equipment.

Now, I know I sound very ungrateful and had no right whatsoever, but as we left Indian Springs I couldn't help but feel deeply disappointed. In the hour we had been chatting away with Paul, airing our feet, he had offered us some berries. That was it. He seemed like a really nice, friendly guy from our conversation. He obviously had carted gallons of water up the mountain to fill the shower but had watched as we slowly hand-squeezed water through a filter. His two giant cool boxes were no doubt filled with food, a fact corroborated by not one, but two grills. The resentment that I had felt towards those women the previous night had grown exponentially.

"How much do they really need an on-trail shower? I mean, they're hiking less than 10 miles a day, and they'll be home tomorrow anyway." I grumbled to Conrad, knowing that was beside the point.

I appreciate jealousy is a very ugly quality and as strangers we were not entitled to anything. But in my defence, it was a particularly sticky day and our packs were so heavy from the last resupply we must have been burning calories like crazy. I would have killed for a cold, sugary drink. Maybe we should have offered to buy a couple of cans. And what about the shower? Wow, it would have felt SO GOOD! Absurdly, I hadn't always been drawn to outdoor showers. I once booked a "glamping" trip staying in a traditional gypsy caravan for Conrad's birthday, but after two nights I'd convinced him to leave a day early as I couldn't face using the primitive toilet and outside shower. I even tried searching online for a nearby gym, purely for showering facilities, but with none around, we went home.

Disheartened and irritated by the heat, we trudged off down the Indian Springs trail, the beginning of the long, 4,000-foot descent into the Columbia River Gorge. Like many other PCT hikers, we had chosen to take the popular Eagle Creek alternative trail into Cascade Locks. Maybe we would have reconsidered this choice if we had realised how horrendous the two-mile connector from Indian Springs would be. It was one of the worst sections of the entire hike, purely because of the rapid rate at which it lost elevation. I had never before suffered with my knees, but they strained under the downward pressure, compounded by the weight on my back. We had to keep stopping to alleviate the pain. The PCT is a well-blazed trail that employs hairpin turn switchbacks to make life more agreeable. This trail did not. The air became more and more oppressive the further we progressed into the dense maze of silver firs. On such sections we could hike for hours without a word, focused on the immediate physical strain. At some point near the end of the connector, Conrad stopped in front of me and turned back to catch my attention.

"No wonder Joel told us to bypass this one and go further onto Wahtum Lake."

"Huh?"

"You remember," he began, taking the paper map out of his side pocket, "we said we'd look into it when we got to the spring. Joel said it was worth the extra few miles."

"Seriously?" I rolled my eyes trying to recall our conversation with Joel, which felt so long ago. "F**k!!! I blame Paul's cookout for throwing us off our game, I was distracted by the food."

Conrad seemed to share my explanation. "Maybe if I had just gotten some crisps in me, my salt levels wouldn't have been so dangerously low and I could have thought straight."

To be fair we probably wouldn't have subscribed to walking a "few extra miles" on just one person's advice without the gift of hindsight, or proper map coverage. But Joel had proven himself a wise man. I wondered where he was at that moment. I liked to daydream from time to time about all the many other hikers, who, like a trail of ants, were scrambling somewhere along the same route as us, possibly thousands of miles apart.

Once we reached it, the Eagle Creek trail was spectacular and *poof*, just like that, my mood was transformed. We continued to shed elevation, passing trees covered in bright green moss, ferns and berries lining the forest floor, and with abundant water cascading from tiny falls into grottoes. The water was heading in our direction, flowing into the powerful creek which snakes through the striking basalt canyon. It was easy to see why the trail is one of Oregon's most popular hikes. Over a hundred years ago, with the help of dynamite – and probably little safety equipment – bedrock was blasted out to create the narrow passageways hugging the canyon's steep walls. We traversed the section called "vertigo mile," with its exposed sheer drop into the gorge floor below, with particular care.

We now stood at around 1,000 feet, the lowest point of the entire trip so far. It was sweltering. In our over-heated state, we decided to stop at a shallow section of water where, stripping off our shoes, we went paddling in the refreshingly cold, but deceptively fast-flowing currents. Only once I was standing in the water, knee-deep, deciding whether or not to dunk my t-shirt in, did I notice rapids bubbling just metres away. Back on the trail, less than a hundred feet from our bathing spot we passed the crest of Twister Falls. I couldn't believe it was so close, given the crescendo created by the combination of streams crossing over each other in a hypnotic spiralling fashion before tumbling into the void. How stupid we had been. We really should have learnt to consult a map before bathing in moving water; a simple loss of footing was all that stood between us and a 140-foot death plunge.

Continuing along the canyon, we reached the famous Tunnel Falls. As it was late afternoon, and with six miles between us and the trailhead, any day hikers had now dispersed. We were alone to marvel at the rainbow forming across the 175-foot cascade. I had witnessed a lot of waterfalls by now, but this one was a sight. Cradled within a natural rock amphitheatre, a single ribbon of water tumbled far into Eagle Creek below. We took it in turns to follow the trail along the perilous edge, disappearing into the tiny arched tunnel that runs behind the falls, while capturing photos of the wonder.

That night we camped alone at an established creek-side spot, where for the first time it felt like a summer's evening. I stayed outside, listening to the calming sound of flowing water and crickets. There, on my log seat, I sat writing my journal until the sun sank and I could no longer see the page.

At first light we excitedly set out for the final five miles to the trailhead. Most of the way we enjoyed the grand, green canyon all to ourselves. With cooler morning temperatures and little incline, we sailed along, following the ebbs and flows of the water gushing far below. Occasionally the trail would cross the currents via old metal footbridges, providing heart-thumping views. High Bridge proved one of many photogenic spots, towering above water being tightly funnelled through vertical rocks a long way beneath our feet. I lost count of the number of times the water swelled into falls. At Punchbowl Falls we took a quick breather to appreciate how the aptly-named cascade filled a deep, cavernous bowl. Conrad remarked the location would make a great bungee-jumping site; I felt a little sick in my mouth just thinking about it.

We had taken a gamble on this alternative route. The Park Service website was reporting a vital bridge had been taken out the previous year by a fallen tree. But all we needed was the word of one person who had been through – cue Joel – to give us the confidence to label it somehow *doable*. The bridge was still there, albeit mangled beyond belief as if someone had fed it into a car crusher. It was taped off to deter anyone stupid enough to attempt crossing it. With the use of some nearby rocks and deadwood, we managed to scramble across relatively easily. Had the water been much higher I wouldn't have recommended it. We were lucky, yet again; as pretty as the canyon was, I wasn't prepared to die there, or backtrack.

Upon reaching the trailhead parking lot, Conrad dashed off to the portaloo to partake in a morning routine that didn't involve digging a massive hole, while I fired up my phone. With one rare bar of signal, a text came through from Dan. It made me bitterly jealous. Conrad caught an ear-full when he returned from the restroom looking particularly pleased with himself.

"You won't believe where Dan is."

"Let me guess, he's in Cascade Locks already?"

"No. Better! He hitched out of here last night, completely skipping these last three miles, and currently has his feet up in a hotel room in Hood River 20 miles away!"

"That jammy bastard," Conrad conceded with a smile while he re-secured his pack.

Feeling hard-done-by I resorted to whinging, instead of being thankful for the beautiful morning's scenery.

"Why can't we just beam to the lock now? I bet we wouldn't be missing much. I could seriously murder a cooked brekkie."

But without a teleporter to hand, we reluctantly joined the Gorge Trail in low spirits. The trail traced a small section of the 80-mile Columbia Gorge canyon, just above sea level. Directly below, loud, bustling traffic zoomed along the highway, the passengers enjoying views across the expansive Columbia River from the comfort of air-conditioned vehicles. We found ourselves hidden in the trees, with only the occasional glimpse of the water beneath. Heads down, we plodded along in the searing heat, mentally clocking off miles while dreaming up our next meal.

20

Washington Calling

Cascade Locks was good to us. The place itself contains little more than a small strip of tourist conveniences sitting on the southern banks of the Columbia River, but in nine waking hours there we achieved everything a hiker could possibly desire: motel room, shower facilities, and most importantly, fuel. For the food we really went to town, fully exploiting the choices of unhealthy American cuisine. My personal favourite was the battered fish and waffle fries from Bingham Fish Market, which aside from being delicious, provided a nutritional change from dehydrated chicken.

Sitting on the deck of the riverside Thunder Island Brewery we toasted to our walking victory while watching tourist boats coasting along the sparkling river. Yes, we had somehow hiked the length of an entire state – well, pretty much – and survived to tell the tale.

Only weeks before, reaching this point felt impossible, but in just a few hours we would enter a new state and (currently) had no intention of quitting.

"You know, Oregon is supposed to be the easiest state," I reflected as we gazed out at a pleasure boat passing beneath the striking Bridge of Gods, which stood like a colossal skyscraper straddling the river.

"Well, we're f****d then!" Conrad smiled back, sipping his beer.

I decided to consult the maps to see whether he was right. I pulled out my phone and searched for an electronic copy of the next PCT *Halfmile* map. The PDF maps are split into small, alphabetical sections, each one ending with elevation charts that give a mile-by-mile visual of what's coming. I studied the pages with intent.

"I don't think we've been in the green before." I observed out loud.

Conrad looked confused. "What are you talking about? You're just like your mum, coming out with random shit."

"The *elevation* profiles. We're basically at sea-level now, the lowest point on the *entire* trail, which is green. Where we started near Ashland was beige, over 4,000 feet, and we've never been below that kinda height, just dancing up to seven and back again."

Something then struck me, tracing the diagonal line up across the screen.

"We've got to climb back into the mountains from sea-level tomorrow. The trail only goes *up*. Steady up. Look at this!"

I handed Conrad the phone and he skimmed the charts, scrolling down to the next page, then the next.

He looked back up and let out a huge sigh, "there better not be any blow-downs in Washington."

Hearing the new state, my mind did its usual seemingly random word-association shift. "Do you realise this is the last stop for tax-free shopping?" Oregon has zero state sales tax.

"Shame there isn't an Apple Store around here then," Conrad replied, still distracted by the maps. But this was *serious*. I racked my brain for what last-minute purchases we might possibly need to distract me from tomorrow's seemingly impossible trek.

I left Conrad finishing off his 4-brew flight sampler and headed back inside the brewery, clutching my credit card. Thanks to my impulse purchases, I wrote a postcard to Concord, which we later posted along with a commemorative t-shirt. I felt excited to think of Chris and Leslie receiving this small memento from our trip, while we disappeared into the abyss.

The Bridge of Gods was not designed for pedestrian foot fare. We knew it was going to be precarious, so we uncharacteristically skipped a hot breakfast the next morning, hoping to beat the traffic. I'm sure it could have been a lot worse, but epic crosswinds battered us as we strode across in single-file, clutching our belongings with a death-grip, the surging river clearly visible through the steel grate below. Lots of lucky motorists got a flash of my knickers each time my skirt blew up. I got multiple hoots – which I took as a compliment. With streaming eyes and dishevelled everything we entered Washington, welcomed by a giant overhead sign. At the trailhead another small wooden sign provided a stark reminder of just what lay ahead: *"U.S.-CANADA BORDER 507.2 Miles"*.

The Washington trail has a reputation for being full of elevation gain but beautiful. That day we totally understood the first part, climbing nearly 5,000 feet back into the mountains, but failed to be won over by the scenery. Thanks to the relentless hills, commencing with a never-ending ascent up and around the flat-topped Table Mountain, the day stood out as one of the most demanding. It certainly provided a shock to the system. The strong midsummer sun fiercely penetrated the forest, and with no air circulating we poured with sweat.

On the western face of the mountain, we found ourselves traversing along our old friend, the lava field, as a pair of bald eagles swooped through the sky above.

"Can you see the eagles?" I shouted to the back of Conrad's bandana-covered head.

"Yeah."

"They're stalking us. They prey on the weak, so they're probably sensing we're about to die."

"That's vultures, these are eagles."

"So what... aren't they all birds of prey? Don't you think they'd pick us clean if we dropped dead?"

Such brief and nonsensical conversation peppered the long day. We stopped only to filter water and eat a pizza-slice lunch on a couple of tree stumps. I spent the entire afternoon scanning the forest floor for snakes after a stripy yellow and black one slivered out of the grassy trail undergrowth at an alarming speed. Due to our lack of snake knowledge, we had no idea whether it was venomous or not.

On one of our water-filtering breaks, I left Conrad scooping water from a small creek to step away for a tinkle. I should have strayed further from the path to somewhere more discreet, but having not seen anyone all day I just didn't think. Mid-flow, with my skirt hitched up and knickers at my ankles, Conrad shouted over from behind a tree "someone's coming," which I naturally assumed was him trying to be funny. But when he followed with another, more urgent prompt I panicked. I tried to stop the flow but couldn't. I was so concerned with exposing myself that I hiked up my knickers while still going, pushed my knees together and let out a meek "hi" with my head cast down in shame as I heard them walk right past. It must have been glaringly obvious I was peeing myself from my half-crouching stance, and the fluid now running down my leg. Mortified, I completed my pee before retreating to the stream for a cleansing bush wash. Conrad found the whole thing hilarious. He repeatedly taunted me with "Pissy Pants" over and over, while I cringed with embarrassment, threatening to do him in with one of my poles.

"Pissy Pants" was, according to Conrad, my new trail name. A lot of thru-hikers on the PCT are known by adoptive trail names. Living so far away from the reality of their normal lives, trail names provide the key to a new identity. Frequently the names take the shape of hippy-sounding monikers, chosen for embodying something of their hiking persona, or their affinity with nature such as "Hummingbird" or "Bear Claw". We heard some fantastic ones, some rude ones, and some downright peculiar ones. [1] Names are traditionally bestowed upon the person, not chosen, but the hiker has the right to decline anything offensive. Following my little incident, Conrad tried introducing his creation, but luckily it never stuck. Instead, we would remain collectively known as "the Brits".

As the hiking day ended, I was proud of how far we'd come on our first day in the Evergreen State. We covered 20 miles of crazy elevation change, concluding with an unwelcome 2,000-foot descent. All those downward steps felt painfully counter-productive given our hard work. It took us 11 sweaty hours to reach a small clearing on the steep fern-covered banks of Rock Creek.

While I attempted to freshen up in the creek as Conrad worked on the tent further up trail, I experienced a heart-jerking fright from movement on the bridge above. After the initial relief of recognising it wasn't a bear or a man pointing a

---

[1] Here are just a few: Jetski Jesus; F**k-It; Fartbag; Willy Wonka; Dilly Dally; Highly Caffeinated; Prancer; Snooze Button; Pinecone Sparkles; Old School; Nipple.

gun – my standard gut reaction – I quickly ascertained the young grimy-looking hiker peering down at the water was not a threat. It's funny how just a small smile of recognition can be enough to tell your intuition a person is safe. Back at camp we became acquainted with our fellow traveller.

"It's Skidmark Steve on the trail," he beamed, with a wide friendly grin. "My friends coined it 'cos of my shirt." He gestured to his shirt, soiled with huge dark patches across the chest: "it used to be khaki, believe it or not!"

The shirt was clearly beyond saving. Steve located a suitable spot nearby from which to hang his hammock, before returning to offer us some pot. Having never been a recreational drug taker, I was a little taken aback, but Steve eagerly assured us that cannabis consumption was now legal in Washington state, as if that little nugget would somehow change our minds. In fact, Washington had, along with Colorado, been one of the first U.S. states to vote to decriminalise the drug for recreational use back in 2012. Since then, over 500 licenced dispensaries had popped up all over the state to provide vital pain relief, and to assist others in simply getting high. Whilst it was now legal to buy recreational marijuana in Washington and Oregon, some internet research later taught me the rules didn't extend to sharing it with anyone (this constitutes *supply*), carrying it over state lines, or enjoying it in public. Seems like Steve was racking up the violations!

Steve was from Reno. He was supposed to be out section hiking with a group of college friends, having all set out a few weeks earlier from somewhere in northern California. But, earlier that morning, as he got ready to hike out of Cascade Locks, Steve's companions had spontaneously opted to go partying in Portland instead. I congratulated him on having the tenacity to keep going alone, sensing he was still unsure about his decision. In return, he revealed an unease about spending his first night alone, so I considered it fate that our paths had crossed.

As the three of us chatted on some logs, Dan's weary figure appeared, having hitched into Cascade Locks, before blue-blazing along a forest service road "alternate" for the last few miles. Conrad and I mocked him, secretly wishing we had discovered the road too. The four of us ended the day hovered around a small camp fire, eating food and exchanging stories, including a classic Dan tale of his hitch from Hood River earlier that morning.

"This guy in a big haulage truck picks me up. He was nice enough, a real talker. We were cruisin' along the highway full-speed when some alarm starts beepin'. The guy casually leans forward, blows hard into some straw on the dash until it stops beepin', and then just carries on as nothin' happened."

I was eager for details.

"Did you say anything?"

"No. We never spoke about it. Eventually we started talkin' again, but it wasn't difficult to figure out it was a compulsory alcohol screening. I'd never seen one of those machines before."

"Just your luck! At least you made it to tell the tale," I mused, leaning over to give the camp fire an encouraging poke.

"Yeah, friendly guy, but didn't leave me with the best confidence."

I loved Dan's dry sense of humour and delivery. His entertaining anecdotes were often unintentionally farcical and showcased a degree of self-deprecation; a characteristic not uncommon in us Brits. Thanks to that morning he now had yet another hitch-hiking story to add to his collection. Another one being the tale of the native American driver who picked him up somewhere in California the previous year and spoke fondly about wanting to hike the PCT the following season, as long as his parole officer agreed to it!

21

Passing It On

With aching and reluctant limbs, we continued climbing through temperate rainforest early next morning, in an unprecedented sweat-fest. Dan passed us by at our first water stop, pausing just long enough to complain about his sweaty knees. I couldn't help but laugh at the wet patches in the centre of his khakis and his unwitting comedy.

After Dan left I was in a huff. You see, filtering water had fast become the most frustratingly repetitive of chores. I would love to know how much time we lost that summer doing it. Many long-distance hikers we encountered didn't even bother cleaning water, or would do it only selectively based on their own risk assessment, like Dan, who was now ahead as a result. I knew it wasn't a race, but I hated losing time. For us, thousands of miles away from home with a once-in-a-lifetime opportunity to reach Canada, the risk of getting sick from contaminated water felt too great. Contracting a water-borne virus, such as giardia, can easily spell a nasty end to a hike, with symptoms including diarrhoea, severe abdominal pain, and rapid weight loss. As much as I was all-for rapid weight-loss, our caution with water significantly slowed our pace, but as I grudgingly told Conrad, "if anyone's going to get violent diarrhoea out here, it'll be you."

A couple of days before, Conrad had amused himself at camp by fashioning a gravity filter with the help of some string and our hiking poles. Being outdoors, with no other evening entertainment was promoting a real resourcefulness in him. The filter was simple genius, sparing us the effort of manually squeezing the dirty water, but was only really effective when we had extra time to wait for the slow trickle. We used it mostly at camp or if taking a lunchbreak.

Once we had enough water to get moving again, we pushed

on the 10 miles to Trout Creek, where we found Dan eating lunch. I was rummaging through our food bag to follow suit when Steve appeared. Last seen in a comatose state that morning engulfed in his hammock, he provided another fine example of how much faster everyone else hiked compared to us; *slow and steady*, I kept reassuring myself.

While polishing off a luxury lunch of bagels with cream cheese and jam – a real treat given their weight – Steve brought up the topic of Bigfoot. According to Steve, we now sat within the hairy creature's territory. Usually I would have automatically laughed off such urban legends, but with a new appreciation of how deep and impenetrable these great wildernesses were, it no longer seemed completely unimaginable to me that Sasquatch could roam covertly in the shadows.

It was far too hot to make miles that afternoon. At a large state-run campsite just off the trail, we found Dan once again, sat in the dirt by the entry stand. He was cooking his evening meal, as he typically did in the mid-afternoon. While it made perfect sense to sit out the heat before continuing on as he intended, as soon as Steve joined us from his afternoon siesta and we had relaxed with our packs off, we just couldn't find it in us to muster up the resolve. Instead, the three of us said goodbye to Dan, venturing off into the campground to see what it had to offer.

Sadly, Panther Creek campsite contained no showers. But it did have picnic tables, drinking water spigots, and portaloos. Such amenities were hard to resist, yet after much debate we strangely agreed that the $18 site fee was extortionate. It was the principle of it I suppose; with no car or RV to hook up, and it being virtually empty, we couldn't believe that a hiker discount wasn't on offer. So instead, we took a very brief dip in the frigidly-cold Panther Creek, then stealthily cooked our food on one of the more secluded picnic tables, before retreating back to the trail less than 30 feet away.

It was nice having Steve's company for another night. Out in the wild our human interactions were limited, so subconsciously we craved additional companionship, and Steve was an easy-going dude. He hoped the experience of hiking alone would be character-building, nourishing him with enough material to

write a successful medical school submission essay. I wasn't sure
if I could see him as a doctor. He seemed very laid back about it
all, including the deadlines. Maybe it was just the massive spliff
we'd watched him roll for dessert that chilled him out, and he
was indeed a focused scholar. A very high-brow discussion over
the nuisances of American "English" ended the evening. We
should all know a cookie is just a *type* of biscuit, the correct way
to spell "Mum", and that a "fanny pack" may not be considered
the same thing in both countries. Had Steve's European ancestors,
just a couple of generations back, decided to sail over to the New
World just to bastardise their common tongue? I teased. I let
him have the word "restroom" though, I liked using it as a polite
way of saying "the crapper", and we made sure he understood
the appropriate use of East London putdowns, including a full
explanation of when to describe something as "slaggy".

That evening we went to sleep for the first time without
the rain tarp on our tent. We figured it was warm enough, and
besides, if Bigfoot did choose to appear, Steve hanging beside us
in a hammock would be the creature's obvious choice.

Steve was remarkably awake the next day, and following
his streamlined morning routine of a coffee and a joint, was
unsurprisingly ready to leave ahead of us. We said goodbye,
doubting we would see him again. He had just nine days left until
he was due to meet his uncle for a ride, so he was motivated to
put in some big miles. I was always sad to say goodbye to people
we met on the trail, especially Steve because he was so easy to
hang with. Having a happy optimist around provided a refreshing
contrast to us cynics.

I concentrated on keeping my oatmeal down during another
slow, prolonged climb. To occupy and motivate my mind, I started
processing some stats. I knew at some point that day we would
reach our personal halfway point of 471 trail miles, so firstly I
calculated that location. I then worked out that it had taken us 32
days of hiking to get there. Upon leaving Cascade Locks two days
before, I had set us the goal of enduring no more than 25 further
nights of camping, because I hated sleeping on the ground that
much. The success of reaching this target now depended upon

two factors. Firstly, and most crucially, how much we could crank up our daily mileage, and secondly, on the availability of rooms on town zero days.

Also swirling around my brain was something troubling me even more. The previous day, Steve had remarked how much he was enjoying Washington so far. As we struggled up a massive pass, blood boiling, I repeated the statement to Conrad and we laughed at the irony.

"Is something *wrong* with us? Why can't we be loving every moment of this?" I asked, suddenly serious.

"Maybe we should have taken Steve up on his offer."

"What offer?"

He smiled. "The POT. I bet this would all seem like one f*****g awesome ride if we were floating along in one big stoner haze!"

He had a point. I still hadn't worked out how to look beyond my own discomfort, and the longing for all the conveniences I missed. Like proper food, a shower, and a bed. All that agonising was making me really question what the hell we were doing out there. After all, we had already established we weren't "outdoorsy people". I started thinking about all the amazing adventures we could be having with a whole summer to explore the U.S., like road-tripping up to Glacier National Park, or discovering Cape Cod, instead of counting down miles in a mental leap-frog between each resupply stop.

I momentarily buried my fears to pull out the phone's GPS and count down our halfway point, which turned out to be an unremarkable spot at mile 2,187.6. I made a makeshift ½ marker point in the ground using leaves and twigs, so we could take some celebratory photos. This, and a couple of party-sized Snickers lifted our spirits.

At Crest Horse Camp 15 miles into the day, we collapsed onto a couple of picnic tables where we lay still. It was painfully hot, and we were low on water. We secretly hoped someone would drive up with a massive horse trailer and rescue us. That never happened. As the deserted camp had no water, we remained lifeless until finally accepting the need to continue.

We trudged a few miles to the next water source at Green Lake to find it more of a green pond than lake. The filmy water swarmed with mosquitoes, so it wasn't a natural choice for a stop, but we were desperate. We sat in the dusty dirt for lack of any logs to perch on and filtered questionable algae water to cook. Mac'n'cheese was becoming tiresome, so the whole experience did nothing to defuse our irritable moods. In these moments it was hard to be at our best. Tensions were high. Snarky words were exchanged, over what I don't even recall. The final five miles up Berry Mountain featured silent, relentless plodding in the still-stifling heat, with me all the time pleading I wasn't about to revisit my dinner.

The light was just about leaving the mountain tops when Blue Lake finally appeared. My feet were so cramped, it felt like I was walking with stones in my shoes. To our surprise, we spotted Dan's easily-identifiable tent set 50 feet from the lake in a small clearing. As camping at Blue Lake was only permitted in designated spots, and nearby road access had brought some groups out there, we had no option other than to set up just inches away.

We had just completed a record 23-mile day. I popped some painkillers for my feet before retreating into the tent. Tomorrow, I hoped things would get easier.

Startled awake by our new, super-early 5 a.m. alarm call, our sole purpose was to reach Trout Lake. Whether we could manage another 23 miles to get there was uncertain, but the promise of real food, our next box, and the possibility of a bed provided good enough motivation to give it our best shot. Only 3,000 feet of elevation gain, an 11-mile water carry, and a predicted heatwave stood in our way.

Tree after tree the morning's hike continued in a bit of a blur. We took very few pictures, instead opting to walk in silence wearing headphones. I listened to *Untold*, a new murder mystery podcast about the death of Daniel Morgan, a British private investigator murdered in the 1980s, amid a tangled web of police and press corruption, in a deliberate attempt to divert attention from a leg strain I had sustained somewhere near Mount Hood. I had initially dismissed the pain in my right quad as a pulled muscle that would go away. But it hadn't. I kept the injury quiet for a few days, not wanting to fuel our negativity, instead just patching it up with stick-on support tape. But ripping pangs and skin-surface tingling were making me uneasy. I knew that if it turned out to be something more serious than muscle strain, I probably shouldn't be walking on it at all. I convinced myself that if we could just get to Trout Lake and take a much-needed day off, it would repair itself.

Washington remained a canvas of repetitive, boring forest scenery. We passed handfuls of mosquito-infested ponds, skirted around small "buttes", which would qualify as "hills" back home, and wet our t-shirts and hats every chance we got in an effort to cool down.

On the positive side, the trail had been freshly maintained, evident by the wood-chippings and felled timber. That was a Godsend; the last thing we needed was a day of obstacle-course climbing in such conditions. It would have finished me off for sure. Dan was just ahead of us. We kept meeting at water sources. At the last one he departed while we sat, trying to psych ourselves up for the final five-mile push.

If we made it, we would have hiked 46 miles in just two days, approximately half the time it would have taken us at the start. This was not a testament to developing super fitness. I didn't even notice a great deal of change in my body by this point. Just when we broke another record, like a high mileage day, something would happen the next day to make repeating the same feat even harder, such as an injury, or greater elevations. Why did hiking never appear to be getting any easier? That day we pushed hard because we just couldn't bear the idea of camping another night. We stank, and with all the added effort we just couldn't satisfy our hunger.

Despite these perceived hardships, I actually think our complaints were being voiced a lot less. Having celebrated our third wedding anniversary just a month before starting the hike, we both hoped to reach the next. So, for the sake of our relationship, we got better at internalising. It wasn't easy to spend so much time together, day after day seeing each other at our worst. A tacit agreement was formed, whereby whenever either of us was in a crappy mood – usually brought on by tiredness – we simply retreated into our own solitude. This way we significantly reduced tension and demonstrated a new level of tolerance. Ultimately, for us to survive this hike, we both knew we needed to function as a team.

At 6 p.m. we emerged onto Forest Road 23 in pieces. The trailhead was still 13 miles from Trout Lake. Physically I felt as though I had hit an all-time low, and by the look of Conrad, he wasn't faring any better. There was no sign of Dan, but he had been there, evident by his sunglasses lying in the middle of the road. We retrieved them as I pulled out my homemade cardboard sign. The road was empty. The sun's heat bounced off the tarmac. Within minutes I started feeling panicky. I gazed across the road to the northern PCT trailhead. The thought we may need to cross the road and re-join it to continue walking in search of water was beyond devastating.

One truck finally passed, going the wrong way. He waved. I sighed. A few more minutes went by, then a red Honda Civic appeared from the same direction as the truck, but it seemed to be slowing down. He did a large U-turn to pull up next to me. Conrad was in the bushes attending to nature's call so I appeared alone. An old man rolled down his window and leaned his head out.

"Were you waitin' for me?" he smiled, underneath his bushy moustache.

I didn't quite know what to say. This was just my luck; I had attracted a weirdo and was about to be abducted. What was taking Conrad so long?

"I'm with my husband, he's over there," I finally replied, lowering my sign and pointing to the bushes. I felt vulnerable in such a secluded place.

Thankfully at that moment Conrad staggered out, zipping up his pants, completely unaware of what was going on.

"Oh, hi there," he smiled. I could sense the excitement in his voice, obviously assuming we had scored a ride.

The man acknowledged Conrad and continued.

"You PCT hikers? I just picked up a couple of you earlier. You wanna ride to Trout Lake?"

I was puzzled. Maybe my sense of direction was off.

"Isn't that the way you just came?"

"Yeah. I got back home from dropping off those other two, and just kept thinking how hot it was – you know it's still 90! I couldn't get over thinkin' there might be more hikers stranded up here so, I thought I'd take a ride."

Seems I had completely misjudged Bill. What a complete and utter diamond! He barely paused for breath as the car glided mile after mile through the twisting forest pass. Washington's Mount Adams, second in height only to Mount Rainier, dominated the east, its slopes coated in the white stuff. Bill spoke vividly of the forest fire that had devastated parts of the region the previous year, and gave advice on the limited facilities in town. This included a detour to drive past the local park so we knew exactly where to camp if we had to. Bill was a gift from the Gods. He was the epitome of the term "trail magic," refusing to accept any gas money, instead simply instructing us to "pass it on."

22

Trout Lake Timeout

A s we entered the small rural community of Trout Lake, my first impression was, *is this it*? Nearly 600 people officially reside within the tiny farm belt, but from the backseat of Bill's car, I wondered whether the Washington census counted cattle too. Don't get me wrong, I love the vast space Americans enjoy compared to London, where each mile is inhabited by approximately 14,500 people, but given our current situation I couldn't help but feel disappointed by the lack of big town amenities.

Bill dropped us outside the gas station, which also doubled as the local diner. Inside, the old Country and Western-inspired timber building was at capacity, revealing where at least five per cent of the local population spent their Friday nights. Various state licence plates decorated the walls, and a classic jukebox with flashing lights stood in one corner while the chef frantically worked her magic behind the grill. I was just eyeing up the pies sat under glass domes on the counter-top when a waitress instructed us to find a seat outside, so we retreated to the yard.

Strangely there was no sign of Dan. We figured he must have eaten and left already. While waiting for burgers to arrive, I darted across the road to the general store to enquire about a room. My heart sank when the lady explained that the last of their three rooms had just been taken by another two hikers who arrived an hour ahead of us – likely Bill's other passengers. She offered us a room for the next night, so I reserved that. Without any further hotel options, it looked like Bill's campground tour would come in handy after all.

Back in the yard, we sat polishing off homemade huckleberry pie *à la mode* while listening to a local teenager strumming his guitar for tips. Then Dan stomped in. He was looking even more frazzled than usual.

"Hey, we were wondering where you were!" I called over.

"I was *abducted*!" he exclaimed, throwing down his pack and taking a seat on the table next to us. Dan never liked to intrude.

"What you talking about?" I grinned.

Before Conrad added, "we found your glasses in the road, we were wondering where you'd got to. Did you get a ride?"

He was still fuming. "Oh, I got a RIDE alright. To the damn arse-end middl' of nowhere! I was at the trailhead by five. Two grannies in a big ol' diesel pickup gave me a ride. I told them where I was headin', and the ol' lady said she was going to Trout Lake too, so I jumped in the back with the horses. I sat there, enjoying the ride, until it hit me: this is a long 13-mile drive. So I turned on my cell, and by the time I got a signal we were way past Trout Lake! Near-on 20 miles south! I was virtually back at Cascade Locks! I even saw this gas station when they turned at the junction, but I didn't have a clue where I was."

Dan was motioning to the junction just the other side of the gas station.

He continued, scarcely pausing for breath. "I started hollerin' and beatin' on the cab, waving my arms frantically in the rear-view mirror, but they couldn't hear shit cos of the diesel engine. I was abducted! By the time they finally figured out I was tryin' to communicate and pulled over, I was surrounded by nothin' but farmland and cows. She thought Trout Lake was still ahead, crazy old biddy! So I'm standin' by the side of the road tryin' to hitch when I should'a been here eatin' already; no one stopped. I ended up callin' the general store, someone came out and gave me a ride 40 minutes later. I just got here."

By that point Conrad and I were chuckling on our mouthfuls of pie, clapping our hands together at Dan's misery. Only Dan could get himself into that kind of mess. With his hitchhiking record to date, he could have gotten his own TV show.

"Maybe they had other ideas for you." I teased.

But Conrad was concerned by another thought.

"How the hell did you get to the road an hour ahead of us? We weren't going *that* slow and we didn't stop once!"

"You remember the trail crossed a forest road, couple'a miles in?" began Dan, "Instead of going up and over, it went around. I took that route, figured it best given' the heat, wanted to catch a ride before it got late."

Damn it. He had gone and done it again! Misfortunate ride aside, I was particularly jealous we hadn't spotted the same "alternative" route, because whilst we endured a brutal end to a long day, scaling up a scenically meagre-forested hill, Dan had bypassed it along a fairly level track.

We kept Dan company while he ate, enjoying the music and the last of the sun, before reluctantly heading to the state park campground for another night under canvas. At least we got to wash off the days of accumulated grime in coin-operated showers, although as the hot water heater in the Men's was broken, Dan and Conrad both had a more *exhilarating* experience. The sound of cars driving in and out of the park all night was disturbing. Next day, Dan left first thing, muttering under his breath about the noise. It had been a sticky night, so sleep hadn't been forthcoming for any of us. I was sure that a decent breakfast, chased down with lots of coffee – or in Dan's case his favourite Mountain Dew – would sort us all out.

We had no intention of hiking the next day. It was to be our first zero since Timberline Lodge, so we looked forward to taking some well-deserved downtime to recuperate and muster up the strength to continue.

As soon as the diner re-opened at 7 a.m., we took up residence at the counter, where we began enjoying endless caffeine refills. While Conrad entertained himself with his phone, I became captivated by the hectic goings on between the chef and her giant hotplate, especially the way she tended to the mound of hash brown. The mountain of eggs, meat, and potato we ordered constituted a proper "greasy spoon" fry-up by English standards. Our taste buds danced to the smell of bacon, anticipating the greasy carbs. When finished, I commenced the American habit of loading my surplus toast with what they call "butter", but is in fact some kind of whitish cream-whip substitute, and jam, which they strangely name "jelly", probably because it contains little real fruit. It resulted in a very pleasing sweet dessert course.

I was just contemplating whether I could fit in a full second breakfast of huckleberry pancakes, when in wandered a familiar face. Skidmark Steve casually sauntered over to us, his beard even longer, wearing flip flops and a backwards cap.

"Skidmark! Good to see you!" Conrad welcomed him with a friendly pat on the back as he sat on the next stall.

"When did you two get here?" He seemed just as surprised to see us, and very tired.

It turned out Steve had been one of the lucky hikers who had scored the first ride with Bill, reaching the general store just before us to secure the last room. Dan was back there now, he told us, taking a shower, preparing to take the room off his hands. He motioned to the waitress for a coffee.

"You're heading out then?" I mused, wondering why he wasn't wearing his usual stained shirt.

"Nah, think I'm done," he sighed, in an unusually downcast mood, "might try to hitch to Portland, not sure yet."

His words stunned me.

"What happened? You were doing so well, and isn't your uncle meeting you somewhere?"

"I dunno... I'm just tired, and all my mates are hanging out back home, I dunno if I can make it that far."

Maybe he had smoked all his weed, but I couldn't stand to see another trail casualty, so tried insisting that he'd come too far to quit.

Conrad agreed, still partly distracted by his phone. "Yeah. We're leaving tomorrow, why don't you join us?"

I pitched in. "Yeah, we should be at White Pass by Wednesday. Why don't you get there at least?"

"Thanks, but I'm supposed to be meetin' my uncle near Lost Lake, he's gonna give me a ride back to Seattle. I think that's..." he paused and shifted his weight to pull a crumpled map from his back pocket, "it's further than White Pass... it's 150 miles."

He trailed off as if his brain was processing the distance for the first time, something he surely already knew.

"When are you supposed to be meeting him again?" I asked.

"Saturday."

"So you have less than a week to hike 150 miles?! Shit. You'd better get your arse in gear!"

He sighed, gloomily starring into his coffee cup. I tried to be more motivating, "make it to White Pass, you could always hitch from there, you can't miss Goat Rocks, it's meant to be the best bit!"

I felt strangely compelled to keep Steve on the trail. Maybe it was because something about him reminded me of my brother Tom, with his dark, unruly hair and friendly face. Or perhaps it was down to the joy I felt upon being reunited with people I hardly knew. Out in the wilderness, with so few faces around, fellow hikers became our surrogate family, and I relished their spontaneous company.

Meanwhile Conrad had been distracted by his phone thanks to the novelty of a Wi-Fi connection. I didn't pay him much attention until he suddenly blurted out some kind of profanity.

"What? What's wrong?"

"My visa card's been *cloned*!"

He showed me a screen showcasing a list of purchases made in Michigan whilst we'd been backpacking through Oregon. What a kick in the teeth, and a royal pain in the arse. The criminal hadn't even shown much imagination, with the largest purchase being something like $25 in KFC! It took a very lengthy phone call back to the UK to establish the fraud, after which the card was cancelled. Given the bank's strict policy of posting replacement cards to only the cardholder's home address, we now had just one card each.

On a more positive note, and somewhat ironically, I believe we managed to convince Steve to keep going, though I had no way to confirm this, as after he exited the diner during the card debacle we never saw or heard from him again. That was until almost exactly two years later. The hiking world would randomly cause our paths to cross once again, hundreds of miles east in Glacier National Park, Montana. Turns out Steve not only made it through Goat Rocks to White Pass, he also made it into Medical School – after two years of trying – though he's still not permitted to enter Canada for reasons only disclosed with his customary wide grin.

The Trout Lake General Store was an archetypal American

country store. The small red and white timber-framed building, complete with sweeping front porch and floorboards that creak as you enter, offered $25-a-night rooms to hikers. We weren't expecting much for the price but knew it would be a step up from the park. Yet having walked through the small office and laundry room out back, we found ourselves pleasantly surprised to find a suite containing a private shower, clean bed and a TV. The room was incredibly hot, but with windows that opened, it was certainly not the worst place we had ever stayed by a long stretch.

After showering and laundry, we crossed the road to check out the Saturday market in the Trout Lake Community Hall. Inside the large room decorated with handmade quilts hanging from the rafters, an array of small handicraft stalls sold their wares. We got chatting to two friendly locals selling raffle tickets, so we bought some of those. We couldn't refuse cookies, peaches, and a giant huckleberry cinnamon roll from the huckleberry-inspired bakery stall either. The locals sure seemed proud of their huckleberries, so it felt wonderful to be able to support the local community by eating them in some form or another. Since entering Washington, I had started noticing that I kept needing to tighten my pack's hip belt. Looking in the mirror I hadn't spotted any visible change, so it was highly possible that the belt just loosened itself each day, but the uncertainty was enough to justify guilt-free eating.

Returning to our room for a short between-meal breather, I received a message from my brother Tom requesting I give him a call. I hadn't heard from him since leaving England over two months before, so something felt amiss. With a weak Wi-Fi signal, I reached him from the tranquillity of the store's garden.

"Where are you? Are you sitting down?" he asked softly.

These are never words that precede good news. Keeping his words very matter-of-fact, he explained how our grandad had passed away a couple of days before. I was dumbfounded. My grandad Les may have been 96, but I naively never considered when saying goodbye before leaving England that it could be for the last time. He hadn't been ill.

I remained motionless as Tom continued, explaining how my grandad had been admitted to hospital six weeks before, on

June 20th, which instantly struck me as the very day we started hiking. This was difficult to process. I had been in touch with home since then, including a few phone calls to my parents, but not once had my grandad's illness been mentioned. The family had deliberately decided to keep it quiet for the sake of our trip. A momentary flicker of anger over the deception was swiftly replaced with guilt – while we had been rambling away on what was essentially a long holiday, my family had been juggling hospital visits with the added task of supporting my nan. And what about all the moaning I had been doing during this time? The thought of my complaints compounded the guilt ten-fold.

Conrad must have seen me sitting on the bench shaking, for the second I disconnected the call his arms pulled me in.

What happens now? I wondered. My first thought was to get home. Conrad instinctively realised this, vowing to support whatever I decided. I wanted to talk to my parents, they would know what to do, but they weren't answering. I slumped onto the bed, and not knowing what else to do, started scribbling down all the things I wanted to remember about my grandad: like the time he thought he'd help out my parents with a bit of DIY in their new house and dropped a hammer in the shower, shattering the tray. Or the time he thought he'd help by cleaning out their cellar, destroying bag-loads of historical documents that detailed the history of the house. He always wanted to help, not always with the best results, but always with good intentions.

All the usual resupply and hiking preparations came to a halt.

The next day was Sunday. Out on the store's porch, I was still trying and failing to get in touch with my parents. The town's main street was silent except for the sound of a lawnmower off in the distance. Conrad had found us potential flights home leaving from Seattle the next day – we just needed to find a way to get there. The guilt of being in this sunny place was festering; I played over and over the details of my conversation with Tom, and my last visit to see my grandparents. I wondered if I had sensed anything on the day he passed, if I had somehow known, or even felt my grandad's presence, but I hadn't. It was a total shock.

At a loss, I wandered alone into the service at the local Presbyterian church. The tiny white building was surprisingly busy, so I sat wedged up against smiling faces, all very welcoming. I felt underdressed for church in my one outfit of black hiking skirt and red Nike t-shirt, but I was pleased to be greeted by a Hawaiian-shirt wearing Pastor, so the dress code didn't appear overly formal. I hadn't been to church for quite some time but being in the presence of such caring, joyful people and the interactive nature of the service was uplifting, making me feel closer to my parents who I knew would have been praying a lot recently. I kept my emotions together, until Pastor Scott gave me a single red flower, at which point I cracked.

Once the service ended I made for a quick retreat, feeling embarrassed for crying in public, but was instead assertively ushered into the church hall. Over coffee and homemade cake, the locals huddled around the stranger with the accent, asking all about England. One gentleman jotted down his number on a paper napkin and demanded that I call if we needed a ride back to the trail. I thanked him whilst explaining that I wasn't sure if we would be heading back to the PCT. Saying that out loud wrenched something inside me I hadn't anticipated.

Back at the general store, I found Conrad hanging out in the shade of the porch with Dan drinking sodas. I had a missed call from home, so I went out back to return it. My parents were at my nan's house. They were upbeat and gave all the reassurances that people in such positions often give. Even my nan, who marvelled at the technology of Facetime, seemed to be coping well. I had the impression they hadn't intended on me finding out the news: not yet anyway, and certainly not through Tom. They were overly apologetic for concealing everything, but the predominant concern now seemed to be trying to convince me to finish the hike. Even my nan joined in, saying she wanted to hear more of the stories and see more of the pictures I had been sporadically uploading online.

"Do it for your grandad," I was told, over and over.

With an uneasy mixture of feelings in my stomach, I eventually promised my nan I'd send her a postcard from Canada.

In that moment a key decision point had been reached. The

hike would continue, but with a fundamental shift. Conrad and I vowed that if we hiked out of Trout Lake we *would* make it to Canada, whatever it took. There would be no misgivings and absolutely NO QUITTING.

It wasn't just the difficult circumstances that made Trout Lake such a memorable place in my personal tale. Just like at Elk Lake before, somehow at our most difficult times, amazing people appeared to lend us their support. My mum would probably call it being guided by angels, and previously I would have dismissed her by rolling my eyes, but you know what – who knows?

Conrad had taken me out for a coffee to discuss the phone call. As we walked back through the gas station's yard, one of the men from yesterday's raffle ticket stall waved us over. This was a small town after all. Ed introduced us to his beautiful wife Becky. The two of them made a dashing couple dressed for church – yes, apparently there was more than one church in Trout Lake. We got chatting, as people around those parts easily do. I'm not sure exactly how it happened, but within the course of 10 minutes we were accepting a sincere invitation to drive us 25 miles to Walmart in Hood River, the very place that Dan had purchased his new phone from. Becky mused that it would be a treat to drive us, which I thought was nuts on such a beautiful day, but the promise of a large store was too appealing to refuse.

What followed was a wonderful afternoon full of kindness from total strangers. After grabbing some supplementary trail food from Walmart, the couple took us to a microbrewery in White Salmon. Had I known they would insist on paying I never would have ordered any bar snacks. On the return drive, Ed pulled into a gas station to pick up a tub of ice cream, which Becky served up with warm homemade huckleberry sauce back at their home. Their house was self-built, something very uncommon in England. A giant, two-storey stone fireplace dominated the main living area, which looked out on Mount Adams through floor-to-ceiling picture windows. It seemed like an idyllic life. I felt honoured to be welcomed into their private space; the homely comfort meant a lot.

Weeks later Ed and Becky would receive a postcard thanking

them for that day, but it was impossible to convey in words what their warm hospitality, and the help from so many other people we encountered along the way meant to us. I hadn't met people like that before. Genuine folk, with no hidden agenda, wanting only to support our efforts. Maybe these kinds of people don't exist in the real world. Or perhaps living in a big city had tainted my view of humanity. On the busy streets of London, I am accustomed to feeling like just another anonymous face in the crowd. On the very rare occasion that a stranger ever approaches me, my natural instinct is typically to treat them with guarded suspicion. I am not used to people wanting to help others purely to be *nice*. My time spent working inside some of London's top banks probably helped cultivate these jaded views. There, I operated like a fish out of water amidst an underhanded culture of competition, where colleagues wouldn't think twice about selling each other out to further their own careers.

Our interactions with people since joining the trail couldn't have been more different. As backpackers, we occasionally relied on assistance from others, but in all those incidences I hadn't yet met an angry person, or anyone with bad intent. And further still, total strangers were volunteering their services completely unsolicited. I remember so many characters, like Becky and Ed, and find myself thinking of them from time to time, forever thankful for the ways in which they touched our journey.

23

Above the Clouds

The next section of our journey promised a lot to look forward to. Beginning by traversing mighty Mount Adams' north-western slope, the trail guides hikers northwards through the Cascades towards Old Snowy, climbing up passes, down into basins, crossing glaciers, and culminating in a nail-biting "Knife's Edge" ridge-walk. The Goat Rocks Wilderness area, as we'd told Skidmark Steve, was widely considered one of the most visually impressive sections of the entire trail. If we managed to survive the rollercoaster ride, in just 70 miles we intended to make our next resupply near White Pass.

On 1st August, day 43 of our trip, we left Trout Lake full of positivity. Fuelling this positive energy were two acts of kindness. Doug Anderson, the local man I had met in church pulled up to the diner to give a ride to five hikers. Conrad, Dan, and I were joined by another hiking pair who had also been staying at the general store – Steve, aka Steve-O-Reno, a peace-loving Buddhist who owned an espresso business in Halifax Canada, and his old college friend Mark, from nearby Bellingham. The duo had helped us out the previous day by picking up some items from our shopping list – a new water filter and socks – from a long mission to REI in Portland, so it was nice we could return the favour with an organised ride.

That morning over a last breakfast, of huckleberry pancakes no less, Mark provided another boost of trail magic by handing over the keys to his car parked at White Pass. He assumed, with youth on our side, that Conrad and I would reach the Pass a day before himself and Steve, so we could drive ourselves 20 miles to the town of Packwood, before returning to collect them the next day.

The prospect of hitching continued to cause me anxiety, so it was a massive relief to know we didn't face it at the next highway. I was stunned that a man who we'd just met would trust us with his car. He didn't even ask to see a licence!

I believe the true beauty of the Washington trail begins in the foothills of Mount Adams. It was a glorious day, visually striking, and mentally peaceful. Departing from the trailhead we soon entered a burn zone. The previous year, in 2015, the PCT had been closed from this point, forcing hikers to take a boring and smoke-inhaling 24-mile road detour. I was thankful to be walking on soil instead of tarmac, through a path that didn't feel stark and miserable like past burn areas. Instead, it was littered with colourful wildflowers and fresh grass, especially a blue-purple bloom which from a distance reminded me of English bluebells. Life had returned in abundance, with butterflies fluttering and chipmunks hurrying themselves over the skeletons of charred black timber. Through the absence of tree foliage, the snow-coated peak of Mount Adams and its many glaciers provided a mighty backdrop.

The draw of Mount Adams meant we bumped into a handful of other hikers, and a few PCT south-bounders. A young French-Canadian guy named No Spoon chatted with us about Brexit. He was an idealistic economics student, who held particularly strong views on Europe for someone so young and geographically removed from the realities of the issues. I treaded diplomatically, not wanting to upset international relations, but eventually pretended to need the toilet so we could shake him off. We had been struggling to climb and talk at his marching pace anyway, and more importantly were unpleasantly down-wind from his glaringly obvious need of a shower.

Dan later told us that No Spoon had just half a jar of peanut butter to eat for the next 66 miles. When I remarked that I would have given him some of our stash had I known, Dan chastised me.

"Hikers like that tick me off! They don't pack enough cos' they know they can free-load off the charity of people like us."

I was speechless. Dan continued. "He coulda stopped at Trout lake for supplies, but for some dumb-ass reason he decided not to!"

Dan's un-Christian response caught me by surprise, given he

was a real life "son of a preacher-man" – as he once rhythmically revealed whilst describing his upbringing. But Dan wasn't being intentionally cruel. His argument was a valid one; it was irresponsible to not carry adequate provisions in such remote environments. According to Dan, it was exactly these types of people who were the ones most likely to end up needing rescuing, and that frustrated him. This was no walk in the park. Still, I thought, if I saw No Spoon again I'd slip him some snacks when Dan wasn't looking.

At Riley Creek, a pretty glacier-fed tributary of Mount Adams, we stopped for lunch, and were caught up shortly after by Steve and Mark. I loved having a chance to combine a foot-soak with lunch, while the sun dried out my sweaty socks. There was just one element that hampered an otherwise idyllic experience: small, biting black flies. The little cretins were unbelievable.

"What a beautiful lunch setting, ruined by nature!" Conrad quipped.

I laughed. "You've gotta see the irony, the little shits turn up just when we shake off the mosquitoes!"

Breath-taking, screen-saver-worthy views were captured throughout the day, but perhaps the greatest occurred as we sectioned across lava boulders on Mount Adams' northern banks. High up on an open ridge, the three-peak panorama of Mount Adams, Mount St Helens, and Washington's highest peak, Mount Rainier, re-appeared, so much closer than our glimpse from Oregon. From this vantage point, the wind-swept detail of Mount Adams' frosty-white glaciers became clearly visible. For a person who typically sees a skyline of grey rooftops, construction cranes, traffic, and tower blocks, these were sights to behold. The colossal splendour of the natural structures rising into the clouds transformed thousands of giant trees into a sea of tiny pin-heads. I felt very small and insignificant.

By late afternoon, the air had cooled. We waved goodbye to Steve and Mark and enjoyed five miles of down-hill smooth-sailing to Lava Spring Camp. Those gentle rambling miles of small streams, whilst listening to Nora Jones, were very tranquil. I shed tears as I walked whenever my mind drifted to my grandad, but it felt cleansing to do so quietly amidst the serenity of the trees with no one trying to soothe my grief. The calmness was centring. I know this sounds very corny, but I was beginning to understand the concept of being in "God's garden" in the great outdoors. Away from all the chaos and artificial edifices of modern day life, a person doesn't necessarily need to believe in God to sense a higher presence. The loss of my grandad signalled a new appreciation for where I was at that moment. It also gave me determination. Guilt still lingered, I didn't think I deserved to be out there when I should have been back home, but in the rustling trees I felt a strange feeling, as though he was somehow there with me. I never spoke of this to anyone – they would have taken this as the final confirmation I was crazy – but if Grandad had been there I knew our ridiculous antics would be making him laugh.

By the next morning my small cotton bandana had been transformed from a sweat cloth to a snot rag. The most challenging days on the PCT were not the ones when we walked the furthest, or climbed the highest, but those spent hiking in the rain. That day we did just that, while I desperately tried focusing on happy thoughts, conscious of how much our moods rubbed off on each other, a phenomenon called "emotional contagion" in the medical world.

"At least it didn't rain last night, we'd have been screwed!" I tried cracking a smile which felt more like a grimace, while alluding to the fact we had slept once again without the tent's rain cover. It was fun to do that when we were alone and it wasn't too cold, because on a clear night I could lie in my sleeping bag and gaze up at the stars through the net membrane.

Conrad barely acknowledged my comment, so I continued.

"Ha! No wonder there are so many bloody 'shrooms in this state! That one looks like something from Willy Wonka's Chocolate Factory," pointing to a patch of bright red mushrooms with white spots, just like the one that Mike Teavee's mum had scooped cream from in the movie. Something told me this variety were not edible.

It was hard to believe how dramatically the weather had turned. It wasn't just wet. Worse than that, it felt bitterly cold.

A heavy mist hung in the air, veiling the tops of the trees. At one clearing we tried hopelessly for some phone signal, eager to check the temperature, with no success. We kept hiking with perseverance, unwilling to stop and break due to the cold. During these times I busied myself clocking down the miles and revisiting memories. At the 12-mile mark we needed water. The packs came off for the first time as we perched on damp logs, squeezing the filters as quickly as possible.

I was looking at the water source waypoints on the *Halfmile* app to calculate our requirements, when I realised we were about to reach the 400-miles-remaining milestone.

Conrad didn't seem impressed. "How long did it take us to walk the first 400 miles?"

I consulted the app to re-crunch the stats and work it out.

"Urm, so 400 miles would have been near Salvation Spring, just after leaving Timberline Lodge, so..." My heart sank and I exhaled, "bloody ages. Probably around a month of solid hiking, and that's without rest days."

He stood up to put his filter away, "so unless we pull our finger out we'll still be going in October in the bloody snow then!"

Now that was a depressing thought. We really weren't equipped for snow, which could frankly fall at any moment in the mountains. Not only that, but is was Chris' birthday on 6th September, which we vowed to celebrate with him back in Concord, and Labour Day – a U.S. public holiday – days before, so we hoped to beat the travel rush. I was just finishing off squeezing through my water when Conrad looked at me.

"Shit! Your lips are *blue*, and look, you're shivering!" He hurried over and took the filter from me, "put your bottoms on, quick!"

I had no idea. My brain must have switched itself off in an attempt to conserve energy. I put my wet gloves back on and awkwardly added my zipped-leg waterproof bottoms which made a swish-swishing sound with every step. It was already pretty obvious our 24-mile goal, which would have delivered us to White Pass the next day, was unobtainable. Throughout the afternoon any remaining hope faded as my feet reached the point of maximum saturation and I started losing sensation in my toes. We briefly met two separate section hikers who warned of a potential storm on the way. With that news we gave up hope things would blow over, making the reluctant decision to call it a day.

Spying Dan's tent at the next designated camp spot, it was clear he had reached the same conclusion. After a disappointing 19 miles, during a brief break in the rain, we fought against fierce wind to pin down the tent. I felt utterly defeated, knowing this now added an extra night of camping to the tally before White Pass. But we had to be sensible and accept the need to warm up, the only route to which was to get out of the wet clothes and the wind. Desperate as we were to get into the tent, dinner became a cold piece of American rubber cheese wrapped in a soggy tortilla. No time was spared hanging our food in the trees. Yes, that night we threw caution to the wind and did something unthinkable: we slept with our food bags! Well, surely bears hate storms, right?

The following morning, we woke in the clouds. Standing at the edge of the Packwood glacier, 7,000 feet high, we gazed down into a deep valley with Mount Rainier dominating the distant skyline. Here, far above the timberline, we had a choice to make. Continuing along the PCT meant traversing a couple of snowfields, which looked steep but patchy from what we could make out. Alternatively, the higher-ground Old Snowy trail would climb steeply up the peak to firmer ground, reconnecting with the PCT in less than a mile. One option seemed possibly riskier, the other involved more climbing. Which one did we take? The shortest one of course!

Grateful bears hadn't attacked us in the night, we left camp wearing nearly all our clothes. Slowly progressing along a narrow ridge, I could see my breath in the chilled morning air. Within a mile, we broke through the mist, and a mighty vista unfolded. We stood high above a wide valley filled to the brim with hovering puffs of cloud. A promising bright blue sky rested above, with the peak of Mount Adams poking through like a floating island in the distance. The land was still and expansive. I have never been a morning person – if I had my way I wouldn't wake up before nine – but seeing the landscape awaken from a position above the clouds felt ethereal. Over the saddle at Cispus Pass a whole new view containing a wide basin and new mountains materialised. Having crossed a number of small seasonal streams, without getting our feet any wetter, we stopped to cook an unusually late breakfast. I threw everything and anything I could find into the oatmeal, resulting in a magic blend which tasted a lot like melted Bounty bars. We enjoyed our breakfast from a well-positioned throne-like log, staring down into the wildflower-coated scene below with the morning sun in our faces. I was just beginning to realise something: moments like this were what the trail was all about. So many passing thru-hikers wouldn't pause to take in their surroundings or even to say hello, intent on making the day's target miles. I appreciated the difference in goals between us and them meant we had the time to enjoy it.

We met one such person at Snowgrass Flats. Well, we didn't really meet her, she was in far too much of a rush to stop and chat, but as she scampered off trekking impossibly fast over a sheet of icy snow Conrad and I couldn't help but stare. Not just at her hairy legs – I know I'm judging again – but at the way she hurled herself across the snow without the help of trekking poles, staying low and occasionally toppling over from side to side, arms there to push her back up again. She must have been travelling at four times our speed.

"So THAT'S how you hike 30-miles a day!" I observed, through green eyes.

Conrad continued watching as she became a tiny dot in the distance. "We'd fall off this mountain if we tried that! Best-case scenario, I'd break a leg."

He was probably right. It was implicitly decided to continue with our usual cautionary pace, yes you got it: *slow and steady*.

Reaching the Old Snowy trailhead decision point, we choose to stay *pure* and keep going along the PCT, an approach based purely on a quick calculation of lowest elevation and shortest possible distance. Having said that, from the limited footprints it was clear to see that ours was not the popular choice.

"What way do you reckon Dan went?" I pondered.

Conrad gave me a wicked smile, "he's not gonna like this."

"Yeah I know," stepping aside, "after you."

The trail clung to the snowy precipice toward Elk Pass with patches of bare jagged rock and a seemingly endless drop-off into the valley. Traversing it was not actually that bad, we slowly followed vague footprints, a little slushy in places, with just a couple of uncertain moments when transferring between snow and rocks where the trail crumbled away and we had to leap to safety. Conrad contends it was much worse than this, so maybe I had unknowingly become infinitely more confident at crossing snow by now; regardless, we survived.

As the Old Snowy trail reconnected with the PCT we entered into the section widely regarded as the highest and most dangerous in Oregon and Washington. Eyeing the faint winding pathway ebbing along Goat Rocks, I instantly recognised the iconic PCT image. It has to be one of the most photographed parts of the trail, widely known as the "Knife's Edge." It wasn't difficult to see where the unofficial name came from; the pointy mountain ridge resembled the spine of a Stegosaurus, its serrated peaks the remnants of an eroded stratovolcano, extinct for over two million years. Thanks to glaciation and erosion scouring the terrain, the sheer drop-offs on both sides into deep U-shaped valleys were alarming to say the least. I considered the two young hikers we'd met near Olallie Lake who must have crossed this minefield over a month before, marvelling at what they must have faced. Spying the immense expanses of Washington's mountain-scape, I would often pinch myself at the rugged splendour, wondering what the place would hold for other hikers, especially thru-hikers who, weeks behind, would more than likely face poorer visibility and unpredictable weather.

Climbing up and down the jagged rollercoaster, I kept stopping to take pictures. It was the very definition of awesome. The previous day, these views would have been obscured by the mist, so I considered it fate that we witnessed the scene in its full grandeur. The trail itself was very exposed, so thankfully clear of snow. Instead we followed the rocky and at times loose track, glad that very few people passed by, and we met no horses. Yes, despite being precariously narrow in places, the trail is somehow open to horses. I was concentrating on my footwork while also trying to take in the deep drainages to both sides of me, when

Conrad decided it was a good spot to stop and point out how his shoe treads were now completely worn away!

The trail quickly descended into a lush, alpine meadow dotted with glacial streams. It was baking hot. We saw no one except the back of Dan's red shirt up ahead when we first entered the basin. On a bed of damp grass beside a small creek we lay soaking our feet and t-shirts, while relaxing over a lunch of tortillas filled with peanut butter, Nutella and jam. Before leaving we stocked up on electrolytes as Conrad asserted people had died of hypothermia up on the "Knife's Edge" due to exposure. I had no way to verify his claims at the time but can now sadly confirm that he wasn't talking his usual garbage.

By mid-afternoon we found ourselves back in forest. The mosquitoes had returned, but they were the accepted price to pay for some shade. The trees also provided some much-needed coverage to finally attend to nature's call, something I had been putting off for at least 10 miles. We passed Dan who was pitching his tent virtually on the trail for lack of any nearby alternative. Predictably, he complained about his nerves earlier in the day when crossing the Goat Rocks. We continued through a couple more miles of blow-downs, then after 12 hours and 18 miles of progress, reached a small wooden trail junction for Hidden Spring. With great reluctance, we took the quarter-mile detour for water and a flat camp spot. Every part of my body ached with tiredness so, unsurprisingly, I completely failed to appreciate how truly *epic* our day had been.

24

Straight Outta Packwood

I peered into the sports store's darkened window. A small handwritten sign stuck inside the glass read: "*At Vern's doing pickles*". I drew back, confused.

"Do you think they mean literally *pickling* veg, or is *pickling* some new thing all the kids are doing these days?"

Conrad double-checked to confirm the door was disappointingly locked.

"I have no idea," he sighed. "Maybe we should ask around and find out where this Vern lives, check it out."

He was just joking of course. But the predicament now facing us was where to find a gas canister in the middle of nowhere.

Packwood was dead, except for the occasional car zooming through to who-knows-where off Highway 12. The place had once been a logging community, until a downturn in the economy closed the lumber mill in the nineties (but hey, maybe Trump will bring them back)! What remains today centres on a section of highway sprinkled with a couple of gas stations and perhaps a dozen stores, whose trade depends on seasonal tourism and passing vehicles crossing the Cascades. Even the mobile phone companies seemed to have neglected the town, we couldn't get any coverage. We pulled up in Mark's car around lunchtime, overjoyed to have found it parked as instructed opposite White Pass' closed ski terminal.

Our morning miles had sailed by. We'd set off before it was barely light, not pausing to cook breakfast, driven by the familiar motivation of a town awaiting our arrival. Passing the distinctively-shaped Shoe Lake, up and over a notch in the ridge, we traced the thin line of trail skirting around a huge open basin. Atop the large craggy ridge, the top of a ski lift was just about visible in the far distance.

I had a decent marching pace going on; I could almost taste

the impending burger until I got caught off-guard by a marmot dashing out of nowhere. I lost my footing and narrowly escaped plunging into the void. As I recovered my composure I instantly forgave the cute goofiness of the fat squirrel-beaver shaped character. Moments later, nature once again tried to obstruct us with a train of horses. We had witnessed many signs of equestrian users out on the trail, mostly in the form of smelly mounds in the middle of the path, but until then we hadn't appreciated what an inconvenience they are when they approach down the narrow trail. Apparently, they own the trail too. Having waited for the unappreciative convoy to pass, we sped down the remaining descent into White Pass, twining along ski runs through steep shaded forest, trying to outrun the mozzies.

Dan joined us in the car after some texts and a quick reroute to the trailhead. During the 20-mile car journey Conrad concentrated on the winding mountain road, whilst I joked with Dan that Mark and Steve were probably just behind us. Sure enough, no sooner had we all checked into the Packwood Inn motel and grabbed lunch, than a text came through from Mark. Poor Conrad. He took a quick shower, jumped into his waterproofs – commando – and left. While he was gone, I ticked off the usual hiker-min of laundry and unpacking resupply boxes, with the ultra-efficiency that comes with repetition.

We later found Mark and Steve sat polishing off beers in the pizza place next to the no-frills motel. They filled us in on their recent escapades, through the rain and the ridge-walks, and all the wonderful people they had met just after us, who through the hiker grapevine gave out trail reports on the progress of the British couple up ahead. It was sad to be seeing them go so soon, but Steve had a coffee shop business to return to in Canada, and stressed how the espresso machines would always break, sending the place into meltdown whenever he went away. He kindly offered to sell us Steve-O-Reno's Cappuccino so he could retire, but we hastily responded that, visa issues aside, we would have been in way over our heads. I have to admit though, it wasn't the last I thought of the idea. My mind on the trail began dreaming of us as coffee entrepreneurs, an exciting prospect, though I think

I found the part about uprooting our lives to work for ourselves instead of some large corporation more attractive than making coffee and dealing with customers.

The guys departed for the large town of Yakima, 70 miles east. After waving them off, we just sort of wandered around the Packwood strip. We idled down the aisles of Blanton's Market grocery store, purely to soak up the air conditioning and entertain ourselves by ogling the local food selection, ironic as I ordered my groceries online back home to avoid these kinds of places. We visited the hardware store, a place where time stood still. It stocked an impressive selection of tools and farming equipment, but more importantly it sold gas canisters. This was lucky, because as the proprietor took our money, he mentioned the owner of the Packwood Sports Hut only opened the store when he felt like it. Due to the sunny weather and the draw of Vern's pickles, it seemed highly unlikely that Conrad would be securing a replacement pair of shoes. At this point I urged him to order another pair online and get them shipped to our next stop just under 100 miles away, but would he listen? This decision would come back to bite him later.

Following an afternoon nap, the only thing that could rouse us from our slumber was, you guessed it: food. Crossing the highway, we entered the Blue Spruce Saloon, a dark *spit-n-sawdust* themed bar, where it always felt like evening, even in the middle of a summer's day. A neon Budweiser sign hung above the large horseshoe-shaped bar which took centre-stage within the dark wooden interior. The place reminded me of a line from that Cheryl Crow song: "*a happy couple enter the bar, dangerously close to one another, the bartender looks up from his want ads*".

Sure enough, a couple of faces sat at the bar gazed over at us with momentary interest as we entered. I smiled, then took in the small selection of memorabilia on sale, including my favourite, a black t-shirt blazed with white cow-boy style lettering which read: "*Straight Outta Packwood*". If only we'd a suitcase with which to transport home such bad-ass souvenirs.

The 2016 Rio Olympics had just begun, so we chose a table at the back of the restaurant where we could watch TV and eat without the need for conversation. Dan later joined us, so I sat there explaining to him why we found the American coverage of the Olympics so fascinating. It was so extremely un-conventional compared with the broadcasting back home. Presenters on the BBC typically give factual, well-rounded commentary, discussing the international favourites, the underdogs, and covering lots of events – even the ones that no one really cares about, like shot put. Not in America. Out there the games are covered from a completely different angle. Sport is celebrated, it's sensational, and you could easily be forgiven for thinking the only team even competing was "Team U-S-A!" If only I had a dollar for every time a presenter heralded Michael Phelps' return from retirement during our time in Packwood. Perhaps the lacklustre British attitude is a deliberate plot to temper expectations given past disappointments, or maybe Americans are just more zealously patriotic. Either way, it was highly entertaining, and for a person who doesn't usually like watching sports I was bizarrely transfixed.

With so few diversions, Packwood ultimately forced us to rest. We took a full zero day in which we did nothing except buy food, eat it, cram even more of it into our food sacks, and use the Wi-Fi to connect with people back home.

My new spirit of positivity had so far prevented me from complaining about my foot-cramping issues. Secretly convinced I was getting early-onset arthritis, I lay on the bed, semi-watching the Olympic opening ceremony while scouring the internet for symptoms. This symbolised a new stage of a difficult relationship with my feet. We had come so far – they had grown a protective hard layer in the first couple of weeks of hiking, beaten off blisters, broken in a new pair of shoes from Bend which hurt like hell for around 100 miles and resulted in a new set of blisters, but now each day by mid-afternoon they experienced severe toe cramping. In fact, I think I had done rather well to not mention this because it was excruciating. Every night, I would take my shoes off and wipe my feet with a wet cloth and a couple of drops of Dr Bronner's peppermint wash to mask the pong, so I could inspect the puffy red flesh and try to massage them better. Combined with the quad issue which I wouldn't describe as painful, more an irritation which I hoped wasn't the prelude to something major, I knew the ultimate solution was to just STOP HIKING!

Foot problems aside, by the next morning we stood dressed and ready to leave. One last check of the weather reports confirmed the storms headed for the northwest coast were still expected to hit the next day. All we could do was hope they would disperse before reaching the Cascades, because even the weather professionals couldn't predict their course. Over in Grant County, about 90 miles east of the PCT, a pick-up in wind had escalated the Lower Crab Creek wild fire from 1 to 10,000 acres in the space of a day. This information felt scary. We had witnessed first-hand the aftermath destruction caused by forest fires, so prayed it would get contained soon or else we could be scrambling for the nearest evacuation point. Stocked with last night's pizza and a hitch-hiking sign made from the empty box, we hit the road.

Our hopes of an easy ride out of town failed to materialise. Perhaps I needed a bigger sign? It took a solid 25 minutes before El Salvador took mercy on us and pulled up his pickup truck. He was on his way from the coast to Yakima with a cargo full of oysters. Luckily the morning was cool and overcast, so there was no fishy smell emanating from the bundles of strung-up shells. Even Mount Rainier had disappeared, completely shrouded in impending-storm-related mist.

25

Turning down a Gift Horse

Had I just heard right? Two complete strangers, who had stepped out their SUV to talk to a couple of scruffy hikers sat in a patch of grass next to a deserted forest road, just offered us a ride? This caught us off-guard, a flutter of conflicting responses raced through my head.

The lady continued, "we'll just be driving up the road to Lester to see where my husband grew up, then we'll be comin' right back this way. If you're still around, we'll happily give you guys a ride to the Pass."

Every being in my body now wanted to sit and wait for the return of the shiny white chariot, and a brief exchange with Conrad confirmed the feeling was mutual. But that really would have been cheating. Right? Would it though? The internal debate continued, but the feeling in the pit of my stomach, call it a conscience, eventually won out.

I hesitantly peeled myself up, heaving my pack back into place.

"Come on, *quick*! If I see that car again I'm jumping in, we need to leave, NOW!"

Conrad was muttering something about a hot shower and a bed. But with me only allowing myself to hear my own wisdom, we scurried off, heading for the cover of the trees, eliminating the temptation.

By this point, 17 miles and a night of camping stood between us and our arrival in the small ski resort of Snoqualmie. Seventeen miles may not sound like a lot, but given the wet weather of the last few days had rapidly pushed us to the brink, those remaining miles felt endless. Everything we carried was a soggy mess. All I wanted was a hot shower and a dry bed. I would have sacrificed my last Snickers for either.

Added to this, those familiar pangs in my abdomen were once

again ready for their monthly visit. F**k the inconvenience of periods in the wild.

The pain was worse than the previous month, without the vast array of home remedies and special stretching I usually adopted. I knew I had to suck it up and deal with it, just like nearly every other woman on the trail does at some point. Armed with a sheet of tinfoil to carry out my used tampons and a shit-tonne of painkillers, I was ready. Oh, and whilst on this topic, if you ever wondered whether bears are attracted to the smell of human menstruation – fear not. This is an urban myth probably dreamed up by men, as proven by U.S. National Park studies in the eighties and nineties. Having said that, results from a similar study involving polar bears were less reassuring.

Before this tantalising offer, amid welcoming cooler temperatures, we had resumed hiking from White Pass days earlier, passing the busy horse camp, into a forest landscape dotted with tiny lakes. It was the weekend, so there were lots of riders to stop and let pass, along with plenty of smoking piles of crap to avoid. Life sure looked easy-breezy mounted on a horse. One female rider was drinking a beer – it was 9 a.m. – and another smoking away while her horse did all the work. I considered asking where they were headed and whether it would be out of line to request they ferry our bags. I'm not sure why I didn't...

The day was brightening up with no sign of storms. Just before lunch another hiker informed us that Dan was an hour ahead, so he must have made it to the trail super-early, super stealth-like. And he must also have gone on to break 20 miles that day because we never caught him. His cunning meant he missed out on a glorious cold pizza lunch, sat at the edge of Snow Lake, watching bright blue dragonflies hovering over the still water. I wouldn't even dream of eating cold pizza back home – I don't really do any left-overs – but on the trail the carb-heavy, rubbery-cheese and thick, doughy base was a lavish treat. Shame it was way too heavy to carry for more than a few hours, or we would have ditched the dehydrated meals and survived purely on the stuff.

By this stage our packs should have been getting lighter as we shed superfluous items, but in reality the opposite was happening. At White Pass we had collected some online purchases, including high protection DEET, foam pads to sit on, and more hiker food. We also continued the trend to pad-out and pimp up our food supplies, opening up the dehydrated meals to add all sorts of extra stuff such as veg and couscous. While it was helping to satisfy our appetites better, it was a Catch 22 because of the extra energy required to carry the bloody stuff! I complained to Conrad that I needed a back brace, but really, I should have either eaten less, or bought a more supportive, metal-framed backpack.

We finished the day camped just off the trail at Two Lakes. A giant speckled frog interrupted my flannel wash which was already pretty undignified, squatting on my hands and knees in the long-wet grass. Everything was still in our little meadow facing Crag Mountain. Nothing but the sound of crickets and the crackle of the camp fire could be heard. I was consciously starting to enjoy those moments of tranquillity when the hiking day was over and all we had to do was relax in the chilled night air. It was enlivening. If only our tent came equipped with a weightless pocket-sprung mattress so we could have enjoyed a proper night's sleep, and it would have been bliss. Actually, throw in bathroom plumbing too, and some headspace for Conrad. In truth, life without constant digital stimuli was now feeling, well, *normal*.

I hadn't grown up online like kids do today. And when internet reached homes, I still remember the dial-up tone and agonising wait to connect to the world of MSN chatrooms. Yet somehow, in the space of just a couple of years I couldn't imagine life without checking my friend's Facebook statuses daily, or refreshing news apps out of pure reflex-swiping. It had taken weeks, but I was slowly beginning to detox from the noise of modern technology and I liked it. It forced me to reset, to think. It heightened my conscious mind, which allowed me to notice and appreciate simple things like the birds tweeting, or the smell of fragrant flowers. And although I didn't want to become totally ignorant, I realised that the 24-hour news cycle we are subjected to these days is harrowing. Taking a break from it offered calm and felt entirely natural.

My last thought before dozing off was a plea to Mother Nature: PLEASE, hold off the rain.

We have already established Mother Nature didn't think much of us. The rains came immediately after lunch the next day, just north of Chinook Pass. Now, I could deal with hiking in the rain – I had expensive rain-proofs after all, and I'm sure it was preferable to hiking in a thunderstorm, or even searing desert heat – but the thing that made it so mightily unpleasant was having wet feet. Once my shoes were wet on the inside it was mentally game-over. Nothing could make me want to be anywhere other than somewhere else warm and dry. A brief rainstorm would also be OK, if once it ended we could dry out our stuff, but days of consistent rain meant socks and shoes never stood a chance.

The day had commenced in typically-chilled Washington fashion with trees cloaked in low-lying mist, except that day, instead of burning off, it lingered. With low visibility we slowly edged closer to the state's tallest peak, Mount Rainier; not that we could see it. In a strange way I enjoyed the dramatic effects the sky was playing with the mountain tops, encasing them in a mysteriously foreboding shroud. Even the pine trees took on a loftier air, towering above us with their pointy tips disappearing into the abyss. The landscape felt fresh and my cheeks tingled with the chill. By Chinook Pass we traversed hillsides carpeted with pink and purple wildflowers, vividly contrasting against the bleak grey backdrop. It was spectacular, but I couldn't escape the thought ruminating in the forefront of my mind: the temptation to hitch off the trail at the highway to wait out the impending rain somewhere civilised. When Conrad suggested this aloud it took great restraint not to. We accepted that the resulting lost time would jeopardise us reaching Canada, so we trudged on towards the pass, hopeful the clouds would blow over, wondering whether Dan had hitched to a hotel.

Chinook Pass was a massive disappointment. Highway 410 may not be open all year round, but for such a busy parking lot in August they were seriously lacking some kind of ice cream van or refreshment stand. Instead, we got a pit toilet and a garbage bin. This we agreed would have been the opportune moment of the entire trip for a "surprise" visit from the Marshmeiers. They could have embarked on a wonderful road-trip, parking up their massive RV, complete with a fully-loaded kitchenette and shower. They don't actually own an RV, and logistically I'm not sure how they would have accurately tracked us there, but nothing's impossible, right? I hope they read this. Instead, we crossed the parking lot, gazing around in case a stranger was handing out trail magic, before disappearing back up the opposite trailhead, saddened it wasn't our lucky day.

The afternoon brought with it a changing myriad of weather, making it impossible to regulate body temperature. One minute it was freezing cold – we enjoyed a high of 10 degrees Celsius all day – then a glimmer of hope was sparked with a hint of sun, followed by spitting, culminating in full-blown rain by 3 p.m. Did I mention that I hate walking in the rain? Countless mid-trail clothing reshuffles ensued, on and off with the waterproofs. It always seemed to be during the times I wore both pairs of trousers and gloves that I needed to pee. We got through the rest of the day by mentally zoning out, listening to podcasts and eating lots of in-transit cheer-me-up snacks because I consciously told myself I shouldn't grumble. My grandparents never did. They belonged to that war generation of no nonsense, using the term "mustn't grumble" without following it with a "but". I even once heard my nan tell an occupational health worker that she "couldn't complain" after breaking her hip at 94! They really showed me.

When we finally couldn't take the rain any longer we pitched the tent in a thicket high above Big Crow Basin. We huddled inside listening to the nylon taking a pelting. Everything felt dirty. For the first time we decided to throw caution to the wind and light the stove inside the tent's entrance vestibule – a move highly discouraged in every camping safety guide ever written – to make some warming hot chocolate. When that didn't result in the whole tent igniting, we got the confidence to cook a freeze-dried meal. In such times hot food was, without fail, the only way to increase morale; surely hungry bears didn't venture out in the rain.

Since the early hours the distinct call of elks echoed around us, but they were invisible, engulfed in more heavy, grey mist. I couldn't feel my fingers or toes as we exited camp at daybreak. Starting or ending the day with cold, wet feet made it difficult not to feel deflated. We didn't complain out loud – well, aside from one "pit of despair" quote from Conrad – instead choosing to internalise our anguish and listen to countless podcasts until our phone batteries looked worryingly low. Tom Hanks sounds like a lovely man. His interview on *Desert Island Discs* cheered me up somewhat, and another episode with Ray Winston, a fellow East Londoner and all-round salt-of-the-earth type.

As our elevation dropped we came down from a foggy ridge into an eerie, moss-coated forest. I occupied my mind counting mushrooms and other monstrous growth-like fungi thriving off bright-green covered trunks, and knocking rain drops from the undergrowth with my poles. I did anything to try and stop my mind from fixating on the food I craved. The cold weather spell was making us ravenous. I decided I mostly wanted banana cake, a loaded bagel, and a really chocolatey mocha. Conrad's list was as predictable as ever: burger, fries, beer, and salty crisps.

Strategically placed at mile 13, we decided to have lunch at the Ulrich wilderness shelter. The dark wooden cabin was sparse and creaky, and contained that damp smell shared by every garden shed. Thankfully it provided refuge from the rain, enabling us to fire up our cooking stove. We had intended to dry out the tent and our feet using the cabin's large iron stove, but the unavailability of dry wood prevented that. The rain was drawing others to seek shelter too. Within a few minutes of our arrival, a lady in a bin-bag-looking rain skirt and her elderly mother joined. We chatted away while cooking and eating a bland Thai yellow curry meal-in-a-bag, and filtering the bright green water collected from the meadow stream outside.

With the rain reaching a new level of downpour, it would have been a lot more difficult to motivate ourselves to leave the shelter, had it not been for the help of the 15 Boy Scouts who flooded the cabin. While completely chaotic to begin with, swinging from the rafters and sending dust flying down as they stomped around on the floorboards in the attic above, they were friendly enough. Many wanted to chat because they liked our English accents. A couple of more confident boys attempted to mimic us, we smiled and laughed, but after a first round of impressions that would give Dick Van Dyke a run for his money I felt my patience wavering.

The boys were accompanied by five adults who wisely decided to distance themselves out on the porch. Whilst heaving my pack back on, I got talking to a couple of the leaders, one of which offered me food. I could have kissed the man; in fact, I most definitely would have done if requested. With a stupidly large grin I triumphantly shared my little feast of homemade cookies, red vines, peanuts, and a packet of Skittles with Conrad, as we braced ourselves for the torrent outside.

Without doubt, this small act of kindness had already made our day.

By day four out of Packwood I was struggling to keep the Canadian dream alive. For a start, I had no dry socks left. Then, going for a wander into the woods for my early morning business I got a massive scare. Someone had decided to discard a large half-eaten roll of some kind of plastic-covered sausage meat into the bushes just metres from our tent. Yes, we had unknowingly just slept right next to the world's greatest cougar/bear honeypot! It looked pretty vile, so I wasn't going to pick it up and dispose of it as I should have. Instead I tried kicking it down the hill-side, only to get sticky dogfood splatter all over my damp shoe. With that little gift, we made a swift exit.

High up on the ridge of Blowout Mountain, everything was coated in a lifeless mist. With a break in the trees, but still no view, we found a rare spot of phone signal and got a text through to Leslie. The message was a plea for her to post another pair of Conrad's shoes Priority Mail, ASAP. I warned him to expect the worst and hope for the best, but he wasn't listening, instead messing around with the phone. I cast a glance at dark clouds menacingly looming low overhead.

"What's the chance it'll just blow over?" I said, in a hopelessly sarcastic tone.

Conrad let out a frustrated sigh and continued trying to load a weather forecast. It didn't work. Right there, feeling an impeding sense that we were about to get wetter, we made a decision to come off the trail. A Dan-style road-walking expedition ensued, a seemingly sensible plan, especially if a storm did hit, but one that rapidly descended into a bloody stupid idea when after countless hours winding down the steep gravel track, we hadn't seen a single passing vehicle. Being miles and hundreds of vertical feet from the trail felt seriously unnerving.

"You know if something bad happens to us, no one would have a clue where we are," I stressed aloud.

"I'd be more worried about our water situation if I were you," Conrad responded reassuringly.

He was right. In my determined marching frenzy, it hadn't crossed my mind to consider our next water source. The high-level Google Map our lives now entirely depended upon was showing a thin blue line right next to us, but in reality, the water was hidden far below in a completely inaccessible deep ravine. It may sound like a no-brainer in hindsight, but that day the safety aspect of being on a defined trail with a topographic map, became vividly apparent. With greater foot-traffic on the trail recently, I was confident potential help wouldn't be more than a few hours away if one of us suffered an incapacitating injury. But there we were, shin-splints rushing up the legs, walking along a path that might not even be the right one. I had every right to feel stupid.

It took around seven miles of road-walking before we reached a steep valley cradling the Green River and saw another person. The sight of the elderly man out fishing with his grandson beside flowing water brought an enormous sense of relief. A few hours and miles of road later, we reached a patch of grass on a quiet forest road. It was there, as we sat in the damp, eating trail mix wishing it were something better, that the SUV pulled up.

A middle-aged couple climbed out and began making their way towards us. After passing my visual threat scanner I waited to be asked for directions. But on the contrary, it transpired the two had just stopped by for a chat, like only Americans do. Perhaps they were religious missionaries ready to save us from a life of drifting, before our hiking story was revealed. Completely fascinated by our trip, they kept using adjectives like "awesome", before, tentatively offering us the remains of their lunch. It turned out accepting soggy, half-eaten sub rolls from strangers, which we ate on the ground in a new Hikertrash low, was no longer beneath us.

Before they departed they offered us a ride to Snoqualmie Pass, our next resupply stop, still 17 miles away. The ride was on the table, they just needed to make a short trip first, and urged us to flag them down when they passed back along the road if we wanted it. Conrad and I debated it briefly, it felt like the devil was tempting us by dangling the promise of hot food and a bed so close we could almost taste it, but reluctantly conscience finally won as we concluded the lift would indeed be cheating. We recommenced our walk, occasionally glancing back, still unsure whether we had made the right decision. It was only after we turned onto a narrow track full of fallen timber, that we knew it was time to give up looking longingly for the car.

When the rocky track finally intersected with the PCT it was early evening. What a relief it felt to see the now-familiar blue and white trail emblem. We sat on a log to eat a cereal bar and consult the *Halfmile* map. I heard a man long before I saw him, coming down the trail south-bound, merrily swishing a traditional woollen kilt. It wasn't your typical hiking attire, providing an instant conversation-starter. The friendly guy revealed he'd left Snoqualmie earlier in the day and warned of rain forecast for that evening. My heart sank. It already felt startlingly cold, so it was only going to get colder. After wishing him safe travels we studied the map for an answer; aka a way out.

We agreed the plan was not cheating; we were still walking to Canada. Just that day we happened to be doing so along dirt roads, having apparently not had enough of them already. The new "alternative" route continued along the jeep road headed down the mountain towards the Snoqualmie Pass interstate. Our prime motivation was not mile-saving for once; instead we fixed on losing elevation due to the looming weather. In fact, that day, after turning down that much-wanted ride we set our all-time personal hiking record of 25 miles! It helped that it was 100-per cent in a down-hill direction.

On the banks of Keechelus Lake reservoir, we ignored threatening government warning signs to keep off, before downing a couple of our trusty antihistamine knock-out pills, amid the hum of the interstate and the sound of thunder raging in the east.

26

Snoqualmie Refuel

At barely dawn next morning, I poked my head through the tent flap. Remarkably our illicit camp was dry. Thick clouds drifted over the lake, yet the air felt noticeably mild. As we'd lost a whopping 2,000 feet of elevation since the previous morning, getting dressed and breaking camp felt far less painful; it didn't even require gloves.

Gathering our gear, we set out along the Iron Horse Trail, skimming the lake's western shore. Back in 1909, the Milwaukee Road railway line, connecting Chicago to the Pacific, was opened right beneath our feet. After the company filed for bankruptcy for the third time in the 1980s, the Washington section of line was converted into a very long, linear State Park. Little remains of the railway itself, occasionally the odd rusted remnants of steelwork could be spotted, chiselled into the mountain, but mostly we kept our heads down and welcomed the flat, easy miles.

The lake lay grey and barren. Its name, "Keechelus" literally means "few fish" in native American, and with a shoreline littered with deadwood it didn't quite hold the appeal of the alpine lakes we'd become accustomed to. Snaking along the opposite bank, the concrete I-90 was ever-present, its buzz echoing off the surrounding rock. The park's interpretive signs dismissed my theory that we were looking at a man-made reservoir. Although now dammed and twice the size, the lake is natural, and is the source of the Yakima River, which flows into the Columbia River and eventually underneath the Bridge of Gods. It certainly wasn't the most scenic section of our hike, but we didn't care, we were crunching down the miles standing between us and our next hot meal!

We exited the trail onto Highway 906, praying there were no drunken motorists out at that time of day. Had we continued, we would have entered the dark, 2.3-mile Snoqualmie Tunnel that runs underneath the ski resort. When it opened five years after the railroad to replace a steep and tortuous temporary right of way over the pass, it was considered an engineering marvel. Today some people choose to hike or cycle through it with torches, a feat not added to my bucket list.

Walking along the non-existent hard-shoulder, we counted ourselves lucky it was still only August. In just a few months' time the closed ski-lifts, empty vacation homes and huge parking lots, without a single car in them, would spring back to life with the fall of snow. It felt strange being in a ski resort out of season, as it had done at White Pass. I walked along imagining how unrecognisable it would become by winter, heaving with people carrying skis. At present it felt kind of lonesome.

Snoqualmie Pass's summit area looked more promising. The half-mile stretch of highway serves as a popular truck stop and tourist rest area for those headed to and from Seattle, a place I was surprised to discover was only an hour away. Our hotel, The Summit Inn was not difficult to find. According to the Trip Advisor community, this place was rated as the number one hotel in the whole of Snoqualmie Pass. Total number of hotels listed? Just the one. I actually struggled to see what justified the two-and-a-half-star feedback score during our stay, because the place ran like an American version of *Fawlty Towers*, albeit a far less humorous one. Yes, The Summit Inn was a no-frills kind of place, but in our new role as hikers, we were not in any position to complain. It's not like we had the ability to jump in a car and drive elsewhere. When I read the reviews of bed-bugs and all sorts of other gross cleaning-related shortcomings after check-in, they confirmed my suspicion that this was not a place we would ever have considered staying on a regular vacation.

A scarf-wearing stuffed elk head complete with antlers hung over reception, greeting us with two watchful eyes. It took a couple of minutes of standing around and calling before a large woman appeared. With raised eyebrows, she slowly sauntered over from the back doorway, glaring at us as if we had just shot her puppy.

"Can you wait a minute," she said forcefully. It was a rhetorical question. She turned her back and talked into her headset.

I scanned the empty pine-clad reception hall. Some chairs were positioned in front of an unlit fireplace, and an old TV screen showing Olympic coverage created white noise in the background. It certainly wasn't rush hour. There must have been perhaps half a dozen cars in the large parking lot out front. I wondered what important business she had to deal with on the headset.

She finally turned back and slumped into a swivel chair at the counter. "Can I *help* you?"

Conrad responded. "Yeah, we'd like to check-in if we can, I know it's a bit early..." She cut him off.

"Do you have a reservation?"

"I think so, I spoke to someone on the phone, it should be under *Nicholas*."

I should explain here the reason we were not 100 per cent confident about having a reservation. The whole experience of trying to book a room had been a painful one. At the time, reservations were only being taken over the phone. The first time I called, just before leaving White Pass, I was told by a hushed female voice that she was busy and I had to phone back. This happened twice more, and it was not easy to get a phone signal. On our fourth attempt, with a lot of huffing and puffing from the same staff member she reluctantly took the reservation, but it felt like I had just asked for a triple deluxe king room in a youth hostel. Had it been any other situation I doubt I would have called back, gauging how much they obviously cared for the business, but as a hiker you take the crap because you just want a bed.

The receptionist was now clicking the keys of her computer with her acrylic nails, whilst complaining how stressed she was. Another guest had come to the desk with a question, so with the three of us there she was maxed out.

"Check-in's not 'til five. If you want a room before it'll cost fifty dollars."

Did I hear right? Five o'clock in an empty hotel? But just before I started an outburst along those lines, Conrad chipped in with a softer approach.

"Oh, we didn't realise. Sorry we're so early; we're hiking the PCT."

She couldn't have cared less. Perhaps she saw a lot of hikers. I had the feeling we were keeping her from her favourite soap opera out back. At that point, feeling tired and irritated, I turned away, leaving Conrad to take the hit, and to try working his charm. I took a seat on the leather sofa, and stared up at a giant antler chandelier, wondering how many poor animals must have died to decorate this shithole.

A few minutes later Conrad came over.

"She said we could try again after twelve and she wouldn't charge. She didn't give any guarantees though. We've *really* put her out!"

I looked at my watch, it was 10:20 a.m. We made for the adjoining diner, where we found Dan tucking into the remains of a pancake breakfast.

"How y'all doin? The eggs are good." He looked content, the way any hiker with a belly full of food does.

We took a seat in the booth, and I judgingly eyed his plate, wondering how Americans can justify coating bacon and eggs with maple syrup.

Over our second breakfast of the day, we held a debriefing session with Dan. The route to his success, it turned out, began with an easy hitch out of Packwood – he stuck his thumb out at the road and immediately scored a lift with a guy from the Fire Department. He then hiked a record 26 miles on the first day, not stopping until dark. Unlike us, Dan never did care about where he spent the night on the trail, so long as he could find a patch of dirt big enough to fit his small tent. It was no surprise we hadn't seen him the entire section.

I was expecting him to feel jealous when we unveiled our elaborate road de-tour. He was certainly intrigued, but it turned out, only because he was trying to work out if we had chosen the same collection of roads! We compared maps and concluded that unusually he hiked more PCT this time around. I was sad to have missed out on Mirror Lake. Dan had camped there the previous night and described the water as "aqua blue". At least that morning it didn't sound like we'd missed out on much; hiking through the dense fog Dan recollected: "Great views, my *arse!*"

Just after noon, following a lot more huffing and puffing and talking into a headset, we were finally allowed to check into a hotel room. Hot, musky air hit us immediately. We borrowed a rattling box cooler as the windows didn't seem to open. Following showers and a nap, we let loose on the town to see what it had to offer. Parked out front of the gas station, we found another popular hiker stop, the Aardvark food truck. Feeling groggy from the sleep, we slumped into some deckchairs and joined the conversation with a small group of older male hikers happily idling the day away.

Most hikers we encountered were friendly, and our common purpose would fuel a community of story-sharing. Unfortunately, we met a strange bunch in Snoqualmie. There was one guy in particular that we both took a dislike to. Mr Smug kept boasting about having a PhD, like a broken record, just in case we hadn't heard him the first 14 times. He also fancied himself as expert on European politics, although I got the impression he just liked the sound of his own voice over everyone else's.

Over hot dogs and bagels, the conversation turned to gun control. Much to our amusement, the intoxicated food truck owner went on a very animated rant about the government, waving around his beer can.

"I shouldn't *hav'ta* register ma firearm." He gleamed, with rosy cheeks, "it's *un-constitutional*! This Obama and the NSA just want'a spy on people. It's against my civ-il liberties! I don't want them knowin' my business!"

Conrad was captivated and began half-jokingly pressing his buttons.

"You don't want them knowing your business with regards to owning a gun? That sounds kind of suspicious."

"Nah, look I'm an *American*! It's my second amendment right to own a God-damn gun if I *choose*. I need'a protect my fam-ily."

Conrad continued in a careful pragmatic, non-offensive tone.

"You have a driving licence, don't you?"

"Yeah."

"So you're registered to drive a car, and a car could kill somebody. So, what's the problem with registering to own a gun? And what about criminals or mental people with guns?"

But in his drunken stupor the owner just wasn't willing to listen.

"It's like the N-S-A. They're all listening to people...." and with that the tirade continued, taking us further into an elaborate world of conspiracy theories involving federal espionage, all spearheaded by the evil Obama.

I didn't get involved. I was tired. Instead I chugged away on a coffee watching the entertainment unfold, until I began to get the distinct impression it was time to leave. Gun control was not an issue the Brits and our American cousins would be aligning on anytime soon. We thanked the owner for his hospitality, wished the other hikers a safe trip, and exited before we got shot.

After securing the world's most expensive replacement gas canister from the mini-mart – and some Pringles and Ben & Jerry's for good measure – we returned to our stifling room to catch up on life elsewhere. Reading through emails, I came across a couple from Toaster and Smudge, the two ladies we shared a cabin with at Elk Lake. The title of the first one made me laugh out loud: "Mustn't Grumble But…" Vicki went on to explain how they had coined the phrase from two Aussies to describe their experiences in early Washington. Similar to us, they experienced lots of elevation gain, a boring green tunnel, and hiking through drizzle. The phrase sounded very British, so we decide to adopt it as a delightful way of launching into a moan. The ladies were about to leave White Pass, so unless something went wrong, we probably wouldn't be crossing paths again.

That evening. we were the very last patrons at the bar in The Commonwealth, a lively place attached to Dru Bru microbrewery. A sign as we entered the bar area stated: "*No Minors…No guns or knives*".

The fact that the owners had deemed it necessary to inscribe such an obvious rule was a reminder of being far from home. We sat at the bar and chatted with the other friendly patrons, the thing I love about American bars. Two road-workers from a little town called Bishop in eastern California, who labelled themselves "Rednecks" – a term I previously thought was derogatory – were especially lively. One of them leaned a little too close for comfort on his stall to repeatedly blast his life motto at me.

"No. Pussy. Shit. NPS." He insisted with vigour. "You know, like National Park Service."

After a long, rambling monologue outlining what deep, spiritual meaning lay behind this phrase, I gathered he wanted me to understand that everyone has their own level of bravery, ability to face their fears, and that each level is personal, but it's imperative we do things that push and scare us. For him it was jumping off a boulder in Yosemite, but for his friend who didn't jump it was OK, because as a Judo teacher to young kids it wasn't worth the risk of injury to him personally. At this point talking to the guy was starting to feel a little scary to tell the truth, but I just kept nodding, throwing in the odd anecdote of some of the frightening things we had faced in recent weeks, until we came to the agreement that all large corporations are evil and the mountains are the best place to live. I have no doubt our two new friends owned guns, probably in their gloveboxes, so I wasn't about to question him, or reveal that I used to work for an evil bank.

As the bar emptied out, the bartender became very chatty, obviously working on her tip. It was a memorable night, aided by the Cosmos I consumed, my first alcoholic tipple in weeks. I again blamed the thin mountain air as Conrad helped me back to our suite.

Zero days never work out to be particularly relaxing. Unlike in the real world, all our life admin was condensed into just a few hours, like preparing the food we would eat for the next five days. The list of chores was beginning to feel tedious. My body woke up exhausted, having slept badly following our day-time napping and night-time boozing.

While Conrad back-flushed the water filters and cleaned out the crusty cook pot, I set about emptying our sixth postal resupply. Leslie it seemed was beginning to get creative. She had packed an amazing citrus-flavoured turkey jerky alongside a small plastic Ziploc bag inscribed with the words "No Trail Babies" containing two Durex. She needn't have bothered with the later – wilderness camping night after night was not proving overtly sexy.

Into the food sacks for this next section went all the good

stuff, including my new obsession, pretzel M&Ms, which I had tracked down and paid a hefty price for in the local store. There was something about the combination of chocolate and salt I just couldn't get enough of. By this point we regularly tossed a large proportion of our resupply into the local hiker box. The hikers further down the trail did very well out of us. These donations included Cliff bars, along with dried pasta'n'sauce and fake mash potato packets. We replaced them with real chocolate, Pro Bars (a much nicer trail bar), biscuits, and the freeze-dried hiker meals we mailed on from Bend.

Back home I knew today was important. I kept glancing at the clock while fussing over these trivial things, and re-calculating London-time. We were having lunch back in the bar when my mum returned my call. I stepped outside to talk more privately. The funeral had gone smoothly. I wasn't surprised to hear it was a big turn-out. Tom read my words to the crowd, who my Mum urged had gathered to celebrate my grandad, not to mourn him. But I still felt disloyal, that I should have been there. I gazed up towards the heavens. They were smiling, casting beaming sunrays down over the mountaintops. There wasn't a single cloud in the boundless blue sky.

27

Going Commando

Between Snoqualmie Pass to the south and Stevens Pass to the north, lies the Alpine Lakes Wilderness. A scan of the maps warned this section would be the steepest, but thankfully not the longest of the mission.

The Alpine Lakes area was designated a Wilderness zone by Congress in 1976, and at nearly four times the size of Oregon's Sky Lakes Wilderness, with over 700 mountain lakes, it's pretty vast. If someone were to ask me to recommend a short section of the PCT to explore, I would be torn between this and section I; the one containing Mount Adams and the Goat Rocks Wilderness further south. Both encompassed an intense colour palette of stunning glacier-carved scenery, with mountains on steroids, but based on our experience of the two – and heavily influenced by the weather – my personal favourite was the one ahead.

We left Snoqualmie with 268 miles to go. Not that we were counting – much. Like Dan, we decided to take the Goldmyer alternative trail for the first 26 miles which reconnects with the PCT near Waptus Lake. Another hiker at the food truck assured us this trail was once the official PCT route before they changed it to include equestrian users. So obviously we wanted to keep things *pure* and go original; the fact there happened to be an eight-mile saving was just a happy coincidence!

Climbing the first three miles up to Snow Lake, things didn't start positively. Sun blazing, packs fully loaded, I couldn't help feeling frustrated by the number of day hikers floating past us up the endless rocky switchbacks. With nearly two months of pretty solid hiking under our belts, it didn't seem logical that young families were over-taking us. I felt truly inadequate, I mean, why wasn't I running up the trail by now? I pondered this each time we had to step aside for another person to pass. And another thing – it had begun to seriously peeve me how few people respected common hiking etiquette. Didn't people know the rules? Conrad and I were very gracious hikers, adhering to the universally-acknowledged rule that colliding hikers should give way to those travelling uphill, yet this courtesy continued to be completely lost on many. We got rule-flouters all the time, especially with passing thru-hikers, many of whom felt the miles they had trodden bestowed on them a sense of entitled priority over all others. Some even acted as though we were invisible as they stepped over us. That said, if these down-hill day hikers could have learnt the very basic courtesy – the words "*thank you*" – I wouldn't have found myself constantly screwing up my face and muttering stuff like: "manners don't cost a thing", a famous one-liner of my mum's, delivered in a typically British passive-aggressive fashion. I'm definitely morphing more and more into Mum with each passing year.

In my Victor Meldrew state, I felt like a cart horse, struggling with every turn. If I had to bet on it, my pack must have weighed close to 40 pounds. Whilst standing at one switchback, trying to regain my breath as more ungrateful people passed by, I decided we needed to shed some of those back-breaking pounds.

"When we get to Stevens Pass we're posting some shit back. Things have gotten ridiculous, I can't go on!"

Not waiting for a response, I continued, "we should check the weather forecast too, if it looks promising I say we ditch the waterproofs, I refuse to carry this kind of weight any longer."

Conrad agreed, before back-tracking, "but if we send back the waterproofs, what will we wear to do the laundry?"

"A bin bag!" I exclaimed, huffing and puffing as I restarted, "and another thing – we gotta stop buying so much bloody food!"

After countless switch-backing we reached the top. It was torturous, but suddenly I was awestruck by what greeted us. It wasn't difficult to see why Snow Lake was the most photographed part of the Alpine Lakes Wilderness. Deeply nestled within a towering, snow-dusted shell, the crystal-clear water looked sublime, graduating from deep sapphire, to bright turquoise the closer it got to the shoreline. We took our own round of photos, before continuing northward over the next ridge.

Once on the Cathedral trail we became suddenly alone. We navigated down a sharp path, one that included boulder fields interspersed with overgrown thick, slippery vegetation, where with each invisible footing I hoped I wasn't about to break something. The complete absence of people and unmaintained conditions made us wonder whether we had made the right decision on a mission to save a few miles. An afternoon of scaling colossal tree debris followed, mile after mile of taking off our backpacks to negotiate another f****r. I couldn't believe this was once the PCT – maybe the guy in Snoqualmie had his facts wrong – it felt so abandoned, with warped bridges and a crumbling trail. I fell over four times, luckily managing to escape with just a few scrapes and bruises.

We didn't see another soul from Snow Lake until reuniting with Dan nearly 12 hours after leaving town. Our GPS stated the distance completed was 17.5 miles; that couldn't be right, could it? I re-checked twice, before glumly accepting it as truth. It looked like hours of persistence, not miles-per-hour would be our ticket to Canada. During those 12 prolonged hours, we climbed the equivalent of the Empire State Building's 86 stories five times over, descending it more than four times. Not helping matters was the fluctuating Washington weather system. It was wreaking havoc. Just three days before, we had hiked in every piece of clothing imaginable. Today, with the thermometer peaking at 90, the forest was transformed into a sticky jungle where it sometimes felt hard to breathe. Loincloth Man no longer seemed so crazy.

It was now day 55 since leaving Ashland. With no accessibility, not even a dirt track in sight, we found ourselves enjoying mountain slopes and unspoilt lakes entirely to ourselves. As we mounted Dutch Miller Gap, Ivanhoe Lake came into view, glistening in the sun below. I felt privileged to be there. I was just pointing out how we wouldn't have even seen this place had we stayed on the official PCT, when something pierced the air. The alien sound was unquestionable, making us grind to a halt. The thumping of two gunshots echoed high off Cathedral Rock.

"That was a gun!" I screeched. "Where did it come from?"

Without realising, I was now cowering, looking in all directions even though I knew it wasn't close by.

"It's probably just hunters in the next valley," Conrad assured me, "don't worry, we're more likely to get shot in Bermondsey than out here!"

But this was no time for humour. "We're in a protected wilderness, surely that means no hunting!"

Without sufficient maps to know what was on the other side of Cathedral Rock we had no way to verify. It could have been a military training ground for all we knew. The sound was an alien reminder of a world I thought was so far away. Hearing it instantly reinvigorated my fears of being killed. Tranquillity quickly returned to the mountains, but I would remain on edge for the rest of the day.

I felt some comfort as we eventually reconnected with the PCT. It was a relentlessly hot day, one us Brits are not attuned to. My feet were in cramping overdrive. I removed my shoes to find a couple of tenderised meatballs where my feet once stood. We took some emergency time-out to soak them in a creek to numb the pain. While drying off with my ever-handy piss cloth, a lump of skin on the top of my big toe fell off and floated away. Surely that couldn't be good. I was wearing trail runners one and a half times larger than my regular shoes, yet my feet still hated me. In an attempt to prevent over-heating, we repeatedly dipped our t-shirts in whatever water we came across; the feeling of the cool wet cloth against my skin was amazing.

We followed the trail to the banks of Deep Lake, where gigantic ridges encased the water making it look like a deep blue sinkhole. We'd arrived early at 5 p.m., deciding not to go any further than 15 miles for self-preservation, knowing we faced another big climb ahead. I welcomed a few hours of downtime, but felt guilty for it all the same. I had to remind myself this wasn't a race. All too often we found ourselves in the distance-hiker trap of making miles on autopilot. How wonderful it was to be able to stop and appreciate the majestic sights surrounding us. We celebrated the end of another gruelling day with Snickers dunked in hot chocolate while the sun's glow faded behind the mountains.

The PCT departs Deep Lake basin for Cathedral Pass 1,100 feet above. With a wet tent – thanks to the two amateur campers who had erected it on a lakeside plot without a waterproof tarp – our bags were extra-heavy. Starting the day with such a steep climb, I felt annoyed by our choice of tactics the day before. You see, whilst we enjoyed a lake-side dinner, Dan had decided to push on, having already eaten. He hoped to make it another mile or two in the cooler evening air. Conrad and I considered following suit, but the thought of peeling ourselves up off the ground after a prolonged rest was unfathomable. I now regretted our idleness. On the plus-side, it wasn't clear where anyone could have even pitched a tent on such a steep slope. Who knows which option was best, but struggling up the cliff face I wished I were Dan.

Rounding the umpteenth switchback, I had to stop. The irritation had gotten too bad. I hoisted up my skirt in the middle of the trail to inspect yesterday's heat rash, which appeared bright red and blotchy all over my inner thighs and was chafing against the edge of my pants. The only solution was to step out of them, going commando, and lather up with Conrad's little pot of Vaseline which he regularly used on his own back-alley area of friction. At least I'd save some effort with my daily underwear bush laundry later.

We caught up with Dan at Deception Lake outlet, following a potentially-dangerous river-crossing earlier that morning which would have involved a perilous drop into oblivion had we chosen the wrong combination of deadwood and stones to hop across. As he left I began filtering water, while Conrad crafted a washing line from string and a maze of tree trunks. We sat on slippery rocks, soaking our feet, eating crackers covered in Nutella, watching our kit dry in the sun. A retired couple out on a camping trip stopped for a chat. I don't remember much about them because I was mesmerised by their dog, a black Yorkie named Apex, who hung cradled against the woman's chest in the kind of sling you see toddlers in. Never before had I witnessed such a sight; I imagined it must be an American thing. The dog sure looked happy from his high human vantage point. I wondered what the maximum weight restriction for one of those things was, sure that Frank "The Tank" – the family Pug Tzu back home – would appreciate adding this bit of kit to his already modest walkies; especially if it came with a snack pouch.

After downing as much water as we could physically stomach, we began another steep climb up Surprise Mountain. The exposed rock face made for fierce work in the afternoon sun, but the views across the valley showcased a spectacular alpine forest nose-diving down into an inpenetrable valley that rose on the other side into a towering fortress. Over the pass a heart-shaped lake appeared far below. The descending trail made my knees shudder, straining against the sheer, granite path and tight switchbacks. Once we got down to the valley floor, guess what? Another climb followed. This time up Thunder Mountain, which had the steepest gradients we'd faced so far – confirmed by checking the *Guthook* app – mercilessly coming right at the end of the day. I was sure this one was going to finish me off. We both staggered along, barely coherent, employing low, shuffling steps, yet somehow it didn't beat us. It took every last ounce of strength I had to reach the top. I looked back down, glowing with the sense of achievement, and a lot of sweat.

By the time we reached "Marmot Camp" it was nearly seven. The camp won this name from the squeaking racket originating from the hillside right above – a sure-fire sign we needed to filter the mountain water cascading from that very direction. We had barely set up the tent's framework in the frigid wind before two solo hikers arrived to set up camps close by. As the sun rapidly dimmed, we congregated by the spring, happy for some different companionship.

While huddled together, a pretty young female hiker with braided hair appeared. Now, I was feeling pretty good about the 19 miles we had just completed, especially given the terrain, until we met Flower. Attempting to break the PCT SoBo record for fastest unassisted hike, she intended to reach Mexico in less time than it had taken Conrad and I to cover a third of the miles. I couldn't even begin to comprehend her 45-mile day average. While she was rummaging for her head torch in her tiny backpack, I innocently offered her some snacks, concerned there couldn't be much space in her bag for anything other than protein powder. With a massive smile she gratefully declined, clarifying what the rules of *unassisted* meant. The whole thing blew my mind.

28

Joy-Ride of Death

Thundering along Highway 2 in the backseat of a stranger's car I wondered if this was it. How ironic it seemed, having survived the unpredictable, unknown wildness, to be killed by something as basic as a speeding car. Maybe it felt faster than it actually was, given the slow pace we'd grown accustomed to. I subtly leaned forward and peered over the driver's shoulder to read the dash. *Ninety miles an hour? What the hell!* I closed my eyes, mumbled a little safety prayer holding my mum's Saint Christopher that hung around my neck, as the car continued hurtling through the twisting mountain pass.

It had taken around five hours to complete the final 11 miles into Steven's Pass. We arrived late morning, having left camp in a hurry after being terrorised by, you guessed it: mosquitoes. I got the inkling they were following us from their Oregon home. At least they forced us to scale the first mountain pass in the cool morning air. Our second reason for hurrying? Conrad was now out of Pringles, so he was feeling extra motivated to make town.

At the top of our next climb we met an unusual character. He was clearly a thru-hiker, based on the traditional scruffy appearance, smell, and oh-so-obvious Hikertrash dreadlocks. From a brief exchange, it transpired he had departed from Mexico exactly a month before we began in southern Oregon, meaning he had hiked 1,716 miles more than us during this time! Could we BE any slower?

We loved any excuse to take a break and chat to people, but this guy had places to be. By the size of his tiny day-pack, I'm guessing the place he needed to be involved acquiring food, and hopefully a wash. I was bamboozled by his choice of footwear. Who knew that you could hike up and down steep mountains in nothing but flimsy sandals over fleece socks?

Following the cables of closed chair lifts, we descended into our welcome destination. Stevens Pass was another closed ski resort, but showed some signs of life. A handful of hikers sat around a picnic table, welcoming us as we got close. The group were in fine spirits, airing their feet in the sun, eating a box of doughnuts which I spied instantly, making my mouth water. With no offer of a doughnut, we quickly exchanged fellow hiker pleasantries before darting inside in search of nourishment and our next box.

Whilst polishing off an essential ice cream – I'm sure we had low sugar and calcium levels – and chatting to another older couple, a young guy dressed entirely in black approached. He spoke the magic words: "Do you guys need a ride?"

Knowing this fortuitous offer negated the need to stand by the side of the highway baring my little cardboard sign, I couldn't have been happier. The guy introduced himself by his trail name, Spider, having completed his hike six days previously. He was in the area collecting his left-over gear from an established trail angel, who ran a voluntary hostel called Dinsmore's Hiker Haven. Hitchhiking still came with trepidation, so hearing Spider was a fellow backpacker instilled a sense of confidence as we gratefully bundled into his car. In hindsight, I was perhaps even more grateful to get out the car at the other end! I am not exaggerating when I say it was one of the top three scariest car journeys of my life. The steep mountain drop-offs from my window hadn't helped the feelings of impending doom.

Somehow we survived Washington's "Highway of Death," as it's been dubbed by the media. There is even a Facebook group dedicated to that moniker, which shares road closures and car crash images. Thanks to a combination of extreme weather conditions, avalanches, and dangerous lane-drifters, an average of five people die on the stretch of road between Everett and Steven's Pass each year. I was thankful we hadn't reset the giant roadside countdown sign that read: "*DAYS SINCE LAST SERIOUS CRASH*" in bright LEDs. Yes, it used DAYS, not weeks as its unit of measure!

The tiny hamlet of Skykomish sits just over a bridge off the highway. A wooden sign welcomed us to a "Great Northern

Town." I would say the term "great" is subjective, and couldn't see how it possibly classified as a "town," because there really wasn't much to it. A few *historical* buildings sat sandwiched between the banks of the South Fork Skykomish River and an active train line. As Washington law requires trains to honk their horns when entering a town, it promised to be a fun night given our hotel's intimate proximity to the rail tracks.

Spider dropped us off near The Cascadia Inn, a simple but friendly timber guesthouse. The owner, Henry, was great, giving us a tour which included a living room area out back, but I couldn't hide my disappointment when he informed us they had run out of homemade pie. What a blow.

I was surprised to not find Dan loitering around the hotel. There was nowhere else to stay in Skykomish, so I sent him an instant chat while waiting for our room. He replied straight back. I read his response to Conrad, completely confused. It stated:

Maybe you're waiting for them to clean my room. Room 14. The trains come through all night and are loud. REALLY LOUD.

I screwed up my face perplexed.

"What's he talking about, HIS room?"

So I replied back: *Why do you have a room?*

Dan answered immediately: *Ops...meant to say my old room.*

To which I typed: *When did you get here?*

Dan: *Yesterday at 6:30 p.m.*

Conrad looked at me, asking the obvious question on both our lips, "how the hell did Dan get here *yesterday*? That's not even possible... is it?"

Both of us were trying to think back to the last time we had seen our friend from Kentucky.

Conrad was working it through.

"He was at Deception Lake yesterday lunchtime, so maybe he *could* have made a couple more miles than us, but I doubt it because we hiked late. How far was it from there all the way to the highway?"

I fired up the *Guthook* app to look at the waypoints and mileages for each.

"What the hell?! It was 18 miles from the lake to the pass!

That's not physically possible in, what, five hours *tops*?"

"He's pulled a sneaky one, I know it."

I couldn't tell if Conrad was impressed, or annoyed.

It transpired that Dan was now staying at The Dinsmore's hostel, a few miles up the road. A brief phone call revealed his record-breaking arrival had been a sneaky one after all. Shortly after leaving us to eat lunch, Dan had bumped into another hiker who he noticed was only carrying a small day pack. Believing it was way too far from any access road to not be carrying camping equipment, Dan quizzed the hiker about this. The guy's response revealed he was out day-hiking, and was just about to take a turn onto the Surprise Creek trail back to his car parked eight miles away. It must have made for a long day's hiking for Dan, but by electing to divert off the PCT he even managed to catch a ride into town with his new friend. It couldn't have worked out better for him.

To be fair, Dan had tried sharing this "alternative" route knowledge by engraving our initials in the middle of the trail next to an arrow crafted in sticks. On hearing this over the phone, I was immediately gutted we hadn't noticed it, resulting in an extra night of camping. But after investigating his route further we agreed it would have been taking the art of the short-cut a little too far, even for us.

By our calculation, Dan had saved a whopping six miles, taking him to a different trailhead approximately five miles further south along the highway. Sitting outside our hotel I indifferently muttered an over-used PCT hiking phrase: "Guess you've gotta *hike your own hike*."

Have I already mentioned there wasn't a whole lot going on in Skykomish?! In less than a day since arriving, we had exhausted all the local cuisine options, which sadly included a walk around the gas station minimart, where the cashier watched us like we were about to rob the joint, and an empty old-world saloon where the bartender doubled as the cook who prepared everything from the menu in a deep-fat fryer visible out back. I was now feeling frustrated by the lack of choice, and a bit bored. This led to a decision (mostly driven by me), to hitch to a larger town to buy food. While we sat eating a bagel breakfast at the liquor-come-deli store I made a cardboard sign. Before long, we found ourselves on the highway wearing big *"you can trust us"* smiles.

It took only minutes for a local named Bob to stop his pickup truck. He was easy to talk to. He described himself as a "university-educated '60s liberal", and vowed to move to Canada if Trump got voted in. *I wonder if he followed through on that?* He dropped us off in the Safeway car park in Monroe, a much larger town nearly an hour west. I can't recall a time when I was more excited to visit a supermarket. We wandered the aisles enjoying the intense air conditioning, ogling all the items we had absolutely no hope of carrying.

Following a long browse and the purchase of some limited fresh food, we crossed the car park to McDonalds. There I was delighted to discover a standard McFlurry is double the size of the ones back home, and that Oreos are among the choice of toppings. While we sat tucking into the ice cream and free soda refills, I mussed how this was our first "Maccy D's" of the entire trip. A trip that already felt so long. I was dumbfounded that Conrad didn't take this opportunity to order a burger, asking with sincerity whether he was feeling alright.

Walking through Monroe's small, historical downtown, posters were hanging for the Evergreen State Fair, which was just a week away. After brunch at the Main Street Cafe, we headed for the post office. I'm not sure why we didn't go back to the Skykomish post office, where we'd collected our resupply box the previous day. Maybe it was the bad memories. Upon opening the additional box from Concord, Conrad let out a not-to-subtle, "oh f**k" when he discovered the Marshmeiers had posted him the wrong pair of shoes. I quickly apologised to the attendant, before pulling Conrad to one side. While trying my best to be sympathetic, I secretly blamed Conrad for the mix-up, as he had stored the trainers in the wrong box at the Marshmeiers, and Leslie (I'm guessing it wasn't Chris), had just read the brand name on the box and posted them out.

"Does it really matter?" I asked naively with a fake smile. "They've gotta be better than walking in those," eyeing his current shoes which were worn ragged.

"Yeah it *does* matter. I haven't even worn these ones in, and they're *waterproof*," he sulked, "it's way too hot to be wearing waterproofs."

My resolve cracked. "Well, maybe you should have been more *specific*. Or even better, ordered a pair online when I told you to back in Packwood! You can't blame Chris and Leslie, and anyway, there's not much we can do about it now."

Realising my words were not helping, I changed tack. "You'll be fine. We don't have that far left to go. You can buy some new comfy shoes in Vancouver, when all this is over."

Conrad closed the box, shoved it under his arm and exited the post office, leaving me to thank the cashier and scoop up the massive resupply box.

Back in Monroe's post office there was some risk-taking going on. The previous evening, we had emptied the entire contents of our packs out onto the bed in a giant kit explosion, before consulting weather forecasts, and conducting what is known in the hiking business as a *shakedown*. Every item was analysed for its usefulness. It was a far-cry from my usual packing MO, which typically revolved around identifying a capsule collection of cute interchangeable outfits and bundling up heaps of toiletries I couldn't possibly live without. Now every carried ounce would directly influence our comfort levels on what was to be our longest section of trail. Anything we hadn't used so far, or which we deemed *non-essential* was placed in a pile. The most controversial – some may say stupid – decision was to include our waterproofs in that pile. At the last-minute I retrieved my jacket, on the basis that I needed something to wear while doing laundry. We lost a few pounds, shedding items such as my penknife and spare batteries.

We rode the local transit bus back to a small town called Gold Bar. From there we assumed it would be easy to hitch the rest of the way to Skykomish. We were wrong. Perhaps without our full hiking gear drivers weren't taking pity, leaving us standing beside the highway for nearly an hour. There were plenty of cars whizzing past too. It didn't seem logical. Why would people be more willing to give a ride to the smelly Brits, verses our new, clean selves?

I was really beginning to panic when finally, a silver Prius pulled up. The elderly driver, Peggy, said she could take us as far as Index. We jumped in, enjoying a ride full of local history and keen recycling discussion. As we approached Index, Peggy had a change of heart, so first swinging past her yard to tell her husband where she was going, she proceeded to drive us all the way back to our hotel, another 13 miles into the valley. We were eternally grateful for her trail magic contribution.

Going to sleep that night, my thoughts turned to the hike ahead. This last section had been stunningly beautiful, with alpine lakes and striking jagged mountains. Yet despite it being the shortest, the elevation changes and extreme heat had also made it the most challenging. Our miles had dropped; we hadn't completed more than 20 miles a day. This lent apprehension to the next leg of our adventure. How could we possibly carry enough food, and sustain the physical effort required for the next six days and 108 miles? But with Canada now less than 200 miles away, the countdown was officially on.

29

The American Alps

"Never, before making this trip, have I found myself embosomed
in a scenery so hopelessly beyond description."

(John Muir, *Travels in Alaska*)

A pioneer of the U.S. National Park system, John Muir
wrote about the landscape he had encountered during an
expedition to an unchartered Alaska, back in 1915. Just as he was
captivated by the living glaciers awaiting him, a hundred years
later we would share these same feelings the further north we
progressed. Words fall short to describe the story-book land of
giant snow-capped peaks, glacial meadows, plunging canyons,
and crystal-clear lakes that awaited us. Oregon seemed to pale in
comparison to the lands north of Highway 20. Some people brand
the area the "American Alps" but having skied in the European
Alps I was beginning to think the label utterly unbefitting of
Washington's rugged wilderness. Even the photographs, as
stunning as they looked, couldn't quite capture the sweeping
splendour of the Northern Cascades. Each day became a feast for
the eyes, a source of wonder and enchantment.

On the first day out of Skykomish, we broke 22 miles, pretty
impressive given the long wait to catch a ride along the highway.
The sun shone long and high, so our gamble with the waterproofs
was paying off – for the time being at least – and with a new-found
sense of physical strength following our rest, I was buzzing. But
it wasn't all plain-sailing; there always had to remain some kind
of challenge, and this time round Conrad was suffering. The shoe
mix-up meant he was now wearing a new, smaller pair which
needed breaking in during gruelling hot days. He popped painkillers like a junkie, keeping quieter than usual as we pushed to
make our miles.

Despite the kit shakedown, our biggest challenge remained:

lugging a decent percentage of our bodyweight up and down mountains. Dan's pack was so full of food he now hung his bright red plastic urinal – don't ask – in full-view, which we watched swing from side to side until he disappeared ahead. We spent the day amid trees, with no breeze to quash the humid conditions. At one lake we passed a lady out camping with her dog. She warned how her camp had been visited by bears the night before. There were certainly lots of berries flanking the trail, so it seemed as likely as ever we would finally encounter my foes – I just hoped it wouldn't be a grizzly, or a protective mama with cubs.

Having just crested Union Gap, we stood aside for a couple of horse riders. They passed by, but within a couple of minutes became the obstacle as the women had dismounted to guide the horses down a steep, rocky, narrow descent. We reluctantly trod behind, frustrated by the slowed pace and moaning to each other whenever the horses dumped their load at our feet. Just as the trail levelled out and the riders saddled back up, a giant tree blow-down spread right across the path stopped them again, ending their planned four-day trip. There was no safe way for the horses to manoeuvre around it; the slope on the hill-side was far too steep. We wished them well, smugly feeling happy to be on our feet for once as we prepared to climb it. But it doesn't pay to be smug. Before they left, one of the horses whacked me around the face with its hairy tail. *Wham!* I didn't even see it coming. He sure told me! It was the last memorable moment of another hot and tiring day. The next day would prove hotter still.

We woke to a dusty pink sky reflecting off the mountains. By the time we began moving the air was full of haze, promising another scorcher that didn't disappoint. At these altitudes, weaving up and down granite rock passes above timberline, the fear of exposure was very real. The advice we had been given by Shroomer back in California was: stay hydrated, cover heads, and do anything you can to cool down your body temperature. This sounds straight-forward, but was easier said than done. On one particularly tiring climb, nearing the top of White Pass, an elderly gentleman stopped us. On discovering our destination was Canada he merrily hailed our trip a "grand adventure".

Through the strain of physical exertion, sweat clouding my eyes, I couldn't quite find the words to respond, so instead forced out a brief, phoney smile before continuing on at a snail's pace. I see it now of course – the man was right: we really were on a *grand adventure*, the greatest of my life, one that would forever change me as a person, and give me fond memories I would often find myself retreating back to in difficult times. That perspective just wasn't there yet.

The trail weaved above the timberline, with expansive views of conifer forest, deep wildflower-coated valleys, and a new white peak. We hiked past a small wooden sign hammered into the ground indicating the boundary of Glacier Peak Wilderness. Looking at our map, Glacier was the last of the giant peaks marked. Sometimes called Washington's "hidden mountain" due to its relative isolation, it remains the least-monitored and least-studied of the five major stratovolcanoes in the Cascade Volcanic Arc despite being believed to be one of the most volatile volcanoes in the entire country. I'm not sure if this is true, but someone told me its peak is only viewable by air or foot because no roads get even close. The mountain is home to eleven significant glaciers, which might explain why in such hot temperatures, pockets of rippled grey and white snow extended below 6,000 feet. I plonked myself down in one such mound for a solitary moment of cool. I needed a breather, having been unable to take any decent-length breaks due to the re-appearance of those pesky black biting flies. They were everywhere, and just to re-cap, they particularly enjoyed attacking faces, especially eyes and ears, and didn't give a flying f**k about insect repellent.

We finally entered forest cover long after the air had cooled. Dan appeared from behind, leaping across a large stream on slippery rocks, while we stood trying to analyse the safest crossing point. As the three of us stood on a bridge over the White Chuck River taking photos of the water cascading through the green-coated gorge, I managed to drop my sunglasses and simultaneously stomp on them, crushing the frames beyond repair. No amount of tape was going to rescue this situation. *Just great*, I thought, if tomorrow is another scorcher I get to add burnt retinas to our long list of trail-induced injuries!

We camped besides Baekos Creek in the flanks of Glacier Peak. The water took the form of a cloudy torrent, fuelled by glacial snow melt, heaped with a patchwork of tree debris resembling a giant beaver dam. As we hit the hay, Conrad's foot problems led him to argue – not for the first time – how this was his toughest day yet. I'm not sure whether I agreed, but it was certainly up there in the top five. I wasn't sure if it was wise to pop more *vitamin I* for my enduring leg strain, given I already likely possessed some kind of heat-stroke, but I figured, *what the hell.*

The next morning, after eating oatmeal wearing a head torch, we were ready. This was going to be BIG. After briefly sizing up the map we knew the day's climb was going to top everything that had preceded it. But it turned out that not everything in the wild can be planned for.

Emerging from a moss-covered forest into a valley containing another large glacial tributary, Kennedy Creek, we stopped to take photos. The broken wooden bridge was a real sight. It looked as though someone had chopped it in the middle, so it now plunged into the water at 45-degree angles from either side. As we made to cross, a girl appeared from behind. Sarah was your typical friendly Canadian, we hiked with her for a couple of miles before giving up trying to match her frantic pace; it was uphill after all and back home in Vancouver she *ran* trails in her spare time! During breathless conversation – from our side – it transpired Sarah had stayed with Becky and Ed in Trout Lake just a couple of days after we had enjoyed their hospitality. What a small world. As Sarah's last resupply box had not arrived, we gave her a few of our rations, hoping we might not require a full day's hike into Stehekin. Either way it was unlikely we'd starve.

There were certainly more hikers coming through now, some from Mexico, some headed south. The south-bounders brought with them vital trail updates, the consensus warned of bad blow-downs on the last 40 miles into Stehekin. Fallen trees were already slowing us down, so if they got much worse we hated to imagine what it could mean for making it into town on our current supply. Stehekin lay 11 miles from the trailhead and was serviced by just four shuttle buses a day. We needed to be on point to make one of those buses or we would be very hungry. And very sad!

As we tackled a bundle of trees to mount Glacier Ridge, a distinct smell of smoke hit. Out on the horizon far away, the sky looked pinker and hazier than ever. In another situation we might have admired the resemblance to a romantic water-colour painting, but considering our position it was rather concerning. We hadn't come across any forest service roads for a quick exit in recent days.

The day before a couple had told us the darkened sky to the east was likely the Idaho fire, which was blazing hundreds of miles away. But slowly navigating a rocky descent down Fire Creek Pass, another hiker told a more likely story. He had a wider coverage map and pointed out the source of the smoke. There was a wildfire ablaze in Buck Creek, which on the map looked close by, just slightly south-east. He assured us the mountain range between us and the fire made it safe. Let's just hope his logic holds up, I thought, because I'm pretty sure that fires can climb slopes.

A loose scree trail, tinged with copper hues, led us winding down the mountain forever. Finally, after what felt like an eternity on the knees, Mica Lake appeared like a mirage from out of nowhere. It was hidden in a small enclave and framed by a backdrop of towering jagged cliffs reflected in the water. Feeling frazzled by the heat, we thought a quick foot soak and an early lunch would be a good plan. We sat on the edge of the bright blue lake eating peanut butter and jelly pita breads, when a voice echoed out from behind a boulder: "What? I thought you'd be up the other mountain by now. I've called for a helicopter! Don't worry."

It was Dan. A few moments later he appeared from around the bend, looking as sweaty as us.

"How's the water?" he asked.

"Nice," I responded feeling unusually relaxed, "you should try it."

But Dan ignored the suggestion, concerned with more pressing matters. "Have you seen the trail over there?"

He was pointing towards the other side of the valley.

"*Guthooks* looks like a seismic reading!" Referring to the elevation-line chart in our dedicated trail app.

"Is that definitely the PCT?" Conrad asked.

If you imagine someone taking a white marker pen and scoring a frantic, sharp zigzag all the way up a mountain face, that was what we could see on the horizon.

Before Dan could answer I chipped in, "yeah, we were hoping that's a different trail."

Dan sounded very serious. "Oh, that's the PCT alright! It's 3,000 feet down from the pass to the valley, and another 2,700 back up again! *Huge* switchbacks. Long way up and looks a long way from here!"

I mustered a resigned "yeah", splashing my feet in the water.

Conrad was calculating the risk while looking at the map on his phone. "It seems ambitious to attempt the climb today. There isn't anywhere to camp for the next seven miles after this next creek. Are you going for it?"

"I dunno what I'm gonna do yet. I'm fifty-fifty... might take on the big climb in the mornin'." He wiped his sweaty brow, took a swig of water and continued, "I'm gonna head down to Milk Creek, cook dinner, and then decide. I might just camp there."

We wished him luck, feeling guilty for being so static, and watched as he disappeared down the trail. By that point we had only covered 12 miles. We sat procrastinating at the lake for a long time. The lack of designated camping options meant if we did press on, we could be forced to complete an extreme climb in the glare of the mid-afternoon sun. Dan's plan to walk the next four miles and then decide sounded sensible, but it assumed he would be able to find an unofficial place to throw up his tent at the creek. I wasn't confident we could do the same.

All this debating with no shade was making me feel light-headed, and I didn't know what decision was the right one, so instead I made a different decision. I stood up, announced I was going to jump into the lake – a pretty daring decision for me with no clue how deep the water was or whether it was teeming with blood-sucking leeches – and began peeling off my clothes. Conrad registering the unusually-daring move, fired up the camera to film the moment my body ungracefully bombed from a natural jetty, sending shock-waves rippling across the tranquil water. Stunning coolness enveloped me, exhilarating my heart as I swam back to shore. It was the closest thing I would get to a hair wash for a few more days. Conrad, not wanting to feel left out, jumped from the same rock platform, before quickly breast-stroking back, wincing aloud at the shock. Look at us, I thought: I like this new, nature-embracing, adventurous us.

As we stood dripping in our wet underwear, a couple of young hikers arrived. I self-consciously grabbed my t-shirt as Conrad greeted them. From a brief chat we discovered they'd just come down the impossible climb, and couldn't recall any camping possibilities where Dan was headed. They both deemed it "crazy" to set out for the pass at this hour, cementing our decision. We got dressed and travelled a fast downhill mile to the next creek where we established camp in an empty meadow. Although disappointing to be stopping short of expectations, eliminating the possibly of reaching Stehekin a day early, having free time to relax in such a beautiful setting proved a real treat. I'd recommend taking wilderness time-outs to anyone. You've made the effort to reach these far-flung places, so why not take the opportunity to kick back your tired feet and just enjoy them?

30

Finding Beauty

Over the weeks I'd become surprisingly proficient at cooking breakfast on autopilot in the dark, eyes barely open. But next morning something lifted me from my usual stupor. Beginning my tasks under a dim splash of torch-light, I watched as the wide sky above rapidly awakened into a magical pink daybreak, warming the air and illuminating the glacial range opposite, all under the watchful eye of a bright lingering moon. In that short window surrounded by nature's glory, I pinched myself. Living in London, my first view of the day would be a repetitive scene of grey clouds and greyer rooftops. To see beauty I needed to schedule a trip to the countryside, which – let's face it – was a massive pain in the arse because driving anywhere from south London is a bloody nightmare. On the trail I began to realise how lucky I was, to awaken to daily natural beauty. I wondered, in a rare moment of mindfulness, whether I would ever rise to a finer view again.

Step by step, we began descending into a deep ravine toward Milk Creek. The closer we got to the bottom, the more overgrown and dense the trail became. It was an untamed jungle, my legs got truly bush-whacked in our frantic race against the rising sun, desperate to beat its glare touching the impending switchback slope. At the bottom we paused for just enough time to collect water, before crossing the long wooden bridge, and pushing through thick brush to commence the dreaded climb.

It took two long, steady hours to reach the ridge. It was a slog, but I didn't think two hours was all that bad, considering. If I had to pick up the pack I carried up that mountain today I bet I could barely move it to the other side of the room. Our strength was growing, and so with it came a new sense of confidence. Having said that, almost an hour into the ascent a pretty blond girl with pigtails came bounding downhill. She cheerfully told us we had 24 switchbacks left to the top. This information gave me something to focus on, though the closer we got to the top, the further apart the countdown seemed to get. It turned out she had miscounted: there were 25 turns. I was outraged.

Washington didn't let up on us there. As we crested Vista Ridge, we immediately began a long descent which lasted hours. The sun was already full-blown by the time we reached the rocky ridge. I fashioned my bandana into a fetching headdress by tucking it under my cap to protect my neck and eyes. Not having a working pair of sunglasses at this point was less than ideal. I kept my gaze low as we crossed seasonal streams flowing deep into the canyon below. As we progressed, the craggy path turned into a narrow channel weaving through bright-green, blooming meadows. Before us, a dazzling string of mountains appeared, the Northern Cascades, maybe even Canada? They loomed high, standing in our way, but they were magnificent. Caught in the moment, I blasted out an off-tune soundbite: "The hills are alive with the sound of *mu-sic!*" I don't actually know the rest of the words, but the outstanding breadth of our surroundings just produced one of those moments that captivated the soul.

I had always assumed with gravity on our side, that going downhill should be a breeze. But in the hours it took to reach Vista Creek I was concentrating hard. Nature had decided to reclaim the land, demonstrated by the number of times we tripped over roots and stubbed toes on hidden rocks. One guy we passed said he had actually slipped off the mountain edge because he couldn't see the path. At least it wasn't covered in snow I told him, otherwise none of us would have been seen again.

Entering a deep evergreen forest, I decided to plug into a podcast to give my mind a rest from trail obstacles. *The Generation Why* guys were discussing the unsolved disappearance of Amy Lynn Bradley, a 23-year-old woman who disappeared back in 1998 aboard a Caribbean cruise ship. The tale was grim, with theories she was kidnapped by a sex trafficking ring who smuggled her off the ship when it docked at Curaçao. Although completely unrelated, something about the sombreness of the story triggered my mind to drift into repressed negative feelings associated with my old job. I'm sure everyone has at least one work horror story, and it wouldn't be called "work" if we all loved the daily activity. Dealing with work crap, one may argue, makes us stronger, but then again, everyone has their limit.

Back in the day when I had a career ahead of me, I worked for a multinational consulting firm who hailed themselves as an award-winning, diversity-abundant, meritocracy-operating, healthy-lifestyle-supporting place to work. Buzz-phrases like "work:life balance" and "women's networks" were batted around endlessly. But sadly, after six years I came to accept it was all just *bullshit* advertising. My personal experience centred around a culture of face time, where my team were consistently expected to sit at our desks for 10-plus hours a day and never paid overtime. We received *urgent* emails on weekends and were never appreciated for going "above-and-beyond" – that was expected, after all – and on a more personal note, I found myself bullied for my East-London accent. You see, I don't necessarily speak the Queen's English, and seeing as the vast majority of the degree-wielding grads who made it into the company came from plummy private schools, I must have seemed like a prime target; not exactly *diversity-welcoming*. My first line manager, one such Oxford grad, once pulled me aside to tell me the way I spoke "undermined" my "credibility" with the client. I was dumbfounded, retreating to the toilet for a cry. In fact I found myself in the ladies crying pretty often, and I'm really not a cry-baby kinda gal; I knew I was better than that, which just made me feel all the worse. That these people could reduce me to tears was still taunting me years later, here in the great outdoors.

With judgement impaired by throbbing feet, we made a rookie decision later that day. Our *Halfmile* map showed an old branch of the PCT, whose dotted line crossed the Suiattle River far more directly than the current trail, which had been re-routed west a few years ago following a series of washed out bridges. Dan told us back in Skykomish that it was a shortcut not worth the risk, due to the likely bushwhack required to trace the path. But did we listen? With a potential five-mile saving, we left the trail to go scrambling through the thick forest. Eventually we found a way through to the banks of Vista Creek, where we paced up and down looking for a safe crossing point near an old blown-out bridge. But the water was far too fierce to ford. It was futile. After nearly an hour of trying we had no choice but to turn back.

Demotivated in the afternoon humidity, we stomped for miles through a dark, ancient grove of giant redwoods in silence until the sound of thrashing water pierced the calm. We came to a stop at the Suiattle River to admire the impressive timber bridge stretching across it. We hadn't seen a wilderness bridge of this length, or one with bends built in before.

"Now that's what I call a bridge," I shouted over the roaring flow, marvelling at how remarkable it was. I mean, from a purely practical perspective, how do they even complete such a large-scale engineering project in such a remote place?

Before Conrad could respond I was barking orders: "Stand over there, I want to get a picture."

Conrad did as he was told, taking position on the bridge. As he stood there posing, a moment of clarity struck him:

"There's no way we could have crossed this river."

I looked down at the water. Conrad was completely right. His comment cemented our stupidity. From a vantage point half-way across the bridge, even the steep muddy river banks looked impossible to scale. There would have been absolutely no way to traverse such a commanding river without a bridge.

By the time we completed a final uphill push to Miner Creek, our poor feet had endured 6,000 feet of elevation gain and over 8,000 feet of downhill pounding over 23 long miles. Content that we had avoided the inevitable drowning our earlier short-cut might have led to, we fell asleep instantly.

On Sunday 21st August we smashed into our final 100-mile countdown. Conrad's foot issues aside, it was a good day, with far less climbing and an ominous-looking weather-front gracefully holding out for us.

The main climbing action was ticked off first thing, with a long, gradual ascent to Suiattle Pass. After that, as the hike became far less physically challenging, it was easier to mentally switch off from any immediate physical concerns and admire the surroundings. Conrad mostly hobbled behind, stopping occasionally to re-medicate.

A few miles after leaving camp, a bright yellow sign with orange ribbons caught our gaze – in the forest such erroneous items stand out like a turd in a punchbowl. On closer inspection, the hand-written sign pinned to a tree was a fire closure notice. My heart stopped. It took a few moments to read the words and consult the attached map before confirming the PCT wasn't directly impacted. A connecting trail heading south to Buck Creek was closed. The highlighted fire zone showed how we had camped only three miles north-west from the impacted area. Lucky for us, Fortress Mountain shielded the PCT from the blaze, but then again it was 11 days since this information had been posted. Direct danger seemingly averted, this was still scary business. I vowed that if, in the (highly unlikely) event we ever felt inclined to take on another ridiculous hike, we would carry wider-coverage maps and have a vague idea about alternative evacuation points, just as Ginger had back in Oregon.

Straddling Suiattle Pass offered up one of the widest panoramas of the trip. Behind us, thickly forested valleys of pointy pine trees seemed to stretch on forever. Once over the spine we started weaving into another deep valley, but this one was rockier, patched with copper-hues. A towering bare ridge with jagged rock formations, one resembling a pyramid, provided a fantastic bowl-shaped backdrop for our pictures. The resplendent scenery was complemented by a vivid blue sky and a string of peaks fading into the distance. From time to time we stopped to pick blueberries, or huckleberries – I'm still not sure I can tell them apart – for the fructose energy-boost. The berries were delicious, but I couldn't help wishing they could have been soaked in sugar, baked in a pie, and served with ice cream.

By late afternoon clouds began gathering above. Initially they provided welcomed relief from the sun, but gradually they grew dark and heavy. Given we no longer possessed waterproofs, the drop in air pressure felt menacing. We swiftly gathered pace along the valley floor, over mildly-undulating terrain quilted by berries and ferns. At an unremarkable, bramble-covered point I peered at the GPS and registered we had exactly 100 miles remaining. We stopped to remove our bags and take a random commemorative photo. As we did, I could sense us both buzzing at the trigger of a countdown that now seemed somewhat feasible. Aside from our decision to stop early the previous day, we were now consistently completing 22-mile days over some of the most difficult terrain faced so far. I felt a tinge of pride at the progress our modest physical competency had made.

A potential storm seemed imminent as we arrived at our selected campsite beside a loud creek. Dan and a couple of other hikers were dotted around with the same plan in mind – a hopefully easy five-mile morning dash to the 9 a.m. Stehekin bus. We tucked the tent under a large creaking tree, hoping if the heavens opened we would be protected, not flattened.

31

Cinnamon-Roll Overload

I barely slept. Listening to a mighty wind storm outside, I rummaged for my watch, hoping the alarm was about to sound. It was 11:30 p.m. I closed my eyes. Perhaps the anxious excitement I felt about reaching *town* was releasing endorphins into my system, because by 5 a.m. I was up and cooking oatmeal. At least I was trying to cook. Since leaving our last stop we had been experiencing stove issues. After 30 minutes of trying and getting very "han-gry" – the phrase coined by Conrad whenever I was tired and hungry – Conrad went and borrowed a gas canister from another hiker called Tower. Thanks to the morning coffee injection, I could finally start functioning like a human being.

There was an intangible buzz in the air as, one by one, people set off towards High Bridge. It was like a race-mentality had taken hold, ensuring no one would miss the morning bus even though there was still plenty of time. We certainly hiked the fastest five miles we'd ever hiked. Had it not been for a synchronised *emergency* bush-toilet stop we wouldn't have taken a single breather. The valley continued to undulate alongside the river, with the first hint of autumn creeping in, leaves of orange, yellow and red flanking the trail. Even the local wildlife seemed restless, sensing winter was on the way. Woodpeckers were pecking, squirrels darted around hauling nut bounties, and chipmunks squeaked at our feet as if hailing our presence.

In what felt like no time at all, we reached a wooden sliver of a sign signalling the "*North Cascades National Park*". It stood in front of a rusty steel bridge over Agnes Gorge. So, assuming we were already at High Bridge, with tonnes of time to spare, we messed around taking photos showcasing the return of Conrad's thick – and arguably ginger – scraggly beard. Finally crossing the bridge, a gravel track revealed a much grander bridge, high up above a steep gorge. Realising our mistake, we scampered on, gazing down at the vertigo-inducing Stehekin River raging far below.

I slam-dunked our half-full gas canister into the bear-proof trash can as we sauntered into the rest stop. That bloody gas purchased at the Skykomish deli store had caused us nothing but grief, so I wasn't going to carry it a single step further. On the first night, we ended up borrowing someone else's cook set and seriously considered whether we needed to turn around and head back to the trailhead, given most of our food was dehydrated and we seemed to have a dud. I'm no gas expert, but for whatever reason, our burner didn't agree with the fuel, so all we got was a small flame which kept going out, at which point I would vigorously shake it – probably a very dangerous move – to relight the flame for a couple more minutes. Boiling water probably took a good 15 minutes by this process, with the flame needing to be watched constantly. If we couldn't buy more gas in Stehekin, we could at least re-think our food strategy.

There was still over an hour until the bus was due, but out in the sticks no one dared risk missing it. Already, half a dozen hikers sat around picnic tables outside the historic ranger station. I spotted Dan straight away due to his distinctive red top. He was joined by Tower and a few other familiar faces. We sat around, chatting the time away until the piercing rumble of an engine caught everyone's attention. The big red bus had arrived on time. Our magical chariot resembled a vintage-style American school bus, with a curved rear and a shiny chrome grill; mini stars-and-stripes flags proudly waved from the cab's side windows. Sixteen hikers boarded the morning bus; never had we seen so many people on the trail at once.

We made the tactical move to sit at the front, eager to get into the bakery ahead of the queue when the bus made its usual pit stop. Dan joined us and managed to sweet-talk the conductor-come-hotelier into securing one of the last available rooms at the North Cascades Lodge. We had already called ahead from Skykomish, not prepared to take such a high-stakes risk when it came to potentially missing out on a bed and a hot shower.

As the bus came to a halt outside a stand-alone timber lodge, the driver pulled a lever that snapped back the doors. We darted off the bus, straight up the stairs and entered the PCT institution that is The Stehekin Bakery. The bakery is synonymous with Stehekin on the trail. For many it puts the town on the map. Hundreds of miles ago, somewhere in Oregon we had received our first on-trail recommendation about the bakery from a fellow hiker. We soon discovered why. A warm and heavy aroma of sweet baked goodness excited the senses as we entered the building. Straight away we ordered coffees – the *proper* espresso kind – and quickly scanned the double glass case of delicacies before making the snap decision to order two of the largest cinnamon rolls I had ever seen. I took a picture of Conrad taking his first bite and couldn't help but marvel at how the bun looked about the same size as his head.

Proudly armed with our coffees and stash of baked goods, which included cookies and carrot cake, we re-boarded the bus to continue the final two miles into town. I sat quietly, completely transfixed in warm cinnamon/ cream-cheese gooiness. The rolls were so delicious I declared them the best I have *ever* eaten, and I'm no amateur when it comes to anything cake-related. I've since tried buying cinnamon buns in London and I'm telling you it's impossible to get anything even close; something that size and sweetness would probably come with a government health-warning over here!

Our bus journey followed the raging Stehekin River before reaching the northern tip of Lake Chelan, Washington's largest natural lake. It was a pretty ride, but one that seemed to take forever. On board, a congenial camaraderie brimmed from the group of travelling strangers, many of whom delighted in sharing their stories. Dan brought us up to speed on his personal tales of strange noises and invisible objects falling to the forest floor after dark. We surmised he had finally lost the plot after spending so much time out there alone.

The tiny community of Stehekin sits on the north-eastern shore of Lake Chelan, acting as a gateway to the Northern Cascades. Only 80 people live there year-round, as despite being on the U.S. mainland it's one of the most off-grid places I have ever been. Without road access to reach it, Google Maps has no idea how to get there if you try the navigation function. Anyone planning a visit will have to either catch a 50-mile ferry ride from the town of Chelan, hike across mountains, or charter a sea plane. So it's not really an easy weekend-get-away type of destination. There's also no phone reception, but all this isolation gives it a relaxed, old-world charm which we could all do with once in a while. Having said that, Conrad was disappointed there was no television when we entered our room, so some things never change.

That day, as we took a short stroll to the post office, it struck me how many people we had met thanks to the trail. In the space of perhaps 200 yards we bumped into Zelda and Tarzan, a married couple we first met back at Steven's Pass, who were about to board the ferry home with their dog. Moments later, we congratulated PCT thru-hikers Aussie Sam and Canadian Sarah for nearly completing their journey, as they boarded the bus back to the trail. Next up, the M&Ms, a set of identical twins from Oregon, who had been hiking the same section as us, and who we had camped with only two nights before. Much to our surprise, they had somehow made the last bus to town the previous night, determined to reach Canada on the date they had agreed to be picked up by their parents. It was heart-warming to see so many familiar faces, and to witness so many stories about to reach completion.

After queuing for 20 anxious minutes in a shoebox of a post office, we collected our last resupply box from the world's slowest USPS post office. Because our parcel had reached there more than a week ago, the elderly post officer had to close up shop and climb a small staircase to the upstairs apartment to retrieve it. Inside the box, a hand-written card from Leslie read: *OMG You are nearly done! Can you believe it?*

"HELL NO!" Conrad responded in earnest when I read it out loud.

I sent a message to Leslie thanking her for the box, not failing to realise the utter absurdity of it all. The Marshmeiers may have doubted we'd make it this far (a feeling shared by most), but we had also doubted their abilities as our support team. With the last of the boxes now safely in our hands, I couldn't help but feel astonished that every box had reached its intended destination on time. I'm sure it was a relief echoed back in Concord too. I had to take my hat off to our distant support crew – they never let us down.

Having arrived in town so early, we got all the usual hiker admin tasks completed, had lunch and a nap, so by late afternoon were twiddling our thumbs. We decided we couldn't miss the opportunity to try out the one other hot-food-serving establishment in town for dinner. The Ranch was a bus ride away, but we swallowed that for the flank steak daily special.

A full busload arrived at the Western-themed cookout, complete with sawdust floor, long bench seating, giant fireplace, and best of all: a self-serve food line. And in true American fashion, there was certainly plenty of food to go around. Conrad polished off a steak, while I tucked into the *deconstructed* – aka put it together yourself – Pad Thai. Watching us shovelling away you could have been forgiven for thinking we had just come off a hunger strike!

Dessert was a selection of pies and cake with around a dozen different varieties to choose from. It was the biggest decision I had made for months, but finally I settled on a slab of the largest chocolate cake known to man, while Conrad had blueberry pie and ice cream. That was the final straw. My brain should have registered my stomach was full long before, because just as we were being ushered back onto the bus I made a mad dash for the toilet. I could almost hear my mum telling me how my eyes were bigger than my belly as I hovered over the toilet puking up. Suffice to say I didn't feel too clever on the return bus ride. I realise now that my downfall was filling up on the comforting warm cinnamon raisin bread earlier; why don't I ever learn?

It wasn't until Stehekin that I knew for certain we would make it to Canada. Up until then, since about Trout Lake, I had been quietly confident, but there had been moments of wavering doubt during the toughest times. In Stehekin, having just completed our longest section, I finally allowed myself to visualise the border-crossing moment that all the months of preparation and persistence had led to. It was now just days away.

Our last zero day was one of the best. We considered crossing the lake to the town of Chelan to hunt down some replacement shoes for Conrad, until we looked up the ferry timetable and discovered the once-a-day crossing would take four hours. The Lady of the Lake ferry was designed to take people on daytrips to Stehekin, not from Stehekin, so we wouldn't have been able to return the same day. With this information, Conrad settled on purchasing more painkillers from the store, before we rented bikes with only one destination in mind.

It was a gorgeous clear day as we cycled along the lake's isolated shoreline. Across the water, towering mountains formed a hard verge, with a softer border of vivid green reeds framing the bank beside us. A handful of tiny log cabins lifted straight from storyland, and an outdoor church consisting of a large wooden cross and a couple of rows of simple pews, overlooked the water. It felt like we were on holiday in a far-off land. Just before departing the lake we had witnessed a bright yellow propeller airplane landing on the water, its humming reverberating around the otherwise still valley.

The bakery was just as good as we remembered. After a sandwich, we sat outside and devoured warm mixed-berry pie. It was completely worth the four-mile roundtrip! Had our resupply box failed to arrive, we would have taken up the traditional PCT thru-hiker Stehekin Bakery Challenge: completing the last section fuelled by nothing but baked goods. Come to think of it, it's a shame the box didn't get lost!

The rest of the day was spent hanging out on the hotel's deck, watching the activity on the lake. With lots of hikers around, it was a very social affair. Our neighbours at the National Park visitor centre provided a solid weather update, which seemed promising, so the only thing left to do was figure out what would happen once we reached Canada. We never really figured that one out, apart from booking a train ticket the following week from Vancouver back to California. It would take nearly two days to make a journey that would have taken just two hours by plane, but after all our time in the woods the idea of joining the Labour Day airport traffic was inconceivable.

I had a lot of thinking-time that day. In the forefront of my mind was an odd feeling of imminent completion. What a mammoth expedition it had been. Walking all day, surrounded by nothing but nature, had become our new normal, simplified way of life. I pondered what would come next, unable and unwilling to comprehend returning to a corporate office where I had always felt like an imposter. I tried to shift focus to the positive, allowing myself to delight in the inherent sense of joy stemming from the knowledge we had just four more sleeps under canvas remaining. I'd never really adjusted to sleeping on the ground.

32

The End is Nigh

We ended our first day back on the trail camped next to a toilet. It wasn't the most ideal spot, but those picture-perfect campsites have a habit of not being around when you need one. Stehekin had proven a wonderful pit-stop, but it was time to leave. Something had triggered a magnetic impulse, pulling us back to the trail. For the first time, Canada truly felt within our grasp. Armed with another bakery haul, we knew nothing could stand in the way of us crossing the border.

The bus set us at the trailhead after 9 a.m., a late start to the hiking day. It provided a sense of urgency, so with Dan we purposefully pushed ahead of the group, following the northern trail along the roaring banks of a steep thousand-foot gorge. The Northern Cascades National Park, which we climbed through most of the day, was not quite what I'd expected. We had been so spoilt with far-reaching mountainous vistas by this point, that the limited valley views and tree tunnels lacked a certain something. It probably didn't help the sun was beating down on us relentlessly, and those pesky black flies were out in force.

After a few hours of climbing through russet-coloured leaves, Conrad and I squeezed onto a verge of the trail close to Maple Creek, enjoying delicious turkey hoagies and cookies – from the bakery of course – the very thing I had been dreaming about for the last 10 miles. As we sat munching away in tired silence, two khaki-clad park rangers rounded the bend. It was a shock to see them both, the first National Park rangers we had seen on the entire trail. Realising our inconvenient location along the narrow ledge, Conrad and I stood up and shifted our packs out of the way as they approached.

The fit-looking woman was carrying a large pack with a hard hat, orange rescue ropes and a giant ice pick hanging from it. She greeted us with a brief smile.

"Afternoon," we both responded in unison, strangely intimidated by their authority.

The woman and her male counterpart, who was dressed the same as her with the addition of a national park service baseball cap, both said hello while looking us over.

"Are you PCT hikers?" the man asked in a surprisingly stern manner, given his outwardly friendly appearance.

I looked at Conrad as if to say *you take this one*, and he quickly confirmed we were.

The ranger continued, "where are you planning to camp this evening?"

This made sense. To limit over-crowding, the park ran a strict permit system for all campers, and due to the resident bear population, among other things, restricts all overnight stays to official camp sites only. We had tried booking one of these sites at the Stehekin visitor centre before being informed all requested sites were already booked: Dan had beaten us to the last space. We therefore had no choice but to make the 20 miles out of the park before nightfall, or else break the rules and risk getting busted by the Feds.

Casually Conrad told the rangers we intended to camp outside the park's boundary. I couldn't help but think they looked a tad disappointed. Once I sensed they were satisfied with our response, I became intrigued.

"Are you camping in the park tonight?" I asked, turning the focus onto them.

The woman's demeanour seemed much more willing to engage in small-talk than her colleague, and we got chatting for a few minutes on their four-day "foot patrol", which basically involved getting paid to hike around checking the occasional permit, while hoping nobody falls into a ravine.

"What a sweet gig", I whispered to Conrad as soon as they were out of earshot. He agreed.

After a long afternoon hiking through dense brush, we reunited with Dan, and together delivered ourselves to Rainy Pass trailhead just before dusk. Upon reaching the highway I was sad to recall how we had turned down probably the best offer of trail magic to date. The previous night we had received an email from Loren, the gentleman we met at South Brown Mountain shelter way back in Oregon. Contained in that email was a generous offer to meet us at this very spot, and drive us back to his house just over an hour away, where he and his wife Becky would host us. It would undoubtedly have involved good food, hot showers and a bed, which seemed like a no-brainer. But no matter how much we tried to justify the diversion, we couldn't make it work. It was logistically impossible to lose any more time having just re-joined the trail with train tickets booked, so we now faced a night camped in a car-park, obligingly outside the park boundary. We hadn't intended on camping in a ditch behind pit toilets, but after stopping to eat dinner and watching Dan set up his tent we simply lost momentum. By the smell of the air, the toilets were over-due a pumping too.

Fate came to play the next morning at first light. Perched on a wall at the back of the empty parking lot cooking oatmeal, I was fully aware of how much I resembled a homeless person trying to keep warm in front of a small flame. That consciousness grew as a white car entered the lot and began gradually crawling towards me. Conrad was out of view behind the toilets packing up camp, so I felt very alone and hoped an opportunist creep wasn't about to try it on. As it got close, the car window slowly slid down revealing a familiar face: Mark, last seen driving away from Packwood with his friend Steve.

We had exchanged a few texts with Mark over the weeks, but it was by a slim margin of chance that our on-trail reunion came to be. It felt like being reunited with a long-lost friend, despite the fact we barely knew the man. Mark had come bearing the gift of raspberry pie, but what distracted me even more than the food donation was the size of his new backpack. Someone had obviously been busy in REI since Packwood. His new ridiculously ultra- lightweight kit made Mark look like he was out for a casual stroll in the park. He proudly revealed how the entire pack weighed just 15 pounds, at least half what us idiots had strapped to our backs!

We said goodbye to Mark's friend Roberta, who seemed relieved Mark was not alone, and made good use of the early morning hours climbing to Cutthroat Pass. As the forest thinned out below, expansive views, some of the best we'd seen in the Cascades unfolded before us. In those five miles we witnessed the rising sun slowly awaken titanic craggy mountain spires. Towards the top a wide open valley dotted with granite boulders, spots of huckleberry bushes, and dark green heather led us to the crest. I always got a buzz from mounting a pass. Not only was there a sense of achievement coming from the knowledge I had completed the climb without a heart attack, but once at the top a whole new landscape unfolded on the other side. That day we completed a series of passes, each one involving a steady climb to a new expanse of scenery before snaking along a thinly-etched trail, visible for miles ahead. The time passed quickly with the new companionship of Mark. I loved listening to his smooth, laid-back North-Western accent, wishing we could talk just like him.

Munching on a mid-trail lunch of cinnamon rolls, I was in my element. Yes, they were ridiculously heavy – I had carried them 32 miles, which I think demonstrates great restraint, if not madness – but they were just so satisfying compared to the usual granola bar! Unfortunately it seemed we were not the only ones drawn to their sweet aroma. Less than a mile later a startled-looking hiker in his twenties came hurtling along the trail from behind. I tried making polite conversation but the guy was not intent on sticking around. Without stopping, in a French accent, he cried out: "did you see the BEARS?"

We all looked at each other oblivious, before he added how a large bear with cub had just, moments ago, surprised him right on the trail. Going against every piece of wilderness advice out there, he took one look at them and ran. I watched as his slender figure disappeared into the distance, before asking the guys whether they thought the strong fragrant smell of our cinnamon rolls had anything to do with the bear's appearance. I bet it had.

I kept my eyes peeled for the rest of the afternoon, relieved to not see any large hairy beasts, other than Conrad, of course. Despite an overcast lunch, by the time we started a 13-mile ascent towards Hart's Pass, what the English would call *sod's law* occurred: the clouds miraculously dispersed. So, under a scorching sun, we each took on the mountain in our own personal hell, weaving round constant switchbacks on the hot, dusty climb. I honestly don't know how I made it. I can still recall the toughest moments like those so *vividly*. When it felt so impossible. All I could do was look down and focus on putting one foot in front of the other, propelling a forward momentum while internally coaxing myself to: *Push. Push, PUSH*, against another voice telling me to give up. The exposed conditions made it brutal. Conrad was somewhere behind with his foot problems; it was each to their own by this point. It felt like an eternity, but after gaining a solid 2,000 feet in a couple of miles, I made it. An enormous sense of satisfaction swam over me at the top, as it did every time I managed to push myself past that evil mental wall. Maybe such feelings of achievement explain why people put themselves through crazy feats, like taking part in marathons or Iron Mans. It made me think of a quote my mum recited shortly before we left England. It came again from Edmund Hillary, the pioneering Everest explorer. After his success he was widely quoted as saying: "it's not the mountain we conquer but ourselves". Now, when mum first told me this I laughed at the trite soppiness of it but, you know what – maybe Edmund was really onto something deep and profound here. Sometimes you've got to "conquer" your own mountain to succeed.

On a patch of grass nestled amid a landscape of scree and rocks, we established camp alongside Dan and Mark. The small meadow, created by a tiny spring, produced an isolated oasis surrounded by the steep barren cliffs of Tatie Peak. As I attempted to wash the day's build-up of caked-on dirt from my legs, the local deer watched on. They seemed rather put out by our presence there, as they grazed in the spring, nervously maintaining stringent eye contact.

As Conrad started clicking together the tent frame, a flurry of short but melodic calls emanated from the rocks immediately behind us. Scanning to see the origin of the commotion, I finally caught sight of the elusive pika. Two of the small, round mammals, which look a bit like a tiny guinea pig-vole hybrid, were darting around like cartoon characters, well-camouflaged against the rusty-coloured rocks. I was captivated by their goofy cuteness, with disproportionally large bunny ears, an egg-shaped body, and no tail. I left them to their important business, hoping they wouldn't get curious with our tent overnight, to focus on preparing food. For the first time on the trail, given the mileage we had been able to knock off so far, we rewarded a massive day's hiking effort with two dinners: classic mac'n'cheese, followed by chocolate oatmeal. Eating breakfast food at dinnertime was a revelation. I couldn't believe we hadn't thought of it sooner.

33

Let's Finish This

Before beginning the hike I had never woken naturally with the sun, yet the next morning I rose to a perfectly glowing sunrise without the need for an alarm call. Going about my morning routine, I watched the deep pink sky slowly surrender to softer, brighter hues, with the trees around me reappearing from the shadows. The sun's warming effect inspired inside me an unusually optimistic sentiment that today will be a good day – something my dad often declares. The positive start continued, with a pika finally pausing long enough for me to capture his photo right before we left camp.

Having completed the hardest seven miles of the long climb to Hart's Pass the day before, the elevation in our initial morning miles seemed to ease up, skimming just beneath a giant rocky notch between two peaks as the sun slowly cast its rays across the mountains. Hart's Pass was the last road before Canada. For PCT hikers logistically unable to cross the border, the unpaved road often serves as the trail exit point, although looking at a map it still remained a long way from anywhere.

As we reached the pass, Conrad and I went ahead in search of the next water source, leaving Mark behind to make use of the portaloo. I'm not quite sure how Mark seemed to survive on such limited fluid intake compared to us, but that aside, we somehow took a wrong turn at the junction and walked the wrong way uphill for 10 minutes before realising. This resulted in us becoming separated from Mark, who upon reaching the pre-agreed meeting point probably thought he'd been ditched. It took us a couple of hours to catch him up.

The chase took place along a particularly incredible section of alpine tundra, weaving high above the trees through the Pasayten Wilderness. We scanned the faint outline of path ahead as it etched along the mountainside. From up there it was possible to see for miles in all directions. Such views of wide green valleys, infinite skies, and changing landscapes I never tired of. After a few miles we caught sight of Mark's all-black, agile figure up ahead. Yet despite speeding up even more it took another 30 minutes to catch him, just in time for a vertigo-inducing section called, no kidding: the Devil's Backbone.

By late afternoon the cramping in my toes was making me miserable. Mark, who had been quietly suffering with his back, and Conrad, who was being far more vocal about his foot blisters – the result of being mailed the wrong pair of shoes, apparently – were already both taking ibuprofen. The body has wonderful ways of telling us when enough is enough, so instead of listening to it, I popped some pills to become part of their pain-doping club.

The walking ceased after another 22-mile day. We settled in a campground hidden amongst the trees on the edge of a large open meadow. Given the huge hiking effort since leaving Stehekin, we now knew, if given favourable conditions, that it should be possible to complete the hike the next day, a whole day ahead of schedule. I tried to not get too carried away though, because reaching Manning Park the next day would still require a mammoth 24 miles. But let's face it – we had every motivation!

With two other couples eventually joining us in camp, Dan was noticeably absent. I had seen him cross the meadow shortly after us, but despite calling out to him I watched as he continued climbing up towards Rock Pass. I wasn't sure if he had seen us or not. It didn't help my already emotional state. Was this to be our final night in the wild? I stepped away from the heat of a blazing campfire into the open meadow. As I crossed the tall grass speckled with tiny white wildflowers, my head swept from side to side, mentally recording the grandeur of my surroundings. The sun was melting behind Powder Mountain, creating a darkened silhouette backlit by perhaps the greatest rose sunset I had ever seen, which I liked to think was put on just for us. So often had we missed the energy of the sun's daily drama by scurrying into the tent just before dark, completely exhausted. I regretted not witnessing every sunset and every star-encrusted night sky that followed. But mostly, at the forefront of my mind was a single thought: how do we return to real life from this?

I had been thinking a lot over the last few days about the world of work, and its associated unhappy memories. My feelings about which had been heightened by talking to Mark, who had just recently sold his own company. Why hadn't I, like him, found a way to master my own destiny, be my own boss? At 33 I should have been well on my way to making something of myself. Since beginning the walk I had perhaps been waiting for an epiphany, a clarity that would tell me what to do when I got home. But I was starting to understand this wouldn't come. For now, it was enough to sit in the dirt and just be. We had set out only ten weeks earlier, yet without even realising it I'd grown accustomed to dirt underneath my fingernails and, more importantly, I felt safe. No longer was I afraid of so many things that used to terrify me – I didn't think an axe murderer or bear was about to pounce on me in that lonely minute – I had instead developed a feeling of comfort from the mountains. A comfort that I sensed would make adjustment back to the "real" world all the more difficult.

The campfire held its usual mesmerising effect on all around. Whilst Conrad and Mark chatted away with the older couple, I stared into the flickering flames with an overwhelming mix of exhaustion, nostalgia, and joy. I cast a thought for Dan, who must have been camped alone somewhere up on the pass, disappointed he hadn't decided to join our ritual. The other, younger, couple hadn't shown their faces, until they wanted something. The girl strolled over and sheepishly asked to borrow our stove. She explained that her own stove had broken and the two still had a few days left of their SoBo section hike. I handed over our still-hot burner which she took with her back inside their tent. Most other hikers we'd crossed paths with typically jumped at the chance of sharing their stories with new company, but these two kept to themselves. They didn't exactly exude a friendly vibe, so I was left stunned when Mark later gifted them his own lightweight pocket rocket gas burner without a second thought.

"Are you crazy, Mark? Those things cost seventy bucks in REI," Conrad challenged him with concern.

But Mark was his usual casual self, simply stating: "they needed it more than I do."

We arose to the now customary daybreak alarm. Butterflies filled my stomach; a combination of nerves, excitement, and anticipation for the miles to come. In crisp darkness we savoured our last morning coffee and oatmeal. Both Conrad and I were contemplative. I was acutely aware of the irony associated with my heavy heart, given the excessive complaining of recent weeks, even so, it felt bittersweet. We said very little. Together we shared an intrinsic sense we'd miss being out in the wild; its unparalleled sense of freedom, and daily exhilaration which we had until now largely taken for granted. I anticipated re-entering a city – containing all the things I had spent hours pining for – was going to feel foreign.

With Mark we began winding up towards Rock Pass in the dim, fresh air. For the first time I was hiking in the thermal bottoms I usually reserved for sleeping. The sun rose the higher we got, the dark blue morning twilight gradually welcoming the golden hour. The trail snaked dramatically, leading us down steep scree slopes, before climbing back up the valley wall to Woody Pass. The Pass was the first flattish area we saw since leaving camp. As it had taken us an hour and a half to reach it, we were still mystified as to where Dan had slept the previous night.

Mounting Woody Pass, a whole new range of mountains appeared.

"Those *must* to be Canadian mountains!" I smiled, eyes wide in wonder. Our first definite sight of Canada.

The valleys around us were so dramatic in size and shape, they looked as though someone had taken a giant scoop to a tub of soft chocolate ice cream – yes, everything still reminded me of food – and scoured chunks out. As we followed the narrow trail through a path of noble fir trees smelling of Christmas, an increasing number of grey clouds gathered in menacing clusters. They dominated the sky against a few blue patches. Surely it wasn't going to rain on our last day?

By midday, the winds pelted our zigzagging path up the Devil's Stairway towards Hopkins Pass. The precarious, steep ridge probably won such a name from the treacherous, sharp drop-offs on all sides. From a pinnacle at the top of the pass, we came to a halt to take in the 360-degree views of nothing but mountains; it felt as if we were standing on top of the world.

Still feeling cold despite all the exercise, I was grateful when we began descending into forest cover. The next miles passed painfully slowly due to the constant anticipation of arriving at the border. The closer we got, the more excited I became, with little teasers along the way in the form of small wooden signs pointing towards the "*U.S. Border*". I found these last miles of forest visually rather unremarkable, but Mark pointed out how rare it was to see pine, Douglas fir, cedar, and blue spruce all growing together. I struggled to show my enthusiasm given my focus on dealing with around a dozen blow-downs, one of which scraped up my knee. Conrad took one look at the blood seeping down my leg and laughed it off as a "parting gift from the U.S."

Finally, after some switchbacks down, we began to make out voices. Through small gaps in the trees I caught my first glimpse of the famous wooden-pillared monument, effectively marking the end of the PCT and the continental United States. As we entered the clearing, we were unceremoniously received by a small group of hikers sprawled out in the dirt. I stood for a moment to take it all in, I mean this was *it*. This was the entry-point to Canada, the place until now so unbelievably far away. But the border wasn't quite what I was expecting; something was missing. Where were the Mounties to check our passports? Or the electric fence to keep out fugitives? Maybe if Trump gets elected, I thought... Instead, we stood surrounded by carpets of generic trees making up a giant forest that had been growing there since long before political boundaries. The monument I had seen featured in so many hiker blogs, the one that's made of five different-sized wooden pillars bearing the PCT crest, seemed smaller than I expected. Just a few feet away stood a silver obelisk called Monument 78, which according to the plaque signifies American-Canadian goodwill. The most remarkable sight in my opinion was the long line shaved into the slope of the mountains, created by lopping trees to distinguish a physical border viewable by air.

We took the photos I'd dreamt of, the ones proving we'd really made it, but the air-punching moment I'd hoped for was somewhat diminished by the presence of strangers. The group of young, dishevelled Hikertrash awkwardly observed our every move, offering up the odd random comment. They teased us for looking too clean to have walked all the way from Oregon, in what was seemingly friendly, but also critical *"you're not proper thru-hikers"* kind of banter. The solo female of the group jumped up and shoved a plastic Canadian flag into my hand, slurring something about the new Prime Minster being her boyfriend. This confirmed my suspicions, first alerted by their distinct smell, that the reason they were all about to walk 30 miles back to Hart's Pass, instead of entering Canada, was something to do with pharmaceuticals.

Reaching the end of the PCT soon felt very anti-climactic. We still had nearly nine miles to trek in order to re-join the civilised world. Why couldn't there be an air-lift service at this point? Or a nice chair-lift up and over the mountain? We sat and ate a power snack on the banks of a nearby river, which included the last two cookies from the Stehekin Bakery. It was a beautiful spot, but we didn't linger, determined to reach the real hiking finish line at Manning Park.

The sky had cleared so it was under hot, humid conditions the two of us and Mark silently blundered our way along the poorly-maintained trail, tripping on roots and over-grown bush. Conrad had ceased rationing painkillers, as he hobbled away in agony. It must have taken him great resolve to continue, particularly when the trail joined a stony jeep road for four miles. He kept telling us to go ahead, but I couldn't abandon him after we had come so far together.

At around 5:30 p.m. we resurfaced. Well, it was a paved road at least. The trail ended at an unremarkable road junction where a large wooden sign signalled *"Manning Park"*. Three elderly ladies hovered nearby; they asked if we had seen their nephew, who was expected to complete the trail hours ago. They seemed concerned, so we re-assured them of the slow-going conditions in the last section. I couldn't help but notice their two cars parked in the lay-by. As no offer of a ride followed we continued along the hot asphalt towards the lodge, sad about the unforeseen extra miles.

With heads hanging low, and legs now less responsive from exhaustion, we trudged on for what felt like *at least* a mile. In reality it was probably just a few hundred feet before a car containing a widely-smiling lady did a giant U-turn to pull up beside us. In his zoned-out state Mark hadn't even recognised the car. It took a long moment for the cheerful lady to register as Mark's friend Roberta. I can honestly say I've never been so happy to see someone. As we piled into the car, relieved to finally sit down, it dawned on me: we were *done*. After a journey encompassing 935 gruelling miles, climbing 166,000 feet – the equivalent of scaling Europe's tallest building, The Shard in London, 163 times – there was no more walking. Our hike was officially *over*.

34

A Friend is Missing

Over dinner it hadn't fully sunk in. Our future held no more miles to count, camps to create, or mountains to conquer. We had walked to Canada! Tomorrow's views would be filled with skyscrapers, not trees.

With burgers and poutine – a seriously satisfyingly-sloppy French-Canadian dish of chips coated in gravy and cheese-curds – we celebrated the heart-warming achievement. Roberta, who offset Mark's laid-back cool with her chatty persona, didn't conceal her relief at seeing Mark in one piece. But, we'd seen him in action, and could have told her she had nothing to worry about. At 65, Mark was a far more accomplished hiker than us. He seemed to glide up mountains, while we stomped, struggling under our weight. His companionship certainly enhanced our experience. Thanks to a brief meeting at Trout Lake, followed weeks later by a chance reunion at Rainy Pass, we had gotten to share many miles and anecdotes with a very amiable and kind-hearted man. As we shared a meal together I hoped we would stay in touch for years to come.

Before leaving the restaurant, I sent a text back home as promised from Stehekin. It simply stated: *We made it. Call you tomorrow x.*

With London eight hours ahead, I wasn't expecting a response anytime soon – my parents are no night owls – but almost instantly my phone buzzed.

I read my mum's simple response and smiled. She must have been waiting up or having trouble sleeping, and in that moment, I released what I had put her through. I cast a thought for all the other mums out there who anxiously await updates from their adventuring offspring. The things we put our mothers through! In retrospect, I could see precisely why she might have been concerned. All those fears I had spent weeks attempting to block out of my system in Operation Just Get On With It, she had probably contemplated daily, with many a sleepless night. I therefore felt a weight must now have been lifted from her, so many miles away.

The sense of comfort from her words was obvious: *I am so relieved, Mum xxx.*

It was time to leave Manning Park but someone's presence was missing. I had been half expecting to see Captain Dan, our hiking buddy from Kentucky, sat at Monument 78 waiting for us. For hundreds of miles he had kept us entertained with colourful stories taken from his days in the military and his road-walking escapades. But there was no sign of him. I felt a real sadness at Dan's absence from the group, and if I'm honest, a little hurt by it. Was I naive to think we had become friends? As we left the restaurant, Conrad suggested we pop into the bar below to double-check Dan wasn't down there. We knew the once-a-day bus to Vancouver wasn't expected until later that evening, so unless he had hitched, he must have been somewhere close by.

Sure enough, we found him sat at a table reading in the darkened bar. He cut a lonely figure.

Conrad congratulated him on completing the entire PCT with a handshake, before I jumped in, "we thought you'd left us."

He responded in his usual calm tone, "nah, I'm waitin' for the bus."

I couldn't help but think he looked sombre, but perhaps he was just tired.

"I've been trying to message you" I continued, "we just had dinner with Mark and his friend Roberta. She's goin' to give us a ride."

"Yeah, I saw you guys in the window, but I didn't want to intrude."

I found this *ridiculous*. The fact he had seen us but chose to walk past, likely to never see us again hurt even more, especially after all we'd been through, but I tried to mask my disappointment.

"You should have come in; we've been expecting you all day; every time we went over a pass we scanned the trail for your red dot."

Conrad changed the subject, probably sensing that I was a bit annoyed. "When did you get here?"

"Ahh, it was early, 'round one-thirty."

Conrad couldn't hide his amazement, "how did you manage *that*? We got here an *hour* ago!" It was already past seven, and there were no road-walking options out there.

"I camped up near Woody Pass last night. Reached the monument at ten-thirty; I wanted to get done early."

"We wondered what happened to you 'cos we didn't see your name in the trail register," I quizzed.

"Well, I signed it," he stated, with classic Dan ease.

We had failed to spot Dan's name in the tatty book at the monument, expecting it to be the last one on the most recent page. Maybe his handwriting was really bad, or perhaps we were just more focused on trying to commemorate the occasion by taking photographs rather than scanning through the pages.

I congratulated him, then added "you scrub up well', noting a woollen sweater which I hadn't seen before.

"Yeah, I had a shower over at the campground. I sure needed it. And I did laundry – I didn't want to be gettin' on the bus stinkin' it out."

A considerate gesture, I thought, as most other thru-hikers wouldn't have given a shit.

There was so much I wanted to ask Dan, like what he planned to do next, but for now we had to go – Mark and Roberta were waiting for us, unaware of our sudden dash into the bar. It felt wrong to be departing that way, an unfitting end to what felt like a long journey together. But I had to accept that Dan had his own travel plans, and we were lucky to be receiving a ride. With an awkward goodbye, half-mentioning something about the possibility of catching up in Vancouver, we left Dan to his book.

It dawned on me later that Dan set out on a solo hike. For him, reaching Canada was the culmination of an epic 2,650 mile-expedition; one that pushed him mentally and physically to the brink. It was a personal accomplishment he'd needed to complete alone.

Falling into bed in a motel 50 miles from the trail, I laughed under my breath.

"What?" Conrad asked drowsily.

"I just can't *believe* it. Who would have thought?"

He sighed. "Yeah, I know. It's weird. I'm not walking anywhere ever again."

"I honestly didn't think I'd last a single night in the woods, I was so scared, that last night in Ashland I couldn't believe what I'd gotten us into, I kinda hoped it was all just a dream."

Conrad closed his eyes, "that feels like a *long* time ago."

"Yeah, I know. It's crazy to think how it all came about – I can't believe how quickly the idea just, *morphed* out of control."

Conrad hummed his agreement, and I continued my little monologue.

"It all got so out of hand, so quickly, to the point that it was too late to back-out, even though I secretly wanted to."

Conrad let out a loud yawn. "My biggest fear was my leg wouldn't hold up," (a reference to his blood clot issues the year before), "and I'd let you down."

This made me smile, recognising that such generous consideration was why I married this man. I cozied in towards him; "I bet there were times back in Oregon where we both secretly wished it would have too! Or when I thought about pushing you off a cliff."

Conrad frowned with eyes still closed as I continued, "but I wouldn't have done it without you, so I guess it's a good job we're both so stubborn."

35

Beyond Canada

I'm staring at a photo in which I hardly recognise the two faces smiling back, triumphant besides Monument 30. It sure looks like us, albeit grubbier, slightly leaner versions, but how surreal and distant the moment now feels. If it wasn't for photographic evidence, I may even doubt whether "the Brits" were ever there, crediting the long journey to a figment of my imagination. But it happened. As fantastical and down-right unfathomable as the experience became, the memories and visual snippets live on in vivid colour.

As promised, this was not a tale of deep, spiritual self-discovery. Our trek sprung from a bit of a whim after all. We weren't experienced outdoorsy folk. We weren't answering a life-long call to nature by embarking on a carefully-considered expedition. It was farcical really, when I think of how we coaxed each other into this absurd adventure, all the time harbouring massive doubts over our capacity to even survive a night. Unsurprisingly, we found it tough. We swore, we sulked, we moaned endlessly, feeling apathy for the wonder staring us right in the face, because it obliterated our comfort zones. It was a far cry from the constant wonder and joy I had read about in so many hiking blogs. No great epiphanies or answers to life's reaching questions awaited us in the woods, but living off-grid for ten weeks also didn't pass without leaving a lasting impression.

For me, a chief outcome was learning to finally disconnect. And once I did, I found being among the trees elevated my emotional state too. Yes, I complained, but for the majority of the time I felt truly content, an anxious weight lifted through solitude.

A popular quote from John Muir makes me think I'm not alone in feeling an intrinsic connection between nature's rhythms and our own:

"Thousands of tired, nerve-shaken, over-civilized people are beginning to find out that going to the mountains is going home; that wildness is a necessity; and that mountain parks and reservations are useful not only as fountains of timber and irrigating rivers, but as fountains of life."
(*Our National Parks*, John Muir)

Only after leaving the trail did I begin to appreciate the significance of Muir's message. On the trail, days felt infinitely longer because we lived in the present. I concentrated on my footwork, I noticed little things I didn't normally, like the birds singing, or wind rustling leaves, as I only needed to focus on a predetermined route. Each day was simple, revolving around little more than eating, walking, and sleeping, completely shielded from the distractions of modern life. It was a refreshing, uplifting existence. I believe Muir was ahead of his time in articulating the "necessity" of immersing oneself in the beauty of nature. It doesn't take a degree in psychiatry to realise that removing the negative ruminating and social pressures of the urban world can be a powerful tool in improving our mental health. Health organisations throughout the world are already responding. A growth in "wilderness therapy" centres for treating dysfunctional children, emotional trauma, and substance abuse victims, bring credence to the theory that prolonged exposure to nature can improve wellbeing and promote healthy living.

With sentimental memories of the trail so often playing through my mind, I was still trying to understand the impact the experience had on me when conversing with Dan over email months later.

I liked his explanation, so I shall share it. He simply believes anyone who completes an extended hike comes away "with a type of confidence and contentment that's difficult to describe to others".

It's true, the feeling is difficult to explain. Although we hiked the same path, each passage was a very personal one, inspired by an eclectic mix of motivations no single person could ever fully grasp. Even so, I'm confident the diverse mix of stories will probably share fond recollections, where months of gruelling hiking, camping, and blister-ridden feet fade, to be replaced with cathartic memories of romanticised trail life.

Something the hike left in me personally, was an unparalleled sense of achievement. It was an accomplishment that felt worlds apart from any other life success I felt in the past. It signified victory. Somehow, remarkably, against all the odds, we hadn't given up, and that really meant something, especially to someone with such raw feelings of career failure. Yes, it turned out that crossing into Canada was about far more than just the physical goal. We disrupted our routine life to enter a perfect test ground for persistence, determination, teamwork, and stamina, all qualities we had previously underestimated in ourselves. Achieving such a positive conclusion not only made us feel pretty good about ourselves, but it brought us closer together. We can now look each other in the eye and say "we walked to Canada!" A demonstration that *anything* is possible, even if we still laugh at the very thought of it.

As the initial post-hike weeks flew by, I found myself in an unusually quiet and withdrawn state. Such a sudden end to our daily hiking routine required time to decompress and sink in. My diary shows how the initial elation stemming from our jubilant finish quickly melted into a deep sense of loss. As anticipated, Vancouver felt worlds away from the trail. The spell was lifted. We both struggled to adjust. Our hike may have been over, but somehow it still felt necessary to go on long walks each day. Of course I saw the hypocrisy of pining for a trail that had witnessed weeks of my whining over a fixation for counting down miles. Yet I couldn't help but miss the daily exhilaration that came from conquering the unknown. I missed being physically challenged to near-breaking point, before being rewarded by the achievement of making a milestone, reaching a pass, or by witnessing nature's plentiful magnificent sights. Never before, or since, have I felt so alive. But most of all I missed the sense of freedom. No longer could I stop and pee whenever or wherever I desired, and to my daily routine returned the conventional female war paint – makeup – to assimilate back into society.

By contrast, the city, including London once we returned

home, offered nothing we really needed. Okay, so we could secure the delivery of any type of world cuisine imaginable in just a few taps, but the multiplicity of choice felt overly stressful. Not to mention the sensory overload that came from being surrounded by so many people, traffic and fumes. It was draining. Each night we fell asleep listening to sirens instead of rustling trees. I cursed myself for having gotten so complacent with nature during our expedition, given how deeply I now craved those natural wonders. For hours, I would sit fixated on our many wonderful photos, wishing myself back into the past.

So, what becomes of a "thru-hiker"? Well, from what I've read and the people I've met, I'm certainly not alone in finding it tough to adjust back to real life. It's particularly tough for those who began the trail without a clearly defined future, those who perhaps hoped that by following one defined path they may stumble upon another. Just like me, the majority fail to find life-defining clarity out in the woods. People have written entire books dedicated to exploring the psychological and emotional struggles involved in thru-hikes,[1] so it's obviously a re-occurring theme. Just like switching off to enter the wilderness takes time, reversing the process isn't easy. I know dozens of hikers who struggled. Many go on to hike another long-distance trail the next season, seeking to regain the heart-warming sense of accomplishment, physical conditioning and immersion "therapy" of scenery so beyond description. Two people we met on-trail returned to hike the PCT south-bound the following year because something in them just didn't want to let it go.

For me there have been some small life changes, but I sense the process is not complete. While I continue to search for my true vocation, I do so with an elevated consciousness regarding the effect my surroundings have on my well-being. I now accept that getting wrapped up in the stresses of city life, such as complaining about the traffic, or how long the next Uber will take, is to a large extent pointless behaviour. I try and walk a little slower, being aware of my reality instead of drowning

---

[1] See *Pacific Crest Trials: A Psychological and Emotional Guide to Successfully Thru-Hiking the Pacific Crest Trail*, by Zach Davis & Carly Moree (2016)

it all out with headphones or the lure of my phone's screen. I also find I need less than I did before. We have prioritised trips and experiences ahead of material goods. I'm not about to start declaring my love for camping and roll around in the mud – I still maintain my nails – but I haven't lost sight of the simpler pleasures either. Like the energy that comes from breathing fresh air, or watching the sun rise.

The greatest challenge remaining is to figure out the million-dollar question: how does one strike a balance between idyllic dreams of escapism, and living a good life surrounded by those you love?

Lessons Learnt

There's a comment I hear a lot whenever discussing the hike, it goes something along the lines of: "I couldn't do that." Yet, each time I hear those words, I beg to differ. I truly believe long-distance hiking adventures are within the reach of any able-bodied person. I don't even think it's beyond the capability of my parents who are in their sixties – given some training and guidance of course. Now for the caveat: it's *not* easy. In fact, I bet the mere fear of failure would probably discourage most from even attempting to tackle something so seemingly daunting. But fears and excuses won't conquer anything, so if you harbour dreams of taking a walk in the woods, or taking any kind of life-disrupting adventure, I simply say just *go*, DO IT. Nobody I have ever spoken to who takes time out to go travelling ever regrets it. Fact.

For those who decide to take the plunge, being prepared is essential. The wilderness shouldn't be trifled with; its dangers are very real.

To a large extent we found ourselves lucky when it came to potential hazards such as extreme weather shifts. Just a year after our hike ended, a devastating forest fire – ignited by youths playing with firecrackers – wiped out much of the Eagle Creek trail in Northern Oregon. Apocalyptic scenes of roaring flames and falling ash led the press to draw comparisons to the mammoth Mount Saint Helens eruption in the late eighties. The wildfires continued further north too. A lightning storm in early August 2017 sparked the Norse Peak fire which closed a 99-mile section of the PCT near Mount Rainier National Park. I only hope that everyone on the trail during these incidents found a way to safety.

Sadly, search parties continue to this day for signs of two lost hikers: Ohio native Kris Fowler, a 34-year-old who was last seen at White Pass in October of 2016, and Irishman David O'Sullivan, aged 25 who came off the trail to resupply in Idyllwild, California in April 2017. Both are feared to have run into difficulty due to snowy conditions. What their families must be going through is unimaginable. Dedicated Facebook groups full of people wanting to help with the searches still operate to this day.

Since leaving the trail we've had time to reflect on our experience. Below I'd like to share some lessons we learnt – most often the hard way – for anyone considering their own similar challenge. It's definitely not my intention to preach; I accept I'm neither a *bona fide* thru-hiker, nor a camping professional, but here are some pointers I wish I had grasped before leaving home...

Mind Games

Endless hours of nothing but walking is, more than anything, mentally taxing. On the particularly special days where we found ourselves cold, soaked and hungry, fighting off mosquitoes, all while coping with painful injuries and climbing over blow-downs, it took serious motivation to keep going. Many of the people we met along the way who abandoned their hikes short of target all shared a similar rationale: they had given up. Think of Loren and his "negative fun" statement. It isn't hard for me to understand how they felt – I shared these lows, wanting to throw in the trekking-poles on a number of occasions. The mind travels to all sorts of places when it's swinging between despair and joy. It goes all-over-the-place insane! That said, to our credit, we endured things many people couldn't mentally handle. Night after night, we slept on the ground, we rationed food, walked mile after mile hungry, and developed the battered feet to prove it. Quitting frequently seemed like the only sensible solution to the repetitive routine of: *walk, eat, sleep, repeat.*

To succeed, it's imperative to come to the game mentally ready to persevere. Expect the journey to involve struggle; you will undoubtedly feel shitty and your resolve will be heavily tested, but you'll also reflect back on those moments later and feel stronger for them.

We found that packing a few morale-boosting tricks really helped fight off the dark times. To ward off the daily mental monotony I liked to listen to podcasts or playlists which I would refresh at rest stops. These would cheer me up, and distract my mind from thoughts of pain, or hunger. I only allowed myself to listen for an hour or two a day, usually in the late afternoon, due to limited battery life, and I always kept the volume low so I didn't totally mute out my surroundings – you'll want to hear the bears approaching! Also, in more desperate times, I found that taking a zero-nutritional-value sugar break worked wonders. In each resupply box was packed a different, random treat from home, which we reached for as required. I recall the satisfaction we felt from sucking sherbet off a Swizzle Stick late one afternoon following a massive lava climb near The Three Sisters, and how a packet of Nerds helped restore our energy levels during the day we trudged through the overgrown Goldmyer Alternate with delight.

Physical Endurance

According to a recent Department for Transportation survey, the average UK person walks less than half a mile a day. Now, set that against our relatively-modest (by PCT standards) average 18-mile day, throw in a 30-pound pack with countless elevation change and it's obvious our bodies were under a lot of pressure. Signs of resistance were bound to appear.

The majority of our whining in the wild revolved around the exhaustion of being physically pushed to the brink. I never expected it to be easy, but it was BRUTAL. And although our fitness improved over the weeks, our bodies becoming conditioned, we were never totally devoid of some degree of pain or affliction. Dan described finishing the hike as his "most difficult physical challenge ever", and I cannot emphasise this point enough. It was a game of stamina, and we didn't even complete half the trail.

For two city-dwellers this challenge was compounded by our lack of *specific* training. Being fit, it turns out, isn't enough. We discovered gruelling gym workouts do little to safeguard the body from the repetitive-strain type injuries most frequently sustained in the mountains. In his unofficial annual thru-hiker survey, Mac – aka *HalfMileToNoWhere.com* – gathered 381 responses from the PCT Class of 2016. Of the 24 per cent surveyed who left the trail early, the results show that 48 per cent did so due to injury. Now, these results reflect only a small cohort of hikers, but it's safe to say that injury can be a major obstacle in the world of long-distance hiking.

With this in mind, and the power of hindsight, we should have completed more training before leaving home, especially carrying weighty packs over elevation. This may have been inconvenient given our hectic London schedule, but looking back on how beneficial it would have been – by toughening up our feet, or getting our shoulders used to carrying packs – I'm sure we could have found a way.

Who knows, with proper training I might have avoided the on-going mystery issue with my right leg, which plagues me to this day.

Setting Realistic Goals

This point relates to the last. Your body doesn't just feel tired on the trail, it gets repetitively hammered. Fortunately, a simple piece of advice was bestowed on us just before we set out, which I believe proved key to our success. Remember Shroomer, the friendly hiker we meet half-way up Mount Diablo, back when we still hadn't cracked a five-mile trek? Well, that chance encounter left us with a simple, but invaluable piece of advice. To paraphrase, it went something like: "If you want to be hiking 20-milers, don't go in guns blazing with 20s, try beginning with 10. No matter how tempted you may feel to go further, don't. Give your body a chance to adapt. Maybe do 10 miles for the first week, then build up slowly from there."

These words make a lot of sense, especially for people who, like ourselves intend to do most of their physical training on the trail. While we didn't strictly stick to 10-mile days for the first week, Shroomer's advice was at the heart of the low expectations embedded in our *sensible* hiking schedule, and motivated us to call it a night in the mid-afternoon on more than one occasion. Gradual progression is probably what helped give our bodies some sort of fighting chance to acclimatise – that and having the ability to take regular zero days to recover.

Packing What's Right

There is nothing thru-hikers relish discussing more than kit. It can feel like a competition when comparing who has the lightest, most cutting-edge and compact gear. As two novices who did all our research online, it was easy to get tangled up in the popular obsession with base weight (the weight of your pack without consumable goods such as food, water, and fuel), as the majority of blogs and vlogs come from young, experienced hikers. This research implied our starting base weight *should be* somewhere around 20 pounds, and this would hopefully be reduced by a couple of pounds over the course.

But surprisingly, out on the trail, we met people carrying an enormous range of weight and gear. We saw full-size guitars, large bottles of booze, and one instance of what I believe was a stoneware urn but was too polite to ask. Brandon from Tennessee somehow carried a monster 70 pounds. The contents included a bear canister, a folding seat, and a crockpot, which all formed key components of his bush-camp. Camping under the stars, he told us, was his very reason for hitting the trail. Yet on the other end of the weight spectrum we met couples who shared a toothbrush!

From talking to people, I learnt that while it's important to enjoy the experience, it's even more vital to strike a balance between light-weight, comfort, and being prepared. Stories of ultra-light hikers being rescued because they didn't have appropriate protections abound. Dan knew one woman who required a helicopter rescue after catching hypothermia. Even so, there are a number of studies that prove a linear correlation between pack weight and injuries. As rookies, our biggest fear was getting lost or held up and not having enough provisions to survive. In the wild, it only takes a spate of bad weather to find yourself in a sticky situation, by taking out a vital river crossing, or throwing up a dangerous storm meaning you need to stay put and hunker down.

From our gear list (*outlined in the back*), you will see various items that many hikers would deem superfluous, but which formed the cautious ingredients to our *safety first* approach. Some of these items we never used – the whistle, compass, emergency matches, iodine pills – but I felt reassured knowing we had them just in case. We did shed some items – mostly towards the end when we had built up more confidence – but others we added, including some "luxury" objects to improve our comfort. The blow-up pillows, foam seating pads, and an extra thick pair of socks to sleep in each made the weight-verses-pleasure edit, because we valued our rest and I hated being cold.

Therefore, it's probably wise to not be too obsessed with carrying the bare minimum, unless you are an experienced hiker, and depriving yourself is your thing!

Pack what is right for you, and test everything out long before you leave. In particular, you may find that sleeping on the ground night-after-night can make the odd creature comfort seem well worth the extra weight.

Teaming Up

Spending all day every day with another person is tough. It doesn't matter how well you think you know someone, or how tight you believe your relationship is, I guarantee tensions will develop during any extended adventure. It didn't take long before spending every waking hour with my husband began to feel a bit, well, claustrophobic, and certain "flare-ups" drove me crazy with rage.

Going into the hike this wasn't something I'd even considered. Conrad and I had always gotten along pretty well, and we had already travelled together through South America for six months without any major incidents other than a broken toe, which wasn't my fault. But out on the trail things were different. Thrown into unusually stressful situations, emotions were heightened, feelings felt all the more intense. We became bombarded with each other at our worst, seeing the full un-censored version of the person we had vowed to spend the rest of our lives with. It wasn't always easy viewing; I can easily understand how so many hikes end with mid-trail bust-ups.

For those considering partnering up for a long hike, I would suggest having "that" conversation before you go, the one where you agree what would happen if one of you decides not to continue. Conrad and I had no choice but to make our hiking partnership work, because upfront we agreed to hike together or not at all. We either found a way to operate as a team, even when tired and irritable, or it was game-over. While I could say that good communication was the key to success, we also undertook a lot of tongue biting and boundary respecting. Essentially, as for marriage in general, it was often far more important to be happy than to be right. Oh, and on a personal note, I had to learn to stop holding grudges, and to improve my levels of compromise – things I struggle with. In return, Conrad did his best to "just get on with it".

During the most trying times of trail life, I struggled to decide if it was better to be part of a team, or if it in fact made life more difficult. As an individual, only I could physically walk my miles, yet our setup was such that we depended on each other for completing daily chores, and for carrying items of kit. If one of us had fallen off a mountain, the other would have been screwed (and devastated too, I'm sure). I don't know what the ultimate answer is, but I recognise there is a fine line between dependency and self-reliance. So, if you choose to hike with a partner, go knowing that while you can support them to some degree, you can't carry them.

Conrad and I both found the hike tough on our relationship. Our usual connection shifted. Call it marriage preservation, but unconsciously we came to operate more as a team than a couple. All passion went out the window. We relished our own space. Luckily, hiking in pairs doesn't rule out solitude. Mostly moving in single-file, we often walked alone for hours, enjoying moments of silent reflection. Yet, as empowering as quiet time felt, I always liked the comfort of knowing I wasn't alone, and over time I came to appreciate the key benefit of companionship: having someone to share the special moments with.

Food Verses Weight

Arriving in Vancouver clad in the same smelly hiking clobber we had walked all those miles in, we agreed a visit to the shops were in order. Picking out a pair of jeans, I was expecting (and hoping) to be at least one size smaller, considering how hungry and active I'd been over the preceding weeks. Yet, much to my dismay, I wasn't. A step on some scales in the hotel bathroom confirmed I had lost virtually no weight at all. My legs might have been firm and muscly – "legs like a mule", as Conrad teased – but that wasn't the look I was hoping for.

Conrad's body reacted very differently. Neither of us noticed it at the time, but he lost 25 pounds over just 10-weeks. OK, so he had eaten a lot of burgers in the three weeks leading up to the trail, so he probably could have done with losing a few, but on seeing these results I felt stunned with guilt. Thoughts I should have *made* him eat more, and myself less haunted me, and that was before my mum gave me an ear-full over how skinny he looked too! Splitting our trail meals pretty much 50-50 had been an error. With the gift of hindsight, this seems glaringly obvious. Conrad is nearly a foot taller than me, and biologically, scientists have proven that men need more calories than women – 500 a day more according to the UK National Health Service.

Some people go to great lengths to calculate what food to pack on hikes using a combination of caloric density, mileage, and body weight. But their calculations hinge upon a degree of guess-work because there is no *definitive* consensus about what calculation to use in the first place – amount of calories per pound being just one – and the optimal values of each. This is probably because the physical demands on your body change over time, and nutrition varies so much from person to person. We certainly could have coped with less food for the first couple of weeks whilst slowly increasing our mileage. Hiker hunger didn't really hit us until then anyway, but Conrad's body needed more after that, though his weight has well and truly recovered since.

On shorter hikes, of up to a week or two, people can probably survive on consuming their recommended daily calorie intake – 2,500kcl for men, and 2,000kcl for women – knowing that if they lose a pound or two they can replenish any deficit soon enough. But on a prolonged hike where the average hiker burns over 3,000 calories a day, food becomes a vital energy source to sustain the body, so it's worth considering the nutritional value of the foodstuffs you carry to some extent. This might be controversial, but I believe it's possible to take a pragmatic approach to diet by monitoring your body (something we should have done more effectively with Conrad's weight), and using trial and error to fill nutritional gaps if they arise.

Despite all the good intentions we tried packing into our food boxes, we unsurprisingly developed cravings for heavy and unhealthy foods, which we began carrying more of towards the later stages. I'm ashamed to admit that we swiftly succumbed to binge-eating in all town stops. I probably would have lost weight if it wasn't for my greedy "guilt-free" resupply feasts, single-handedly polishing off more than one tub of Ben & Jerry's without a second thought! Compared to Conrad I am an emotional eater, so it came naturally to use food as a reward – something I realise is neither healthy, nor an easy habit to shift. If I did take on another long-distance hike, I would make greater efforts to view food as fuel and avoid this kind of yo-yo eating.

Do it Your Way

Anyone researching the PCT will most likely encounter the phrase: *hike your own hike (HYOH)*. Despite initially dismissing it as a bit cringe-worthy and trite, I now embrace the sentiment. People decide to take on adventures, such as long hikes, for many reasons, each with varying expectations and abilities. For many, the target focuses on a set end-goal, while others just need a method of escape, but whatever motivates a person to take such a leap, the story is often very personal, so there cannot be a one-size-fits-all prescription for *how* each step must be walked.

Take Dan, for example. He was no hiker when he started out,

yet – unlike us – he manged to complete the entire trail. Despite the odd road de-tour and time-out, he can still proudly say he's hiked all the way from Mexico to Canada!

On completing his hike, Captain Dan gave the following wise advice to his YouTube followers: "Do everything possible to tool yourself for the best chance of success."

Conrad and I fully agree with this message. While eager to prove our doubters wrong, our chief aim was to reach Canada as painlessly as possible, by whatever means necessary. We were certainly no *purist* hikers, and I'm okay with that. We did everything within our means to make it; from spending a small fortune on light-weight hiking gear, to getting hotel rooms at regular zero stops, to using electronic navigation apps. This also meant we didn't rule out the odd road diversion, and we didn't succeed unaided.

The point I'm trying to get to is that by having time on our side, and being relaxed in our methods, our experience was enhanced through a collection of memorable encounters with people who blew us away with their eagerness to help. From having initial fears of getting attacked by an opportunist criminal, I instead only witnessed lessons in kindness and compassion. This is not something I experience back in a city where guarded strangers remain strangers.

It was only weeks into our expedition that I recognised the experience was about so much more than reaching the final destination. We had always set out intending to take regular zero days to recuperate and lighten our food resupply, but those random places where we spent time off-trail actually became pivotal memories themselves.

Many thru-hikers generally have to skip and choose which resupply stops to visit, meaning they miss out on unique locations, such as Trout Lake with their friendly people championing huckleberries, or Stehekin with that legendary bakery. So, if you're going hiking, perhaps put some thought into exactly what it is you want from your hike, and set your own expectations and methods based on it. Maybe you don't complete a full thru-hike, or maybe you do bits of one over the course of many years, it really doesn't matter

Enjoy

This brings me on to my last point, the keystone I wish I could have grasped before it all began... *appreciate it!*

I shake my head in shame thinking just how much I focused my attention while hiking on the difficulties I faced, when I should have slapped myself into the reality of the experience. I may hate camping, but there I was in the great Wild West living out a once-in-a-lifetime opportunity that many will only ever dream of. Ordinary life can get very routine, but on the trail each day is an adventure, maybe not always a rosy one, but never are two days the same, and you know what: it feels pretty damn *wild* to *let things be*, topped off with an unexplainable, intoxicating feeling of personal triumph upon crossing the finish line.

It may have initially taken us time to disconnect from the city, unscrambling the brain noise, but once we did, the tranquillity was exhilarating. I enjoyed the quiet. America's wilderness, so impossibly vast, constantly exceeded our expectations. Ingrained into memory is a slide-show of fantastic marvels, mountains higher, lakes clearer, canyons deeper, and tree canopies denser than I ever could have imagined. I close my eyes and feel invigorated by the majestic images, even whilst packed like sardines into the London Underground. My imagination has been sparked. Back home, I now look up at the stars and sunsets, and although they are not as glorious as those illuminating the Cascades, they offer me hope.

All those hours, days, weeks on the trail are now wound together in an irrevocable memory. The people, the views, the agony and the laughter, all held in a place that will stay with me forever. I hope to one day return to complete some of the remaining 1,700 miles. The mountains are calling. But until then, I share excitement for, and wish safe passage to anyone embarking on their own outdoor adventure.

Happy trails.

Epilogue

Less than five months after leaving the trail, Steve from Halifax passed away following a sudden but short illness. Mark sought sanctuary in a desert trek weeks later, paying homage to his dear friend amid the spring wildflowers.

Dan is still out hiking and living an enviable life as a professional nomad. He regularly volunteers advice to other hikers through PCT Facebook groups, and has been known to hand out trail magic from time to time. In the summer of 2017, he ventured across the pond to the UK to trek the Scottish and Welsh coastlines. We reunited in London where he stayed with us for a few nights before flying home. Over tea, Dan made a remark that made me smile: "I haven't figured you out yet… you strike me as a girly girl… a city girl. Yet you yearn to be out in the wilderness".

Dan is a very perceptive man. Conrad and I are not settled in London. We're itching to return to a more natural environment; one where we live in the present. We just need to work out where, and how to incorporate this into a viable life without simply running away. Re-living the memories of our big adventure has helped me to appreciate how special those months of freedom were. It was an experience that many people can only dream of, but one which we are fortunate to cherish forever.

Glossary

Base-weight:
The weight of your pack excluding food, water, and fuel. Often the subject of intense debate and unyielding opinion.

Bear Can/Canister:
A portable container that bears have not *yet* figured out how to open. Protects the *bears* from getting at your food. It's compulsory to carry in some areas in California, such as Yosemite. Hikers hate having to carry them because they're bulky and heavy. Ideally they should be stored 100 feet from your tent with something noisy on top so you can hear if something is trying to steal your food.

Bivy:
A waterproof sack that goes over your sleeping bag to add warmth and protection from the elements. Some hikers carry them as an emergency shelter, while others use them as their primary shelter because they're lighter to carry than a tent.

Blaze:
Trail-blazing is the practice of marking paths in outdoor recreational areas with coloured signs or markings to show the direction of the trail. On the PCT, the markings (when you infrequently come across one) are a white and cyan emblem depicting a tall pine tree against mountains. Useful to see at confusing junctions.

Bonus Miles:
Extra miles which aren't part of the official trail. Includes: additional miles walked to resupply, side-trails to water/campsites, and getting lost.

Bush-whack:
Finding yourself off the trail without a defined path, meaning

you have to force your way through forest or an overgrown area, typically getting cut up as a result.

Cairn:
A man-made stack of stones indicating the direction of the trail.

Camel Up:
Drinking as much as you can at a water source, reducing the need to carry as much water.

Day Hiker:
A hiker who is only hiking for the day, returning home to a hot shower and food.

Dry Camp:
A camp site without a nearby water source. This requires more planning to ensure you have enough water for the night and following morning.

Ford:
A water crossing where you are guaranteed to get wet feet.

Giardia:
A reason to always treat and filter your water, and wash your hands after you've had a poo. Giardia is an intestinal parasite which lives in faeces; it is often transmitted through untreated water or poor hygiene. It causes severe diarrhoea, bloating and flatulence, often leading to dangerous dehydration. It's treated with antibiotics and rest.

Glissade:
To slide down a snow-covered slope on your butt, like sledding without a sled. Gets you to the bottom of a snowfield quickly, but care is required to control your speed and direction so you don't slide into a tree or off a cliff!

Hiker Box:
A box where hikers donate unwanted food or gear for other

hikers to use. Usually found at resupply points like hostels, inns, and with trail angels.

Hiker Hunger:
Intense hunger as a result of burning so many calories compared to nutritional intake. Results in hunger pangs, food fantasies, and in-town binge eating to make up for the physical and mental shortfall.

Hiker Midnight:
Around 9:00 p.m. The time when it becomes impossible to keep your eyes open, and your body officially gives up.

Hiker-min:
Another phrase you can expect to be absent from *The Oxford English Dictionary*. A term Conrad and I coined to refer to the enormous amount of hiking-related admin tasks we needed to perform just to walk, such as securing permits.

Hikertrash:
A term used to distinguish a hiker from a homeless person, who may look similar given a distinct lack of washing and limited set of clothes.

HYOH:
"Hike Your Own Hike". An often-used term to acknowledge that people are all different, so come to the trail with different methods and expectations. One person's goal may not match another's, so it's best to appreciate there's more than one way to successfully achieve the same thing.

Kit Explosion:
The process of emptying one's hiking gear out in one place to help assess your load, the first-step in a thorough gear shakedown.

Leave No Trace (LNT):
The 7 key principles of outdoor ethics: 1. Plan ahead and prepare; 2. Travel and camp on durable surfaces; 3. Dispose of waste

properly; 4. Minimise campfire impacts; 5. Leave what you find; 6. Respect wildlife; 7. Be considerate of other visitors. Basically, leave the wilderness in the way you would want to find it.

Nero:
Nearly a zero. A day when you only hike a few miles, often when you are coming into, or heading out of town.

NoBo:
Northbound hiker; the most popular choice in direction for hiking the PCT.

PCT:
Pacific Crest Trail, one of 3 national scenic hiking trails in the U.S., spanning the entire length of the country from the Mexican to Canadian border. (Hopefully obvious by this point!)

PCTA:
Pacific Crest Trail Association: The organisation charged with protecting, preserving and promoting the PCT. Find out more @ https://www.pcta.org/

Piss Cloth:
A piece of fabric, in my case a micro towel, used in place of toilet paper after urination. A versatile piece of kit that can also double-up as a bandana or snot rag.

Postholing:
A term used to describe sinking a limb into snow. It expends vast amounts of energy, reduces speed, and can be dangerous depending on what lies beneath the snow.

REI:
Recreational Equipment, Inc. – a national American outdoor retailer, that has remained a membership co-op since its founding in 1938. Amazing locations, no-quibble product guarantees, and lots of friendly staff on-hand to give us less-than-experienced adventurists a helping hand. They also run outdoor skill courses

if you're ever in the right area at the right time! Shame we weren't...

Resupply:
When a hiker has to leave the wilderness for somewhere with access – such as a post office or small resort – to get more supplies of food and fuel.

Section Hiker:
A hiker who has the intention of hiking a section of a long-distance trail.

Shakedown:
The process of reviewing all your gear with the goal of removing unnecessary items and reducing pack weight.

SoBo:
Southbound hiker.

Switchbacks:
When the trail zig-zags, using hairpin turns back-and-forth up a very steep section of terrain. Loathed for adding distance to a trail, loved for making it easier to hike – like walking up a ramp instead of stairs.

Thru-Hike:
A continuous hike from one end of a long-distance trail to the other end, usually undertaken in one season.

Trail Angel:
A person who provides trail magic to help hikers, free of charge and out of pure kindness, without expectation of repayment. Though sometimes people do seem to expect payment...

Trail Magic:
A random act of kindness gifted to a hiker. Ranging from a water cache to a bed for the night.

Trail Mix:
A nutritious(?) blend of snacks all thrown together in a bag – typically involving nuts, dried fruit, and goodies such as M&Ms. An easy, usually satisfying, protein-rich snack, but heavier to carry than dehydrated tripe.

Trail Name:
A nickname used as a unique identifier on the trail. Usually given by another hiker after a memorable experience. Can be a way for thru-hikers to dissociate their "real" identity back home with their antics on the trail.

Trail Register:
Sometimes an official book, sometimes a piece of scrap paper located at various points along the trail. Useful for leaving messages for others behind you, or reading trail conditions up ahead. Also useful for search and rescue if someone goes missing.

Trailhead:
An access point to the trail.

Triple Crown:
To complete thru-hikes of the Appalachian Trail (AT), Pacific Crest Trail (PCT) and Continental Divide Trail (CDT), collectively known as the Triple Crown.

Ultralight:
A hiker who has a base weight of under 10lbs/4.5kg, though this varies with people loving to claim they are going "ultralight". We were not in this category!

Vitamin I:
Ibuprofen. Generally taken far too liberally on the trail, and when combined with anti-allergy tablets massively aids sleep.

Zero:
A zero day is a day of rest where no miles are hiked to help recover or wait out bad weather.

Gear Lists

MY KIT

Shelter + Pack + Sleep System

TENT/ Big Agnes Fly Creek UL3 - I carried the poles & pegs /
574g
PACK / Gossamer Gear Mariposa 60 (S with hip belt) / 870g
SLEEPING BAG / Nemo Nocturne 15 (Reg) / 1060g
SLEEPING PAD / Nemo Astro Insulated Air Lite (Reg) / 590g
PILLOW / Sea to Summit Aeros Ultralight (Reg) / 56g

What I Wore

HIKING SHOES / Merrell Moab Ventilators / 726g
INSOLES / Superfeet Orange / 136g
GAITERS / Dirty Girl gaiters / 40g
TREKKING POLES / Black Diamond Trail Ergo Cork / 510g
SOCKS / Darn Tough Quarter Cushion Hiker (2 pairs) / 65g (per
pair)
TOP / Nike Dri-Fit Knit short-sleeved top / 200g
HIKING SKIRT / Purple Rain Adventure Skirt (black with grey
waist-band) / 127g
BRA / Patagonia Barely Sports Bra / 57g
UNDIES / Exofficio bikini briefs (2 pairs) / 35g (per pair)

Clothing I Carried

CAMP LEGGINGS / Patagonia Capilene thermal-weight leggings
/ 140g
CAMP TOP / Icebreaker Oasis long-sleeve crewe / 193g
WARM JACKET/ Rab Alpine microlight down jacket (hoodless)
/ 330g
WATERPROOF JACKET / Mammut Methow jacket / 476g
WATERPROOF TROUSERS / Outdoor Research Aspire pants /
277g
LONG-SLEEVED TOP / Nike Element half-zip running top / 198g

HIKING LEGGINGS / REI base-layer leggings / 200g
CAMP SHOES / Teva Verra sandals / 453g
CAMP SOCKS / REI Merino Wool hiking socks / 85g
SUN HAT / Brooks Sherpa hat / 25g
GLOVES / Outdoor Research Outdry mittens / 28g
WARM HAT / Arc'Teryx Rho LTW beanie / 30g

CONRAD'S KIT LIST

Shelter + Pack + Sleep System

TENT / Big Agnes Fly Creek UL3 - Conrad carried fly sheet &
inner tent parts / 922g
PACK / Osprey Exos 58 (size L) / 1050g
SLEEPING BAG / Nemo Salsa 15 (L) / 1190g
SLEEPING PAD / Nemo Astro Insulated Air Lite Sleeping Pad (L)
/ 652g
PILLOW / Sea to Summit Aeros Ultralight (L) / 74g
GROUND SHEET / Gossamer Gear polycro footprint (L) / 45g

What Conrad Wore

HIKING SHOES / La Sportiva Wildcat Trail-Runners / 709g
GAITERS / Dirty Girl gaiters / 42g
TREKKING POLES / Black Diamond Alpine Ergo Trekking Poles
/ 567g
SOCKS / Darn Tough Quarter Cushion Hiker (x2) / 70g (per pair)
TOE LINERS / Injinji Run 2.0 Lightweight socks / 50g
TROUSERS / Columbia "shants" / 400g
TOP / Nike Dri-Fit Knit short-sleeved top / 200g
UNDERWEAR/ Jockey Microfibre Active Trunk (2 pairs) / 65g
(per pair)

Clothing Conrad Carried

CAMP TROUSERS / Patagonia Capilene Thermal Weight
bottoms / 129g

CAMP TOP / Patagonia Capilene Thermal Weight crewe / 129g
WARM JACKET / Mountain Hardwear Ghost Whisperer Down Jacket (hooded) / 221g
WATERPROOF TROUSERS / Outdoor Research Helium pants / 160g
WATERPROOF JACKET / Marmot PreCip Rain Jacket / 312g
LONG-SLEEVED TOP / Nike Element half-zip running top / 226g
CAMP SHOES / Xero Shoes Barefoot-inspired Sport Sandals / 312g
GLOVES / Outdoor Research Gripper Gloves / 88g
SUN HAT / Columbia Bora Bora Hat / 80g
NECK BUFF / Buffwear – original buff / 35g

Additional Kit We Carried Between Us

CAMP KITCHEN

STOVE / MSR Pocket Rocket / 85g
COOK PAN / Snow Peak Titanium Trek 1400 / 210g
SPORK / Snow Peak Titanium Spork (x2) / 17g (each)
MUG / Snow Peak Titanium Single 450 Cup (x2) / 68g (each)
FIRE LIGHTING / Lighter and waterproof matches
FOOD SACKS / Ursack Minor Critter food bags (x2) / 150g (each)
WATER FILTER / Sawyer Squeeze original (x2) / 85g (each)
[DIRTY] WATER RESERVOIR/ Evernew 2l water bladder (x2) / 42g (each)
[CLEAN] WATER BOTTLES / Smartwater 1l plastic bottles (x4) / 42g (each)

ELECTRONICS

HEADLIGHT (Me) / Petzl E+Lite headlamp / 27g
HEADLIGHT (Conrad) / Black Diamond Storm headlamp / 110g
CAMERA / Canon PowerShot G7 X Digital Camera / 278g
PHONE (e) / iPhone 6S with Lifeproof FRE case / 143g + 100g
PHONE (Conrad) / iPhone 5 / 112g
HEADPHONES / Bose in-ear (x2) / 18g

CAMERA MOUNTING CLIP / StickPic / 18g
BATTERY PACK / Anker PowerCore+ 13400 / 306g
EXTRA CABLES / Petzl E+Lite headlamp / Approx. 150g

MISCELLANEOUS KIT

STUFF SACKS / Sea to Summit Ultra Sil Nano Dry Sack (2l) / 16g
STUFF SACKS / Exped Ultralite Waterproof Compression Bags (13l) / 40g
MULTI-TOOL / Leatherman Style CS Multi-tool / 41g
POCKET KNIFE / Gerber STL 2.5 pocket knife / 42g
HEAD NET / Coghlan's Mosquito Head Net (x2) / 20g
PACK COVER / Osprey Ultralight Raincover / 90g
PARACHUTE CHORD / REI PMI 3mm Utility Cord (50 ft.) / 113g
SEAT PAD / Therm-a-Rest Z-Seat Pad / 57g
CARABINAS / Gossamer Gear mini (x2)
SHOULDER POUCH / Zpacks Backpack Shoulder Pouch
FIRST AID KIT / Misc. / Approx. 80g
WATER PURIFICATION / Katadyn Micropur MP1 Purification TABLETS / 20g
TOWELS / PackTowl Ultralite Towel (L) / 99g
TOWEL / PackTowl Ultralite Towel (S) (x2) / 14g
SOAP / Dr Bronner's Peppermint Liquid Soap (2oz) / 57g
HAND SANITISER / Purell Advanced Naturals 2oz pump bottle / 57g
MOISTURISER / SUNSCREEN / Neutrogena Healthy Defence Daily Moisturiser with SPF 50 / 28g
DEET BUG SPRAY / Ben's 100 Max Tick & Insect Repellent 3.4oz / 96g
TOILET PAPER / N/A
PACK LINER / Waste Compactor Bags / N/A
PASSPORTS / PERMITS / MAPS / N/A
CREDIT CARDS / CASH / N/A
SHARPIE PEN / N/A
SUNGLASSES / Cheap polarised ones (1 pair each) / N/A

Food Tips

When working out a resupply strategy, make sure you factor in lots of variety. You don't want each box-opening to get stale and predictable. Cravings will change, so if you can, don't pack more than a dozen boxes at a time. If doing a longer distance hike I wouldn't have packed all our boxes in advance, as it's impossible to predict what you will find tolerable months down the line.

If you have a friendly person helping to send your boxes, keep them unsealed so they can add in or remove items as required.

Pack spare Ziploc bags to help you decant food out of heavy packaging. Use the freezer Ziploc variety for freeze-dried meals, as not only are they lighter in weight than foil sachets, they can also hold hot water, meaning food can be cooked in them without the need to wash up the pan afterwards. *[This is unofficial knowledge, not endorsed by the Ziploc company!]*

When packing supplies, try to aim for a daily dose of slow energy-releasing ingredients, such as oats and chia seeds, both of which make easy breakfasts. We always ate a decent breakfast, accompanied by a Starbucks Via instant coffee to get us moving in the morning. It may have meant extra time leaving camp, but it worked for us and gave us a solid start to the day.

Plan on buying some fresh basic foodstuffs from local stores along the way, such as lunch items like tortillas, cheese, and crisps.

Fat – especially the "good" kind – can be difficult to obtain from dried packet meals. We used full-fat milk powder (including coconut powder), hard cheese, sachets of peanut butter, and a small bottle of olive oil.

We quickly tired of grocery store mac'n'cheese, instant mash, and dried pasta sachets, so instead we purchased more dedicated dehydrated camping meals. While these are more expensive (around six to nine dollars a meal), they are cheaper if brought in bulk online and contain far more protein. We favoured the brands Backpacker's Pantry and Mountain House.

Despite buying camping meals labelled as "2-3 people", they were not enough to satisfy two hungry hikers – Dan ate the same size by himself! A hiker we met in Big Lake Youth Camp taught us how to supplement these by adding couscous, dehydrated vegetables and other grains to cheaply transform them into a heartier meal.

Tiny portions of pepper, dried herbs, and garlic salt go a long way to making dehydrated meals taste less bland.

My Favourite Oatmeal Recipe
(serves a hearty portion for 2 people)
1.5 cups rolled oats – the instant variety
0.5 cup dried coconut milk (or any other powdered milk)
2 tsp chia seeds
1 tbsp brown sugar
Handful of dark chocolate chips (or any chocolate bar melted down)
Top with dried banana chips/nuts/trail mix - anything crunchy tastes amazing

To prepare: Boil 3 cups of water, then stir in the mixture. Leave a couple of minutes – covering with a lid if you have one – to cook. If running low on gas, or time, the dried ingredients can be added to water the night before and left to soak, removing the need to cook the next day.

Digital Resources

Here are some recommendations for anyone contemplating embarking on a long-distance hiking adventure. There is a world of national scenic trails out there, so while some of these are PCT-specific, many are full of useful general tips and advice.

YouTube Channels

Captain Dan – our friend and hiking buddy Dan from Kentucky. Dan's video blogs of the PCT are special because they show an unfiltered view of life on the trail. It's not all roses, but Dan's appreciation for nature shines through.

CleverHiker – Dave Collins provides fantastically concise "how to" video tutorials for surviving in the wilderness, and ultralight backpacking. Look out for: *Backpacking Bear Encounters – Truth and Myth*.

Darwin onthetrail – a regular guy who quit his job back in 2014 to hike the Appalachian trail and hasn't looked back since. Great gear reviews, AT vlogs, and ideas for shorter U.S section hikes.

Favourite Hiker Blogs

BikeHikeSafari.com – all-round nice guy Brad documents his thru-hiking and long-distance bike touring escapades in an easy style that it's impossible not to be captivated by. He also shares lots of gear reviews and has a talent for capturing great photos. I loved his daily 10 a.m. trail shots.

FollowingTheArrows.com – fellow Londoner (via Australia), Kat shares her experiences hiking Caminos and trails from around the world. She hiked the PCT the year before us and met up with me in the city beforehand so I could try her hiking skirt on for size!

HalfwayAnywhere.com – follow the tales of adventure travel and hiking enthusiast, Mac in his charismatic journeys along some of the world's greatest trails (including the PCT and CDT). The blog provides useful tips, trip ideas, and feeds any vicarious travel desires.

Pacific Crest Trail Information

For specific PCT information, including current conditions and permit applications, visit the Pacific Crest Trail Organisation @ https://www.pcta.org/

To view and download free PCT *Halfmile* maps, go to: https://www.PCTmap.net

For current North American snow information: http://www.nohrsc.noaa.gov/interactive/html/map.html

Guthook's Hiking guide app is available for purchase, and in our opinion was worth the cost:
https://www.guthookhikes.com/apps

About the Author

Aspiring writer, entrepreneur… adult. The one vocation Kathryn has successfully nailed so far is Daydreamer. Her varied ambitions and overall life trajectory has taken a bit of a turn of late. A born-and-bred Londoner, Kathryn is discovering there is more to life than the corporate rat race. It began with a six-month trip through South America whetting her travelling wanderlust, which led to the decision to quit her job as a management consultant.

More recently she upped the adventure ante, swapping city life for the wilderness, on an ambitious walk hundreds of miles along America's Pacific Crest Trail. The plan raised eyebrows from all who knew her - an uncharacteristic leap for a girl who refuses to sleep on the floor. The results were both brutal and awe-inspiring.

Kathryn has never been an 'outdoorsy' person. But the simple, reflective, time spent in the natural environment left a deep imprint. She still (reluctantly) resides in London, but the mountains are calling. She may even camp again. Someday.

For the latest information about Kathryn visit:
www.ALifeToWander.com
www.instagram.com/a_life_to_wander/

Acknowledgements

A special mention needs to go out to the man of the hour, the one without whom I never would have even considered this crazy adventure: Conrad. Mosquito-bites aside, I honestly don't think there is another man on the planet who possesses the patience, sense of humour, and all-round mental resolve required to haved lived this trip with me. I hope we experience many more adventures together – perhaps just not camping.

I would like to thank my mum for her encouragement to write this book. She spent hours reading my blog updates to family, and later, reviewing the many iterations of my manuscripts. She is my champion. Sorry about all the swearing Mum!

Thanks to David and the team at Hornet books for taking a chance on a first-time author. Apologies for all my last-minute notes and zealous feedback.

Thank you to all those wonderful people, of which there are too many to name here, who aided our safe journey across America. Your welcoming spirit, kindness, and compassion toward a couple of scruffy Londoners made our trip possible. I will forever be in your debt.

And how could I forget them – Leslie and Chris, aka the Marshmeiers. I'd like to thank them for hosting us in their home, and for remembering to actually post all those life-line boxes! And to Leslie especially: thank you for taking the time to create the wonderfully artistic map illustrating our special memories.